I0755363

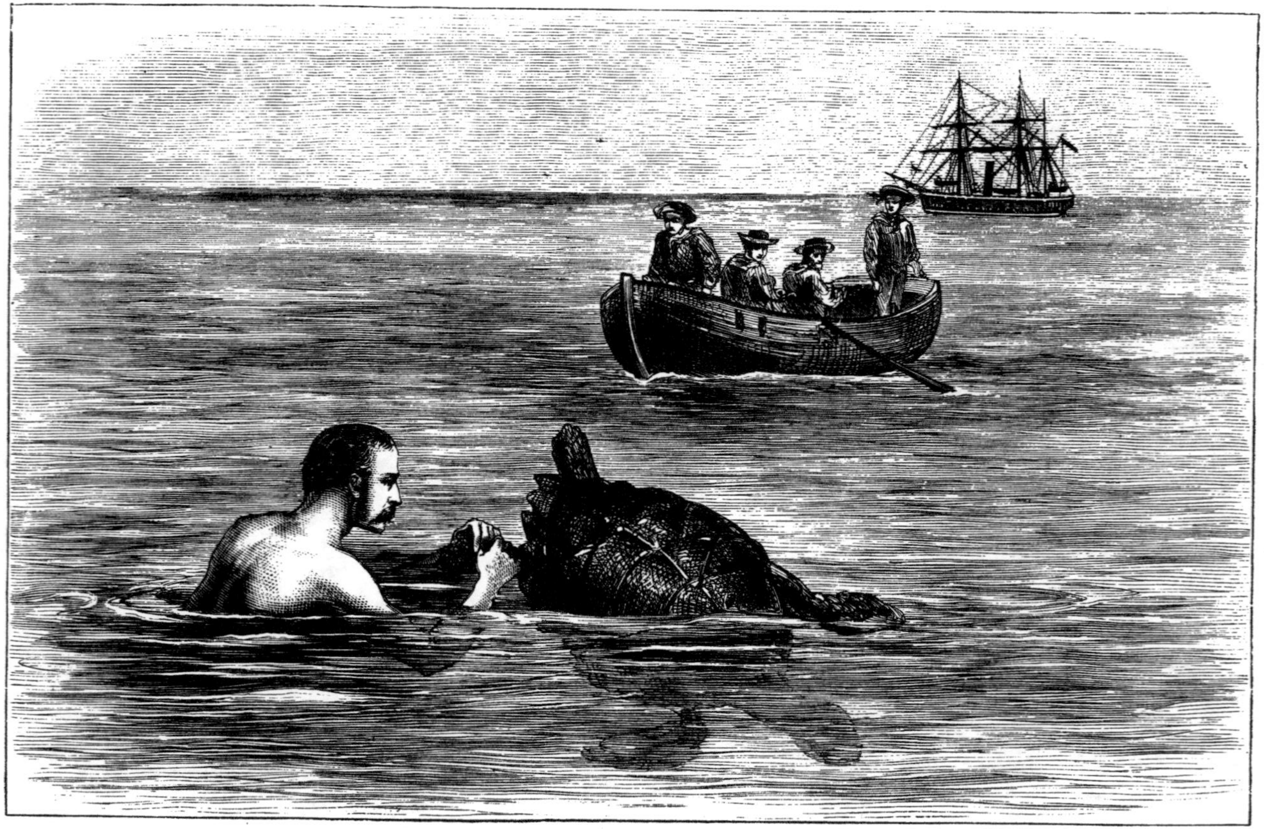

Frontispiece.

TURTLE-TURNING 'AU NATUREL."

THE TWO AMERICAS;

AN ACCOUNT OF SPORT AND TRAVEL.

WITH

NOTES ON MEN AND MANNERS IN NORTH AND SOUTH AMERICA.

BY

MAJOR SIR ROSE LAMBART PRICE, BART., F.R.G.S.,
(LATE R.M.L.I.)

WITH ILLUSTRATIONS.

PHILADELPHIA
J. B. LIPPINCOTT & CO.
1877.

TO

MY COUSIN,

GUSTAVUS LAMBART BASSET

OF TEHIDY,

THESE WANDERINGS ARE AFFECTIONATELY

Inscribed.

B H Swales.

CONTENTS.

CHAPTER I.

CHAPTER II.

CHAPTER III.

CHAPTER IV.

CHAPTER V.

CHAPTER VI.

CHAPTER VII.

CHAPTER VIII.

CHAPTER IX.

CHAPTER X.

CHAPTER XI.

CHAPTER XII.

APPENDICES.

THE TWO AMERICAS.

CHAPTER I.

Leave England—The inducements—Slow progression—An awkward cropper—Fishing at Madeira—The English cemetery—A sea waif proves a sell—St. Vincent—Quail shooting—Shipwrecked mariners—Quail *à la* banana—A good evening's sea-fishing—Soap-fish—A porcupine fish—Eels—Leave St. Vincent—Crossing the "Line"—Neptune's visit—Curious coincidence—The ceremony—Night in the tropics—The Argonaut—Effects of a bad cook—Anchor at Rio Janeiro.

On Sunday, the 4th of October, 1874, I took up my quarters on board H.M.S. *Rocket*, a double-screw composite gun-vessel, 464 tons, and 120 horse-power, bound for the Pacific station, where she was to relieve H.M.S. *Boxer*, then stationed at Esquimault, a small harbour containing a dockyard, in Vancouver Island.

Lieut. H., who commanded her, had been with me in Beauchamp Seymour's "Flying Squadron," where he was first lieutenant of the *Volage*, after F. got promoted; and very kindly offering me half his accommodation—a cabin opposite his own—prevailed on me to sail with him for the cruise.

The inducements were considerable; including a trip through the Straits of Magellan, a look at the

Patagonians, and several places on the Pacific coast of America; possibly some good salmon-fishing and shooting in British Columbia, and an undoubtedly interesting journey home by the Union Pacific Railway from San Francisco, visiting *en route* the celebrated Yo-Semite Valley, the Salt Lake City of Brigham Young and the Mormons, and the Falls of Niagara. I took with me a tent, canteen, and india-rubber boat, besides my guns, rifles, and rods; and with a good-looking young retriever, called "Major," felt tolerably prepared for anything that might turn up on our arrival at the "happy hunting-grounds" of the far West.

Within half an hour of my arrival on board we were under weigh, and, passing Mount Edgecombe and the breakwater, soon left Plymouth behind us; night rapidly cast her dusky wings around, and the last shadowy visions of old England soon faded from our view.

Our voyage to Madeira was varied by light winds, foul winds, and gales of wind; one of the latter, off the Bay of Biscay, being unusually severe. Many of the young hands were very sea-sick, and Martin, a queer kind of factotum of the captain's, and a most original character in his own way, looked the perfect picture of misery and unhappiness, as he crawled with uncertain shambling footsteps and pallid woe-begone countenance about the upper deck, his short neck and square under-sized frame considerably resembling a disconsolate turtle.

Before long we discovered that, though an excellent sea-boat, the *Rocket* was by no means a clipper, and that a very strong inducement was required to prevail on her to go more than four knots an hour under either sail or steam, and that, unless running before the wind, her average lee-way was seldom less than two and a half points. Slowly but steadily we plodded onward, and on the 20th of October anchored at Funchal, having taken sixteen days to get there.

The scenery of Madeira when viewed from the ocean entirely depends on the time of year and state of the atmosphere. To do it simple justice, both were on this occasion unfavourable, and the appearance of the island may be described in a somewhat graphic remark of Martin's, which lost none of its quaintness through being delivered in his broad Devonshire dialect. Seeing him watching the island which we were now rapidly closing with a strong wind right abaft, I said, "Well, Martin, what do you think of foreign lands?" "I don't see noa land," replied he; "I only sees a monsterous rock a-raising of itself out of the sea." And such indeed it appeared on this occasion merely to be, and had I not seen it at other seasons a mass of verdure, its high, sharply-outlined mountains, in bright relief against the clear blue sky, its plots of waving sugar-cane, and terraces of vineyards, I also might have thought it but "a monsterous rock, a-raising of itself out of the sea."

H.M.S. *Albatross* was in harbour. She had left Plymouth a week after we did, and arrived that morning.

Few places pall on one more than Madeira. On my first visit, I thought it a paradise; on my second, not a bad substitute for one; three years back, a pretty little place for a very short visit; and this time it seemed merely commonplace and decidedly slow. H. and myself planned a shooting expedition to a distant part of the island, which was to have extended over three days. It required eight hours' riding to reach the ground, which necessitated an early start; but on getting out of bed on the morning of our intended departure, we found such a storm raging, with torrents of rain, that to start in it would have been simple madness, and so, reluctantly, we had to give it up, and content ourselves with the usual thing that everyone seems to do, *i.e.*, the Little Curral—a slide down a steep hill from the convent in a basket-sledge, and a gallop along the new road.

Our ride to the Curral gave exercise to our dogs, who had been for some time cooped up on board, and they certainly enjoyed their gallop as much as their masters. The scenery, when once well up the mountain, was very lovely, and my enjoyment of it was only marred by the pony I was riding having an awkward trick of stumbling at the worst places; and once coming a regular "burster" on the top of his head at a spot where he might have shot me a few hundred feet down a ravine, had good fortune not tumbled him over on the safe, instead of the unsafe side of the pathway.

Another day we visited a small fishing-village, just as the boats arrived to unload their cargoes of scaly monsters, conspicuous among which was a huge ugly shark, with teeth strong, large, and sharp enough to have bitten a man in two with one snap of its powerful-looking jaws. Most of the boats had a few albicore, the largest about a hundredweight and a half, and quantities of other fish which I knew not the names of, and probably had never seen before. We were much struck with the rapid and dexterous manner the albicore were cleaned and prepared for salting; and after inspecting the lines and different paraphernalia of the fishermen's gear, and cross-questioning them as to the means of capture, came to the conclusion that albicore-fishing must be rather good fun.

The Consul put our names down for the club and reading-room, and what with studying old newspapers and feeding at Miles's Hotel, we managed to get through our visit.

The English cemetery has a certain sad interest about it, from the dreadful number of consumptive victims whose graves lie thick around, the average age on the tombstones being only about twenty-two; poor C.'s, a midshipman I met out here last time I visited the island, being among the number.

On Saturday, the *Albatross* steamed out of harbour, and on Sunday, the 25th of October, we "again urged on our wild career," taking with us as much stock as we could bring, and some of the dirtiest washing, from an old Portuguese hag, a Madame Rosa, that I ever remember carrying to sea.

Next afternoon, while meditating with my eyes closed,—a very usual occupation with idlers on board ship after luncheon,—the quartermaster on watch awoke me to say a large spar was in sight, and that the captain thought I might like to see it. On reaching the bridge I saw a long spar (forty-eight feet, it turned out to be afterwards) some short way ahead, and which, lying but a little distance out of our track, we had altered our course to inspect. The captain, first lieutenant, and chief carpenter, were in solemn confab, and on the carpenter pronouncing judgment that the spar was a good one, it was determined to get it in-board without delay. Shoals of fish were round it, (a bad sign, I thought, for its utility,) and half-a-dozen lovely dolphin, leaving the barnacle-covered attraction, sailed, as if on a tour of inspection, round the ship. Two hours' hard work of all hands secured the prize, but darkness having set in before it could be examined carefully, we could only speculate as to its probable value, until next day determined the result. H. was delighted. "It must be worth from 20*l*. to 35*l*." "He would sell it at Rio." B., the first lieutenant, "thought it would fetch much paint;" and the lowerdeck thought, that perhaps an appropriate splicing of the main-brace, with the proceeds of Neptune's gift to his children, would not come in amiss on some future festive occasion. Alas! daylight next morning rudely scattered all visions of money, paint, and grog; the spar was discovered to be so thoroughly honeycombed by sea worms, as to be utterly useless for all purposes of sale or barter, and on removing its thick coating of barnacles, nothing but fire-wood could be thought of as a use.

We expected, shortly after leaving Madeira, to have found the North-East Trades. which should have taken us within 5° of the Line on our road to Rio Janeiro; but as day after day we steadily steamed onward, without the slightest trace of a wind approaching, and our consumption of coal was gradually making our balance look unpleasantly small for so distant a journey as that which still lay before us, H. determined on touching for fuel at St. Vincent, one of the Cape Verde Islands, which lay almost in our track.

On the 3rd of November, we sighted St. Antonio at daylight, its high peak, 7400 feet above the level of the sea, just peeping out of the clouds by which it was surrounded, and at one o'clock were safely at anchor at Porto Grande, the chief town and coaling station at St. Vincent.

Few places are more uninviting than the town and harbour of Porto Grande. The ground is parched, sandy, and arid; hardly any vegetation is perceptible from the anchorage, and the entire place looks dismal and woe-begone in the extreme. The island is of volcanic formation, and the mountains, though high, are not sufficiently so to attract the clouds and receive their moisture as in the neighbouring island of St. Antonio, which, only a few miles distant, and of similar volcanic origin, possesses a fair amount of vegetation; sufficient, at any rate, to provide fruit and vegetables for their own consumption, as well as enabling them to send a few boat-loads to Porto Grande, not a single thing of any kind being produced in St. Vincent.

In the afternoon, H. and self, taking with us our guns and the dogs, went to call on the Acting

Consul, Mr. J. V. M., who, hearing that it was our intention to try for some quail, kindly lent us horses to ride to the ground and a guide to show us the way. After jogging along for about a mile and a half, we came to a kind of thin scrub partly cleared, and planted with young Indian corn. Among this stuff, the guide, and a couple of niggers who had joined him, commenced beating for quail, and in a short time put some up. They were a very small sort, generally known as "button quail," and being the same colour as the ground, and flying low through the scrub, were as difficult to knock over as hard to find afterwards, there not being an atom of scent for the dogs to work by.

Next morning, before daylight, taking Martin with me, I started from the ship; and, landing about three miles from the town, steadily beat up a large open plain, scantily covered with some green substitute for grass, but bearing a plentiful crop of loose angular stones, in many places as thick and sharp as those on a newly macadamised road, which I had been recommended to try. Not finding anything here, we crossed over a mountain-ridge to the ground we had beaten the previous evening, and where we soon got several shots. A negro milking goats told us the birds lay higher up; but the heat of the sun had by this time got so intense, that, had we continued our sport, the dogs could not possibly have stood it, so, after getting a drink of new goat's milk, which was uncommonly good, we turned our steps towards the town and got on board again for breakfast.

At some seasons of the year the quail-shooting at St. Vincent is really excellent, an average shot being known to kill over twenty brace in a few hours.

In the afternoon we went on shore to prospect the town, and found it a wretched place almost entirely populated by niggers. Some shipwrecked mariners were loafing about, one of whom, a sailmaker, H. endeavoured to persuade to join the *Rocket.* Shipwrecked mariner had, however, once before been her Majesty's servant, and did not seem at all inclined to covet the honour of serving again.

One of the crew, a very decent fellow, appeared considerably distressed at what he told me was a common custom in the Merchant Service, but which nevertheless appeared to me as a rank injustice. It seems that the owners of a vessel stop the pay of the crew from the date they hear their ship is lost. The wives therefore of the men who happen to be married, and who have their husbands' pay allotted for their support during his absence from home, are suddenly rendered penniless, through no fault of either themselves or the father of their children. Piece by piece their household comforts are converted into bread, each visit to the pawnshop bringing them nearer starvation.

As nine times out of ten the ship and cargo are amply insured — that often vessels are purposely wrecked, burned, or founder at sea, through dishonest owners seeking to defraud the insurance companies, is unhappily a well-assured fact—and that rarely any well-managed firm of shipowners suffer from a wreck, their insurance covering all losses—it does indeed seem hard, that the wife and children of a common sailor, who from his position must be entirely blameless for the disaster, should be the only sufferer by the affair.

While I was shooting in the morning, H. made one of those accidental yet valuable discoveries, that so often lead to great results. From a culinary point of view, he had achieved greatness in a no less remarkable manner than by inventing a new method of cooking quail, which only requires to become known to completely supersede all others.

Having ordered for his breakfast some of the birds we had shot the previous evening, he remembered that there were no vine-leaves to cook them with; and looking about him in despair for a substitute, saw a plate of bananas. It suddenly occurred to him to try the peel of one over the slice of thin bacon which envelopes the bird; he did so, and the result was one of those marvellous successes which for ever after render their discoverer famous.

Joking apart, the birds thus cooked were far superior to any I have ever tasted dressed in the conventional vine-leaf, and the receipt may prove a useful wrinkle to travellers, who, like myself, may have frequently enjoyed capital quail-shooting in places where banana peel was plentiful, but vine-leaves scarce.

Mr. M. took us in the evening to a large rock at the entrance of the harbour, called Bird Island, where, being provided with rods and bait, we commenced fishing shortly after the sun had gone down.

The native boats had just given up as we arrived, which was a pretty good sign that the best part of the day was over; however, we went to work, and as M.'s black boat's-crew instructed us in the piscatorial art as practised at St. Vincent, I will try and describe their operations.

The rods, stout bamboos about fourteen feet long, with the lines fastened half-way down and leading to the top, having been taken out of the boat, an active darky commenced spearing small crabs; quantities of whom were running over the side of the rock, as the waves rising and falling exposed them momentarily to the quick eye of the sharp-sighted negro, whose unerring dart seldom failed to secure its aim. Having killed a couple of dozen, he commenced mashing them up with a stone into paste, which, formed into balls, he immediately cast into the sea to attract the fish; and then baiting our hooks with legs of crabs or barnacles, we watched the result of his mode of attack with some anxiety.

We had not long to remain in suspense. "I've got one," was soon the cry, and shortly all the rods were bending at different angles according to the weight and resistance of their various captures.

Nothing could have been more exciting than this sport, which for over an hour was steady and unceasing. Nearly all the fish were of different varieties, and had we been unattended by M.'s "darkies," I am confident some of us would have been hurt, if not seriously injured, by the fish in unhooking them, as nearly all were armed with some description of prickle. Many of their prickles were poisonous, and all of them bit like mad at everything within reach on coming out of the "briny."

A handsome red fish, about two pounds in weight and something like a perch, called by M. "the king of the seas," was the best eating of the lot, and well merited his proud appellation, as a finer flavoured one I have seldom tasted. A black ugly-looking thing, about a pound weight, was called "the soap-fish," and was uneatable; but on being stirred about in a small pool of salt water, soon caused it to lather like suds. A porcupine-fish (*Diodon hystrix*), weighing about seven pounds, one of the Plectognathes, was perhaps the most curious one we caught. The men treated this gentleman with the greatest possible caution, evidently regarding him as a dangerous brute. A more awkward one to handle it is quite impossible to conceive, as he was entirely covered with small spikes, dispersed over sides, back, and abdomen, in such a manner as to prevent effectually anyone touching him. On being hauled up he came grunting loudly out of the water, and as he lay on the rocks, commenced swelling himself out by successive gulps of air, which he inhaled with such noise and vigour that he soon resembled a cross between a distended football and an angry toad. Its skin was so tough that it resisted easily the pike-thrusts which saluted it, and only after several efforts was it dispatched with a sharp and strong clasp-knife. Its maxillary and intermaxillary bones are soldered together so as to render the upper jaw immoveable; its entire mouth appeared plated with some hard kind of enamel, and M. told us that its powers of crushing were so great, that when fresh from the water one of them could easily crumble any of the lumps of scoria lying about, were a piece placed between its powerful jaws.

We caught several large eels, which caused more alarm than anything else—the niggers skipping away like monkeys the instant they were thrown upon the rocks. They certainly were formidable brutes, and the bare-legged boatmen were amply justified for the activity they displayed. Their jaws, shaped something like a duck's bill, were capable of great expansion, and their teeth were strong and sharp as razors. One that we had speared turned viciously round and bit a large piece out of his own tail, and then, seizing a bamboo he had been struck with, severed the tough cane as if it had been a simple carrot. We afterwards spiced and pickled our ill-tempered friend, and found him excellent eating; but though the flesh was perfectly white and delicate, his bones were all deep purple, and strong as steel. The vertebral bone was marvellously formed for strength, having a kind of extra flange through its entire length, which must have given the brute an amount of power I have never seen developed in any other kind of eel, or in any skeleton of snake or viper. All the small bones terminated in a kind of fang or fork which I never observed in any other fish.

We killed many other varieties of fish which it would be tedious to describe, and got back to the ship when it became quite dark, after having enjoyed an evening's sport—as unusual as it was interesting.

On our return we found H.M.S. *Basilisk* at anchor. She had come in for coal, on her way to England, after a commission of nearly four years in Australia.

On the 5th of November we steamed out of Porto Grande, H.M.S. *Coquette* standing in as we left.

The heat at St. Vincent was intense, and though Europeans find it healthy according to their account (half of them never show out for a moment during the heat of the day, and running no risk, are not likely to get ill), we were all precious glad to get away. I lost a new and excellent purse there, which tumbled out of my pocket while shooting; this annoyed me a good deal, and as we evidently had not hit off the cream of the quail season, I was delighted that our stay was of no longer duration.

On the evening of the 15th of November, Neptune coming on board, announced his intention of next morning visiting the ship in a more formal manner (which would by that time have arrived at his own particular dominion), and that he would require a toll from all those who had not already paid their footing. The engines were stopped, sides piped, and his Majesty received by the captain on the quarter-deck, who, after expressing the delight he felt at again making his Royal Highness's acquaintance, asked, "What kind of weather are we likely to have?" "Stormy weather," replied Neptune; "and I also prognosticate much wet very shortly;" which prophecy was almost instantly fulfilled by the donkey-engine, which had been secretly rigged for the occasion, immediately commencing to play on the mob of "greenhorns" who had come aft to see the ceremony, not knowing exactly what they might expect; and shortly afterwards, Neptune having received a bottle of cold tea from the captain (very strong, and smelling suspiciously of rum) for Amphitrite his wife, took his departure over the stern in a chariot of fire, which was seen long afterwards floating miles behind us.

"Reed," a huge boatswain's mate over six foot, and "bearded like a pard," represented the great sea god, and really made a most excellent illustration of the mythological deity. His chariot of fire was manufactured out of a tar-barrel, which was ignited and cut adrift, as he disappeared over the stern to unrig out of sight of the youngsters who were gazing open-mouthed at the interview with H., which had just taken place, and whose mouths were only closed again by the judicious application of salt-water already alluded to.

Next morning, the 16th of November, we crossed the line in Long. 25° 34′ W. A very remarkable coincidence here took place. Shortly after divisions, the hands went to "fire quarters," as being the most convenient method for filling, by all the pumps, a large bath made out of a sail which was to be used for ducking Neptune's victims in, after their being shaved.

The bell had not been rung two minutes, which summoned the men to their stations, when a *bonâ fide* fire was discovered in one of the coal bunkers. The bath had to be taken down, and the fire engines were actively employed for some time in extinguishing the smouldering coal, which threw out volumes of smoke during the operation. In less than an hour the danger was reported over, and not to be done out of their fun, again the hands commenced rigging bath and platform for the coming ceremony.

All preparations been duly made, Neptune, Amphitrite, and their son, (a sturdy little Triton,) attended by a brilliant staff, having promenaded round the quarter-deck to the soul-inspiring strains of a penny whistle, three pot-lids, and a banjo, took up their position on a dais raised for the occasion, and conveniently placed to the bath, which was some four feet deep, and large enough to contain half-a-dozen lusty bears, who, bedaubed with paint like red Indians, growled and disported themselves gaily in the huge tank while waiting anxiously for their prey.

His Majesty, being provided by the assistant paymaster with a list of all hands on board who had not previously crossed the line, commenced in a stern tone of voice by demanding that his first unpresented servant should be brought before him. Immediately the individual was seized by some myrmidons, blindfolded, and led up a ladder to the dais, where he was handed over to the tender mercies of a barber and doctor, well supported by a staff of assistants sufficiently numerous to render resistance quite out of the question.

He was then placed sitting crossways on the extreme end of a bench, close to, but with his back to the bath, which was about eight feet below him.

The doctor at this juncture, fearing that excitement might cause ill effects to his patient, kindly administered his smelling-bottle, a most odoriferous stimulant, the cork being well provided with sharp pins, which—as a description of counter-irritant—was considerately rammed in his nose. This naturally caused him to ejaculate "Oh!" and immediately a pill, the ingredients of which we will not inquire into, was dexterously popped into his open mouth.

The amount of medicine depended to a great extent on the popularity, or otherwise, of the initiated; and the words "Scrub him," and "Werry obstreperous, your majesty—resisted hawful!" hinted to the executioners the amount of torture they were expected to inflict.

The barber then commenced, and having completely enveloped his patient's head, nose, ears, and eyes, with a thick coating of soft-soap and soot, shaved it off with a huge razor of either rusty iron, or jagged wood, according to Neptune's mandate for No. 1 or No. 2 weapon to be used; and then having entirely finished, at a sudden signal, the novice was tumbled over backwards into the bath, where he was seized upon by the expectant "bears," and soundly ducked and belaboured, until he crawled out at the other end, heartily glad, I have no doubt, that his initiation into the mysteries of the deep had at length been completed.

About five-and-thirty "tyros" were operated on, and though much of the play was somewhat rough and boisterous, there was not a single instance in which any of the men lost their temper, or looked upon the whole affair as other than a good joke.

Night at sea, while in the "trades" is always

delightful, and I frequently slept on deck, or lay there watching the stars, so refulgent and glorious, that I often wondered vaguely what they really were, almost ready to believe in the faith of the ancients, who peopled them with creatures and gave them gods. The brilliancy of Venus at times equalled that of the moon. I don't know whether her transit taking place about this period had anything to do with her illuminating powers, but she often threw regular and distinct rays across the water, and gave sufficient light to read by. Sirius and Orion's Belt seemed vivid, and even the overrated Southern Cross grew brighter.

On nights like these, a gentle balmy air stealing along the bosom of the deep—countless stars sparkling in the firmament—the pleasant ripple of the water making music as the ship glides almost motionless through it—and all around, save watch and helmsman, hushed in sleep, one feels thankful to be away from cities or towns—from their fœtid atmosphere and discordant noise.

Shortly after crossing the line we saw a most lovely "argonaut," or "Portuguese man-of-war," as nearly all the nautili are called by sailors. It was the largest I had ever seen, its sails being over a foot above the water, and of a bright violet colour. It passed quite close to the side of the ship, and as we were going very slowly at the time, had opportunity of admiring its excessive beauty. With the exception of the Spirula, it is the only one among its species, the *dibranchiate cephalopods*, who possesses an outward shell, and was supposed by the ancients to have been the model from which man took his first idea of navigation.

A passenger on board ship must *make* occupation. To a man devoid of resources in himself I can honestly say—avoid ship life; and perhaps we had much to be thankful for, in that it pleased fate to bestow on us, in the shape of cook, one Thomas Smith, the most utter fool and spoiler of food I ever came across. His extreme incapacity gave us plenty to do, as not wishing to be poisoned we always made the bread. From bread making we soared to other flights, and if all trades fail, I think that either of us might take the billet we trained for in the *Rocket*.

Time somehow passes more rapidly at sea than in any other place: so little occurs to mark the days by, they seem positively to fly; and on finishing a journey, one is lost in astonishment at the manner it got so soon over.

We jogged quietly along, seldom averaging over seven hundred miles a week, and on the 1st of December, 1874, anchored in the harbour of Rio de Janeiro, the capital of Brazil.

CHAPTER II.

Description of Rio Janeiro—Recent improvements—The Corcovado—A Brazilian forest—Villa Isabella—Botanical gardens—The market—Stupidity of the post-office officials—Opposition of Brazilian priests to public education—Growth of Romanism in England—Leave Rio—Cobwebs on the La Plata—Monte Video—Hotel del Prado—Santa Lucia—The country—Extravagance of cleanliness and the price of soap—The Gaucho—Wretched misgovernment of Uruguay.

It would be difficult to do adequate justice, in merely attempting to describe the magnificent harbour of Rio de Janeiro. The artist only has power to convey an idea where mere description fails, and to the brush of a "Bierstadt" lies the task of truthfully delineating a harbour that, for size and beauty, is generally supposed to be the finest in the world.

Those who have seen Queenstown can get a faint idea of its general character, by magnifying the Irish harbour about ten times, diminishing its entrance to less than half, studding the vast expanse of sheltered water with innumerable palm-clad islands, surrounding it on all sides with lofty mountains covered to near their summit with the rank luxuriousness of tropical vegetation, and throwing up against the azure sky so fantastic an outline, that one becomes lost in amazement while contemplating a scene so full of beauty and yet so weird.

These distant mountains are called the Organs, possibly from their similarity to the pipes of that instrument, and are of extraordinary formation; the peaks running almost like the teeth of a comb, up and down the entire range. They are several hundred feet high, and quite inaccessible to the foot of man.

We found H.M.SS. *Albatross* and *Dart* in harbour, the former having only got in five days before us in her passage from Madeira. The *Egmont*, an old storeship, was in the act of being abolished, and H. did not feel particularly delighted when Capt. B., the senior officer, ordered him to send a working party for two days to assist in clearing her out.

Improvements much needed had been going on at Rio since my last visit, and that energetic monarch Pedro the Second was still busy in further utilizing and doing good.

Facility of locomotion had been increased, by the laying down of trams in all directions for street cars. The line of railway had been pushed on a considerable distance from its then terminus, and public schools had been opened for free education in more places than one.

The morning after our arrival, we were made aware at daybreak, by the most terrific cannonading, that it was the Emperor's *fête* day; at noon we were again reminded, and at sunset it was once more dinned into our tortured ears. However, the Brazilians have a worthy good monarch who unceasingly and unselfishly works for their benefit, and few crowned heads deserve such thundering applause more than the one for whose honour our slumbers had been so prematurely disturbed.

He opened a new stone pier at the principal landing-place in honour of the event, thus supplying a want long neglected, and much felt by all maritime visitors to his capital. We found letters waiting for us on board the *Egmont*, and among mine I discovered the purse I had lost while out shooting at St. Vincent. Before leaving, I had offered the contents as a reward should the purse be discovered and sent me. Twenty niggers had scoured the country after we sailed, and the Consul forwarded the result of their diligence by post.

The Navy and the British Merchant do not seem to "hit it off" at Rio. Whether the latter are too humble to take the initiative, and call on men their superiors in station, or whether they be so wedded to their dollar-bags that dinner-giving and gaiety might incommode them, it would be hard to say, but certainly no cordiality exists between the classes; and the latter seldom attempt the slightest hospitality or politeness to men who in their interests are compelled to serve for years on one of the most unhealthy and uninteresting stations we possess.

Mr. T., the Navigating-Lieutenant of the *Egmont*, was kind enough to put H. and myself down for admittance to a reading-room, with billiard tables and a bar attached to it, called "The English and American Club." It was well supplied with the periodicals and newspapers of both countries; but not being able to get either luncheon or dinner, it was rather an undertaking to go there, as it was at least two miles from the town, and three from the landing-place where we embarked. I visited it some three or four times, but only saw one member, who appeared astonished at a stranger's entrance, but who did not honour me with either attention or remark, after apparently satisfying himself that I was not likely to steal the papers.

One morning, shortly after daylight, I walked to the top of the "Corcovada," a small but exceedingly steep mountain, from which in clear weather the most perfect view of the harbour and surrounding country may be obtained. B., a Sub-Lieutenant, but occupying on board the proud position of "First Lieutenant" of the *Rocket*, came with me, and after being put down by a "tram car" near the foot of the mountain, we commenced our ascent.

The path led in a zigzag manner almost to the summit, by the most gradual of inclines. It was most beautifully kept, and completely shaded from any sun by the trees, whose branches, covered with creepers, orchids, and vegetable parasites of all descriptions, met far above our heads. A deep humming but not unpleasant sound, caused by the myriads of beetles, bull-frogs, and flying insects, sc prevalent in all Brazilian forests, accompanied us on our way, and occasionally a butterfly, of a size and brilliancy only to be met with in South America, fluttered gaily before our eyes.

Dense walls of vegetation, through which occasionally we got a glimpse of the distant sea, rose high on each side. Palm-trees of every variety, reared their tall and stately heads above the deep masses of green, bending gracefully to the sea breeze, just setting in, as if almost bowing it a welcome. The broad-leafed banana peeped modestly from the jungle, and the tree-fern struggled for existence mid the thickly piled masses of growth. Huge giant-like trees, towering above their fellows, were covered with a profusion of creepers to their highest boughs, from which they dropped in pendants, like long leaf-clad ropes, to the verdant depths beneath. A faint odour of musk and orange-blossoms seemed to float through the atmosphere, and the general sensuous influence of the whole scene made one instinctively long for cooling drinks, a grass hammock, and a fragrant cigar.

Half-way up, we came to a reservoir, prettily situated, and laid out with ornamental skill of no mean order. A cool and crystal torrent dashing down the mountain side, taking its last plunge over a large boulder of rock, was here arrested in its career, and from six large tanks made to receive it, conveyed through a covered aqueduct along the path we had come up, to the town of Rio, a grateful and wholesome supply for its many dwellers.

Farther on, we met a well-built and commodious summer-house, and from this spot the climbing part of our ascent commenced. It was nothing very dreadful, and we soon reached the top, 2272 feet above the level of the sea.

Fortune had not favoured us in the day she selected for our ascent, as a heavy mist drifting in from the ocean just as we arrived at the top pre-

UNIV. OF MICH.

A LIVELY SALMON.

See page 223.

vented our seeing much beyond our own noses; and had it not been for the exquisite beauty of the forest scenery we had passed through on our way up, our toilsome walk of over two hours would have finished with unmitigated disgust at our bad luck.

The city of Rio Janeiro being in itself somewhat low and crowded, its suburbs stretch in many directions. Among these, Tjuca seems the most favourite abode for business men, who gladly resort from their stores and counting-houses to its cool and shady heights 3316 feet above the level of the sea. Several hotels are generally in the hot weather quite full, and as there are charming swimming-baths, and the temperature is many degrees lower than in the town, it is not surprising that the people flock there. H. and myself went one afternoon, and half meditated on taking up our quarters at "White's Hotel," where we dined; but I got so bitten by a vicious blood-thirsty beast of a fly, called a "borrachuta," far worse than either Canadian "black fly," or African "mosquito;" and my friend, the captain, got so badly-cooked a dinner. that neither of us was inclined to carry out our half-formed intention.

Owing to work that had to be done on board, H. was unable to leave the ship for any length of time, and not caring to travel alone, having on a prior occasion gratified my curiosity by a couple of hundred miles' trip into the interior of the country, I remained during our whole stay in the vicinity of the town, amusing myself by drives on the various tramroads which radiated for many miles round Rio.

Villa Isabella was one of the places thus visited. An interesting drive of about six miles along a road, at times abounding on each side with daintily laid-out gardens and villas of the Brazilian gentry, while at others, it passed through parts of almost primitive jungle, affording a pleasing diversity of scene exceedingly charming.

A "matadero" which we passed, though hardly embellishing the beauty of the landscape, was singular in appearance and not devoid of interest, on account of its entirely un-European-like character. Long before we reached it, my attention was attracted by the thousands of vultures which seemed to be hovering over one particular spot. This turned out to be the establishment where all the animals required for the use of the town are executed. It occupied a considerable space, and in places large heaps of heads and horns lay drying in the sun.

The sky was darkened by these horrid birds, but not the slightest unpleasant odour tainted the air, though we passed sufficiently close to the ghastly heaps to have easily found it out, had these hideous yet most useful and necessary scavengers, failed in doing their duty.

The town of Villa Isabella, except in being beautifully situated, some height above the sea, exactly resembled Dickens's "City of Salem." Not a single house was to be seen, but a large plot of ground was laid out and staked off for future building. The names of the different streets in contemplation were already painted in a conspicuous manner on large boards, marking their position, and the distinct site of every edifice in this most embryo of towns was already most carefully and accurately put down.

It seemed to me that the ground selected was somewhat swampy for building, but with regard to effect and charm of position, hardly anything could have been more perfect, and I have no doubt that but a short time will elapse ere the young embryo will burst forth in full life, strength, and vigour.

Rio does not possess many places of much interest to the traveller. The Botanical Gardens are fairly kept, and have a fine avenue of cabbage-palms, but perhaps the market is best worth seeing of the whole, though much necessarily depends upon the time of year at which it is visited.

All kinds of tropical productions, and almost every variety of fruit, may here be obtained, but by no manner of means for nothing; indeed, the price of provisions, vegetables, fruit, and every kind of necessary, is most exorbitant.

A small mean-looking fish, of dark colour and about five pounds in weight, but whose Brazilian or Portuguese name I forget, they asked 12,000 Reas for (about 27 shillings), and most other things were pretty well in proportion. The prawns were the finest I had ever seen, many of them being over six inches long, and exceedingly delicious in either curry or salad. The small crab, with sharp spikes on the shoulder of his shell, large prominent eyes, and colour a light blue before boiling, can compete for excellence with its celebrated brother, the West Indian land-crab; and the *avocado*, or alligator pear, arrives at a perfection here not to be met with in any other part of the world.

Some of the hotels had fairly good cooking; the Hotel de Globe, where I generally dined, probably the best. For the rest of the town there is not much to be said. Everything is exceedingly dear. The beetles and humming-birds exhibited in the shops you can buy cheaper in either London or Paris. The best diamonds go to Europe, and those exposed for sale are generally "off colour'd" and most unmistakeably "Cape," and all things that are of interest, as being either peculiar to Brazil or manufactured in Rio, are to be had cheaper out of it.

The streets are narrow and crowded, the places of amusement, the Alcazar, etc., very second rate and French, and I was not sorry when our visit drew to a close.

We had much trouble with the post-office people, who were without exception the most utterly inefficient, useless, insolent, and ugly set of officials I ever came across. We had the very greatest difficulty in getting our letters from them, and the cool manner in which they lied was absolutely bewildering.

The tidings of an insurrection stirred up by the priests in the neighbourhood of Parahyba, and the fear of a demand for an English war-vessel near the seat of action, made us still more anxious to quit.

It appears that the Emperor, among his numerous improvements and reformations, has encouraged and fostered the growing demand for education among the lower classes, which the Roman Catholic priesthood have for so many years successfully suppressed and neglected. This has caused the latter gentry to kick rather over the traces, which his Majesty promptly endeavoured to arrest, by placing two of their ringleaders, who happened to be bishops, in durance vile, and has consequently raised a perfect clerical wasps'-nest round his royal ears.

He has also, with the full consent of his people, put the curb on many other priestly abuses far too numerous to enter upon.

We were getting very tired of the place. The scenery was certainly very lovely, but looking constantly even at the finest harbour in the world, with the thermometer at 85° in the shade, and not a breath of air before the arrival of the "doctor," a name given to a sea breeze which in the hot weather sets in every afternoon regularly, is apt to grow monotonous, and we were quite ready to clear out, which we eventually managed to do on the 11th of December, 1874.

Our run to Monto Video was for H.M.S. *Rocket* a good one, our best day being 143 miles.

On the afternoon of the 19th, we sighted the low coast of Uruguay, as it extended for miles and miles in one unbroken plain, with a few ranges of hills in the far off distance. The land was thickly interspersed with cattle and horses, and occasionally a low-built *ranche* betokened the habitation of their owners, but not a tree was to be seen anywhere.

After passing the little town of Maldonado, which we did early next morning, we were fairly in the great river La Plata, one of the largest in the world.

Rising in the far off Andes, 2210 miles from its mouth, it wends its way through some of the finest and most productive lands on the great continent it waters, and debouches into the South Atlantic at the part we had now entered.

The water became muddy and the current strong, but the most singular and peculiar characteristic of the river was the strange manner with which our rigging became completely covered with long gossamer-like cobwebs, betokening, according to some of the authorities on the subject, the close approach of the much dreaded "Pampero."

On the 20th of December we anchored off Monte Video, finding there H.M.SS. *Amethyst* and *Cracker.* A considerable quantity of merchant shipping lay in the harbour, many of them moored close to the shore, while others were anchored at least four miles off it. We were about to pick up our quarters among the former, but the senior officer in the *Amethyst* signalled for us "to close," and take up a billet close to him. We had to obey the order, and were consequently located at the inconvenient distance of almost two miles from the nearest landing-place, though only drawing eight feet of water.

Monte Video, a name taken from the small solitary hill overlooking the city, is a clean, well-built town; it possesses a few handsome buildings, and is laid out in blocks on the American plan. The principal streets have tramways in them, the cars four horses, and the fares moderate.

Why this system of cheap passenger traffic should

not be more generally adopted in our large towns I cannot conceive, as, if managed with the smallest amount of care, it would certainly pay the proprietors a handsome profit on their outlay, and be a considerable boon to the poorer classes of pedestrians into the bargain.

The English merchants have a comfortable club house, provided with papers, periodicals, billiard tables, and a bar. They invariably invite all officers of H.M. ships to become honorary members during their stay in harbour, and the officers on the station speak highly of their hospitality and kindness. At Buenos Ayres, the same good feeling exists between the classes, and it appears that only at Rio Janeiro is there any difference of opinion.

In a handsome square overlooked by the club, ornamented by trees, and possessing a fountain, every night, from eight to ten, plays a military band. The music is very dreadful, chiefly consisting of cymbals and big drum; but as the people are pleased and satisfied, what does it matter?

All the fair damsels put on their best attire, and thus armed for conquest in costumes varied and numerous, bright eyes glance, and looks are thrown such as the daughters of sunny Spain alone can send, and it is with regret one listens to the final crash of execrable torture, which warns the promenaders that the time has come for them to return home.

I had intended visiting Buenos Ayres, but our stay was so very short, and the weather so unsettled, it could not be managed; so with regret I had to relinquish the idea, and instead of taking my passage in the *Villa del Saluto*, for the capital of the opposite Republic, went with H. to the Hotel del Prado, a few miles from the town instead. This is the Uruguayan "Star and Garter," and was designed and built by a German, who amassed a large fortune in the country, and at that time inhabited it himself. After his death it became an hotel, and is now the chief resort for the upper classes of the town to dine and lunch at during the summer months.

The house was situated in the centre of a well-kept garden, and was approached by a handsome avenue of trees; but the general effect was to a certain extent marred by the quantity of execrable statues in stucco of all the gods and goddesses in heathen mythology, who displayed their misshapen limbs and features on every pedestal and at every corner it was possible to place them.

Next day I took the train to Santa Lucia, a small town some twenty-five or thirty miles from Monte Video. The engine and carriages were English, the former provided with a cow-catcher, a necessary appendage where the line is quite unprotected, and cattle as numerous as in Uruguay.

After leaving the town, we passed for some distance through the picturesque suburban residences of the gentry. They were flat-roofed villas, gaily decorated with the brightest colours, had pretty little well-kept gardens, with generally a statue or large ball of coloured glass by way of ornament, but which in reality spoiled, through its tawdry vulgarity, an otherwise very pleasing effect. They seemed quite toy-houses, beautifully clean (outside) and brilliant with paint, but far too small to be compatible with an Englishman's ideas of comfort; indeed, by no amount of ingenuity could one swing a cat in any of them.

The slowness of our progression gave ample time for inspecting the country, which extended far as the eye could reach in one vast gently-undulating plain, studded with cattle or cornfields, but bearing on all its uncultivated spots enormous crops of thistles

The abundance of this weed was quite surprising, and consisted chiefly of two kinds—one a species of creeper or undergrowth, and the other a large plant over six feet high, bearing a head with a bright blue flower on it as large as a moderate-sized artichoke, which indeed it greatly resembled.

Aloe, or cactus hedges were the only kind of protection the fields under cultivation had from cattle; and the corn, which was being gathered, was taken without a particle of straw, which remained on the field, fine stubble over two feet high, as cover for the partridges which abound here during the season.

The soil, where exposed by any cutting, was both deep and rich, and as from the excessive flat and level nature of the land all kinds of agricultural machines might easily be applied, any farmer with skill and capital could shortly acquire a fortune, the purchase of land, or mere rent of the farm, being comparatively speaking nothing; and the soil being so rich, that superphosphates, guano, or manure, are things unheard of.

Santa Lucia was a scattered sort of place, chiefly consisting of hotels. I got a fair luncheon at the Hotel Oriental—a capital omelet and an odd-tasted preserve of tomato. The water supply for Monte Video comes from here; but I was so plagued by flies that, finding no good-natured Moses to drive them away, I returned by the next train to my original quarters at the other Hotel Oriental in the Calle de Solis. It is a comfortable hotel, fairly clean, at least in comparison with other foreign hotels, and by far the best in Monte Video.

Cleanliness out of England, or away from hotels frequented and chiefly patronized by Englishmen, is simply not to be had in the world. I have been in many parts of it, entirely round, and in most of its corners, but have never yet met cleanliness of habits, person, and habitations combined, away from our egotistical selves.

Why this should be the case I cannot even hazard a conjecture. In some lands I have sojourned in, cleanliness is a part of the inhabitants' faith; but if they are clean in person, owing to the frequency of ablutions prescribed by their religious tenets, their other habits are filthy; while in others, the extraordinary value placed upon soap and water (for outsiders) shows that at any rate they recognise a virtue they do not seek to attain themselves.

On paying my bill at the Oriental I found I was charged two shillings and ten pence for a very small cake of scented soap, and three shillings and four pence a day for my cold bath.

Two singular and picturesque characteristics of

Uruguay must not be overlooked. Her military officer, and her *gaucho.* The former is chiefly noticeable for the excessive pegtopiness of his trousers. Red or white, they are alike bowed out to such an extent by some virile kind of crinoline, that, either coming or going, he resembled a young balloon, which his very small feet seemed quite insufficient to anchor to the ground. His appearance, though singular and almost grotesque, was hardly incongruous with the muliplicity of habiliments here met with, embracing as they do every costume in South America.

The *gaucho* really is a picturesque fellow, whether mounted on his mustang in ordinary working attire, his loose trousers fluttering in the breeze, his poncho streaming behind him, as galloping in full career he swings the lasso; or when, got up for purposes of effect, he comes into town a pompous dandy for his three days' spree. On the latter occasion he is very grand indeed. His hair, long as a woman's, is carefully combed out; his poncho is of the finest and most costly material; his sombrero of the smartest and most cavalier-like style, and his saddle, harness, stirrups and spurs, one mass of solid silver. I have never yet seen a costume more picturesque and graceful, than that of a well-turned-out *gaucho.*

Uruguay, though at present uncommonly shaky, may one day become a desirable country to live in. Its climate is healthy and temperate, its land fertile and cheap, and its chief products of hides, tallow, cotton, and wool, much sought after, yet most abundant. All European fruits and vegetables thrive under cultivation, and its water communication, both by river and sea, is almost the most perfect in the world; and yet with all these advantages, a resident of nine years' standing, a shrewd and sensible man, singularly capable of forming an unprejudiced opinion, told me that he would as soon think of throwing spare capital into the country, situated as it is at present, as he would dream of pitching it into the sea.

Notwithstanding all its natural advantages, which are numerous, it is so handicapped by a miserable Government, that industry becomes paralysed and life insecure.

The people to whom one looks for protection are the greatest robbers, and its rulers so many legalised thieves. Discontent prevails on all sides, constant rebellions are the consequence, and on either side the foreign settler, like the man between two stools, falls to the ground.

Should the party in revolt approach the Ranche his neutrality as a foreigner is an unavailing plea. The "he who is not with me is against me" style of argument prevails, and his cattle and horses are swept ruthlessly away. Should the Government troops be the visitors, his property is quite as certainly harried, on the excuse that it must be prevented from falling into the enemy's hands. An acknowledgment to that effect is invariably tendered with a promise to pay attached to it, but as the reimbursement is quite as invariably refused or indefinitely postponed, on the ground of there being no available funds for that purpose at present, the unfortunate settler is bound to lose on both sides.

Patriotism among Uruguayan legislators is as extinct as the dodo in Madagascar, and each man during his tenure of office merely seeks to feather his own nest.

This state of things cannot go on for ever. Brazil has had longing eyes on the rich provinces watered by the La Plata, and ere many years elapse she will certainly stretch forth and seize the ripe fruit only too willing to drop into her mouth; and the Uruguayans will surrender their nationality and insecurity for amalgamation and peace.

CHAPTER III.

Leave Monte Video—Coast of Patagonia—Port San Julian—Wild ostrich—The Tchuelches, or natives of Patagonia—Early discoverers—Stalking guanaco—Description of guanaco—A bad shot—Patagonian partridge—Wild fowl—Wide-awakes—Tale of a skunk—Leave San Julian—Possession Bay—More guanaco and ostrich—Death of a guanaco—A successful shot—Terrific effects of Express bullet.

On the 23rd of December we left Monte Video, and next day picking up a rattling fair wind, logged our greatest number of knots in an hour, *i.e.* ten: a very unusual rate of speed for the old "dummy." We were in great glee, and anticipated a wonderful run to Magellan. However, next day we had a gale in our teeth, a regular "pampero," or violent wind from across the pampas, and for the next four days we were knocking about under close-reefed top-sails in a heavy cross sea, that reminded us most unpleasantly of the weather we had experienced in the Bay of Biscay.

On the 3rd we sighted Cape Blanco. The weather was most unsettled; barometer low, and even the standard compass affected to such a degree that the needle jumped about in an erratic and uncertain fashion, which rendered it most difficult to steer by. The wind came strong from the south-west, and we shaped our course for Port Santa Cruz, to get shelter until the gale should have moderated.

Next morning, on approaching the land, we found that we would be unable to fetch the harbour, and being utterly incapable of doing anything against the strong southerly wind, ran up the coast for Port San Julian, a well-sheltered uninhabited inlet on the east coast of Patagonia, Lat. 49° 15′ S., and Long. 67° 42′ W. The seaboard here very much resembled that of Kent between Ramsgate and Margate. Perpendicular white cliffs, about three hundred feet high, form the coast line, and where any indentation occurred we were able to get glimpses of the country, which consisted of gently undulating plains, covered with short herbage, something similar at a distance to park land at home. A few small patches of short thick scrub were the only cover, and not a tree or mountain was to be seen.

As we neared the inlet, several distant mountains of considerable magnitude appeared in view, all singularly flattened out at apparently the same elevation above the sea. Some extended in long ranges for miles, forming plains of table-land on their summits; while others ran up in conical forms, but with the apex of the cone cut off, to make a diminutive plateau in uniformity with the longer ranges about them: but every hill, no matter how rugged or precipitous its sides might be, invariably exhibited the same flat-topped peculiarity.

On the 5th of January, 1875, we reached Port San Julian. It was rather ticklish work entering the harbour, no chart of it being supplied, and the weather still squally and uncertain. A long reef uncovered at low water ran for about a mile across the entrance. after which we had to work over a bar of sand on which at one time the leadsman reported only ten feet of water, *i. e.*, one foot more than the *Rocket*'s draught.

A heavy squall, against which the engines were powerlesss to force us, suddenly broke down, and, though not at our intended anchorage, we were compelled to "let go" until it was over.

In half an hour it cleared up and we were again able to get under weigh, and again a severe squall compelled us to anchor before we had steamed two hundred yards. Again we made an effort, and this time anchored off "Sholl point," so called from a monument being erected there over the grave of a lieutenant of that name belonging to a surveying ship.

The weather with unusual capriciousness suddenly cleared up, and four ostriches being seen close to the ship, H. and self got our rifles and set out after them.

The ground was most unfavourable for stalking: we not knowing exactly where the birds were, they saw us before we saw them, their long necks enabling them, even when lying down, to command a very considerable extent of country. They did not appear much alarmed, and looked at us for some time before they moved slowly away, leaving, however, one of their number to keep a watch over our movements. So unembarrassed, indeed, was their exit, that I fancied, if we waited until the sentry had crossed a little ridge to which he was slowly making, that by running hard after he had disappeared, we might get a shot at him before he had gone many yards. We accordingly waited patiently until he had got over the ridge, and then ran as hard as we were able for our shot, expecting to find him close to us. However, it was not to be, as, much to our disgust, we saw he had joined the main body, who were by this time quite half a mile away and still going on, their long necks poked clumsily out before them, as they covered the ground at a pace which put all idea of pursuit out of the question.

A little further on we saw a herd of guanaco, but too far off to do anything with, and as it was rapidly getting dark we retraced our way to the ship. On our way back I got a snap shot at some animal about the size of a wolf; but he ran into some scrub, from which it was useless at this time of the night and without dogs to attempt to dislodge him.

Though devoid of either water or inhabitants, Port San Julian must always command a certain interest, as being mixed up with the early discovery of the country.

Magellan, three hundred and fifty years ago, anchored at and named this port. Starting from it, the pilot Serrano explored the coast to the southward and discovered a river, which he named Santa Cruz, where also he unfortunately lost his ship. Magellan remained at Port San Julian and Santa Cruz from April till October, 1520, when he sailed southward and discovered the straits that bear his name. Two months after his arrival at Port San Julian, a man of gigantic stature appeared on the beach, larger and taller than any of his crew; and shortly afterwards eighteen natives arrived, dressed in cloaks of skins and shoes of guanaco hide, which made huge foot-marks, whence they were called "Patagonés," or "Large feet," by the Spaniards; and thus originated in a nickname, the name of the country of Patagonia.

The "Tehuelches," or Patagonians, have not by any manner of means feet in reality so extraordinarily large as those ascribed to them by the Spaniards. All Indian races have naturally small feet; and Musters in his interesting work states that on exchanging boots he found their feet to be smaller and better shaped than his own. On certain occasions, and in wet or snowy weather, hide overshoes are worn similar to our galoshes, which so disenchanted Leech's lover in *Punch*, that seeing his fair one's foot-prints in the sand,—horror-stricken he exclaimed, "Beetle-crushers, by Jove!" and fled incontinently to distant climes; so might the early Spaniards have been mistaken about the Tehuelches, and the term "patagon," or large feet, as applied to the inhabitants by their early discoverers, really be a complete misnomer, owing to the extra covering on their "potro" boots.

Drake next visited Port San Julian in 1578, and, curiously enough, as Magellan had in this place put to death two, and marooned a third of his captains who had mutinied, so also Sir Francis Drake executed Mr. Doughty, who chose rather to be beheaded than to be put on shore.

In the year 1581 Sarmiento was sent from Spain

with two thousand five hundred men, in twenty-three ships, to found new colonies in the Straits and Patagonia. On his way back his ship was captured by the English, the colonists were forgotten, and five years afterwards Thomas Cavendish, visiting the Straits, found at Port Famine twelve men and three women alone surviving. Starvation and disease had killed the rest.

In the reign of Charles II. Sir John Narborough took possession of the country near Port Desire in the name of the king. In the eighteenth century Byron and Wallis visited Patagonia, and again Spain made an effort to colonize; Francesco, and Antonio Viedma were sent in command. Antonio selected Port S. Julian as the site of another colony, and from it explored to the foot of the Cordillera. No further knowledge was gained of the interior until the survey of the *Beagle* described by Fitzroy and Darwin, and lately the manners and customs of the natives by Musters.

The morning after our arrival I started at daybreak, taking with me Martin and Major, the former happy in carrying my gun and the latter delighted at once more being on shore.

We had a long and tedious walk for many miles, over sandy and pebbly ground thickly covered with small prickly shrubs and stunted evergreens. I had selected this line of country the previous evening; having perceived from the top of a high hill that it contained the only cover of any extent within reach, and that being apparently rushy in places, it might probably hold a little water.

The ground was covered in all directions with the tracks and droppings of many animals. I picked up several lamellated shells of armadillo, and some ostrich eggs, and though we saw no spoor of any carnivorous beasts, we perceived most unmistakeable evidences of their occasional presence, from the skeletons of guanaco, whose bones were scattered in a manner that showed quite plainly what had been the way they perished.

Finding that it was hopeless to continue in this valley and that the rushes only grew in sandy patches and were quite devoid of moisture, we ascended to the higher land, and shortly after discovered a herd of guanaco quietly feeding about a mile off.

The ground was dreadfully unpromising for approaching them; however, the herd was to windward, which gave me a slight chance, and, leaving Martin in charge of my dog, I commenced to stalk, crawling on hands and knees, and taking advantage of every bush, though none of them were much larger than a cabbage. Gradually and with the utmost caution I worked my way within four hundred yards of where they were feeding. There were five females, four young ones, and one very large male, whose head was fully nine feet from the ground. He was a noble-looking fellow, large in the body as a fair-sized cow, and meat enough on him for the entire ship's company, could I only succeed in bowling him over.

I saw there was not a twig to conceal me any further; so, taking out my field-glass, I watched quietly in hope that they might take it into their head to feed up to where I was lying hid. My rifle was an Express, and very uncertain at anything over two hundred yards.

The guanaco (*Auchenia Huanaca*) is a singular-looking animal, and may perhaps be best described by analogy. The legs are like a deer; his feet like a camel, only very much smaller; his barrel (that of a full-grown male) as large as a cow's, but resembling in shape a sheep, and covered with a long light-red wool; his neck rises straight and somewhat ungracefully from his shoulders, like a llama's; and his tail is bushy, like a Cape sheep's. Their action when galloping is clumsy, and though they cover the ground at a great pace, from the straight and awkward way they carry their long necks, which are poked clumsily out before them, and their lolloping stride, they appear to be going much slower than they actually are.

They are, however, fine animals, not particularly shy, and well worth a sportsman's attention, though I believe when mounted it is easy enough to kill them.

All this time the herd were quietly feeding away from me, so my only chance lay in trying to wriggle within shot. I commenced my crawl, got about forty yards nearer, and was then found out. The does immediately formed group, placing their young ones in the centre, and commenced neighing fiercely, while the buck, detaching himself from the herd, reconnoitred my position, neighing and chattering most vociferously the whole time. The does then moved slowly away at a gentle trot, halting from time to time and looking round, the buck remaining well in rear guarding them from the danger, and rather circling round, as if to get my wind, evidently being bothered to make out what so unusual an object on his feeding-ground could possibly be. The chances are a hundred to one he never saw a human creature before, the country being, as far as we could judge, entirely devoid of water, and consequently unable to support the wandering tribes of Tehuelches who inhabit Patagonia. As for vessels, nothing but the stress of weather while in the absolute vicinity of the port would ever induce them to call here.

The herd soon trotted away over the brow of a little hill and were out of sight, and as my inquisitive friend was about to follow their example, I let drive, and; much to my satisfaction, saw him go over. He immediately recovered himself, and, at a slinging gallop, made for the herd, now some distance ahead. My feet, unaccustomed to much exercise on board ship, were blistered from my long walk; my right leg, which I smashed two years ago, had broken down, and I was quite unequal to following up the wounded guanaco; however, I mustered up a "spurt" for the occasion, and ran on as fast as I was able, to cut him off; the rest having circled to my left, and the buck being quite unable to reach them.

It was hard work, but I succeeded; and turning away for a line of his own, he gave me two more shots, at from five to seven hundred yards, both of which I missed, and, to my inexpressible mortification, saw him go away, slowly ceitainly, but still much too far for a cripple to think of following him up, and much to my disgust I hobbled away towards the ship, not at all certain of getting there without assistance.

On our way back Major found and put up some very large partridges, one of which I managed to bag. He was of a dusky-brown colour, had short wings, long neck, remarkably small head, no tail, and about the size and weight of a well-fed hen pheasant, and proved excellent eating a day or so afterwards.

On getting near the coast, I picked up a goose, a few wild duck, and several banduria, the latter a large and handsome species of ibis; but I was precious glad of a pair of slippers, and enjoyed my bath uncommonly when I got on board.

In the afternoon a party went away with the seine, under charge of the gunner; but not appearing to understand the business they caught no fish, though there must have been quantities about, judging from the number of birds we saw diving after them, and the shoals of porpoise cruising inside the harbour. H. and self, after visiting the seining party in the galley, sailed down to a small island about five miles from our anchorage, which was literally alive with sea-birds.

The quantities of wide-awakes even exceeded those at Ascension, and anyone who has ever witnessed the celebrated "wide-awake fair" at that most abominable of islands will be able to judge what numbers of them must have been here. The ground was so thickly covered with their eggs, that it was quite impossible to walk about without treading on them, and the sky was absolutely darkened by the clouds of birds who, alarmed at our approach, were wheeling and screaming in frightened circles round our heads.

They are pretty, graceful little birds; pure white body, with a black cap and forked tail, about the size of a golden plover, and have a flight not unlike them. Their eggs, both in size, colour, and taste, resemble the lapwing's. We took away about a bushel, and found them excellent for cakes and omelettes, as well as eaten cold, hard boiled. They are a species of tern, and it was interesting to watch them dashing from a height into the water, throwing up a splash like the rise of a large trout in their headlong dive after their fishy prey. Another island was inhabited by shags, both black and white breasted, and quantities of geese, duck, and all kinds of wild fowl, were to be found everywhere. We killed a good many different kinds during the afternoon, and fired at a couple of magnificent black-necked swans (*Cygnus nigricollis*). On our way back, H. landed with the dogs to look for guanaco, and my feet being still tender, I remained in the boat and shot wild fowl of various descriptions as we coasted along.

Failing to get within shot of some guanaco which he saw, he vented his rage on a skunk, which he made Martin carry down to the boat, and as long as I live never shall I forget the odour. Major, who was with him, had been permitted to retrieve it, and smelt as badly as the "varmint" itself, and everything that even went near the brute became tainted with its dreadful smell.

The whole ship stank, as he very foolishly brought

it on board, and the galley retained its stench for days, though carbolic and other disinfectants were freely used. In the cabin we burned brown paper, pastiles, and sprinkled carbolic acid. Poor Major was rubbed with train oil and sulphur, to, if possible, deaden the smell; but it was weeks before the "bouquet de skunk" became entirely eradicated.

Early next morning we went after guanaco again. H. got a shot, which he missed, and they did not come near me. I was much struck with the enormous quantities of huge fossil oyster-shells which we saw everywhere; on all the hills they were strewn thickly, and even on Mount Wood, nearly a thousand feet above the level of the sea, they were lying in hundreds; while in the sea, at the very lowest water, we were unable to find any live ones. On the 7th of January we left Port San Julian, and after experiencing all kinds of unsettled weather, the wind often shifting all round the compass in a single day, we anchored in Possession Bay, off Tandy Point, on the 10th of January, about thirty miles from Cape Dungeness, and well inside the Straits of Magellan.

The aspect of the country was somewhat similar to that in the vicinity of Port San Julian, except that the herbage was thicker, more luxuriant, and evidently far better feeding-ground. The land was undulating, and consisted of a succession of small hills, with occasional patches of what would be in winter swampy ground, but which were now perfectly dry, and only marked by the luxurious growth of grass, which was at least four feet high in parts of them.

Not a single tree was to be seen, and far off in the distance, across the pampas, were lofty ranges of mountains flattened into table-land on the summit, and of similar appearance to those we had already remarked more to the northward. H. and self went on shore as early as possible, and after some little difficulty in landing, in consequence of the long extent of beach and shallow water occasioned by the tide being out, succeeded in settling our camp for the day, and lit a fire for the boat's crew to cook by during our absence.

We had not gone many hundred yards before the innumerable paths made by guanaco (whose disposition in this respect, *i.e.*, that of following a leader on the line of march, strongly resembles that of sheep) convinced us we were in a country abounding with game, and almost immediately afterwards, by way of corroborating the idea, we saw a large troop of ostriches, who were however far too wary to allow us to get within shot. As we went farther inland guanaco appeared all round. Singly and in herds they were grazing in all directions, nor did those who saw us seem particularly alarmed at our presence, for, after having apparently satisfied their curiosity by a prolonged stare, they recommenced their grazing as if nothing had happened to disturb the usual serenity of their existence.

We got within four hundred yards of one herd before they showed any alarm, and on lying flat down were surprised at their actually approaching us, an old male neighing fiercely, stamping his feet, and always some distance in advance. He was much larger than any of the others and of a darker colour, his head in particular being more massive and coarser in appearance.

We remained quiet, hoping their curiosity would induce them to come still nearer; but something happening to alarm them in another quarter, some of the herd took to flight, and fearing we should lose our shot, we both fired, and both missed, when they were about three hundred yards distant.

Men missing a fair shot invariably find an excuse for their clumsiness, and I certainly ascribe the fault to my Express rifle, whose shooting at anything over two hundred yards is faulty in the extreme.

I aimed with the greatest care and caution, resting on my elbows, and can only say that with an ordinary service rifle I have more than once put twenty shots running on a smaller target and at a greater range. An Express is the best of weapons for a short range at dangerous game, but is not to be depended on at anything over one hundred and fifty yards.

On returning to camp for our breakfast, we heard that another party from the ship had been more successful, and had succeeded in getting a guanaco, and catching a young ostrich alive; so sending some men to assist in carrying it to the boats, we started off in an opposite direction to try our luck anew.

The game on our fresh beat was by no means as numerous as on the ground we had travelled over in the morning; and though we saw several guanaco, they were generally alone, very wary, and seemed to be young males, not yet sufficiently dignified to be trusted with the duties and responsibilities of a harem.

After walking some miles without being able to get close enough to risk a shot at any of them, we agreed to separate at the foot of a range of hills, so that by each taking a different side, one of us might get a chance at the quarry disturbed by the other.

For over an hour I tramped along without seeing anything except a couple of wolves and some foxes; the latter were very numerous, and later on we saw still more of them at all the harbours along this part of the coast until we reached Punta Arena.

The spoors of many wild animals crossed my path, chiefly puma and wolf, and somewhat despondent from our bad luck in the morning, and seeming to starve in the midst of plenty, the traces of game both from tracks and droppings being so very plentiful, I was thinking of retracing my way to camp, when through my glasses, on a distant hill, I observed a guanaco feeding by himself, and on examining the ground carefully, found that it was tolerably favourable for a stalk.

Leaving Martin with my spare gun and Major, I set off; and having taken bearings with great care, managed my ground so that I got within one hundred and fifty yards of him, without either seeing the guanaco or being suspected myself, and then lying quite flat I wriggled on both elbows to a slightly rising ground where I expected to get my first view, and where I got it.

The ground was covered with small but needle-like thorns, which went through my light tweed shooting-coat as if it had been paper; elbows and knees were like a pin-cushion and bleeding freely, but I do not think I knew it or felt the slightest pain, as I watched this noble-looking animal quietly grazing at little over one hundred yards from where I lay panting with excitement and fatigue.

To get an inch nearer without discovery was an impossibility, and not daring to risk a shot in my present breathless and excitable condition, I remained motionless watching his movements and hoping he would come a little nearer.

He was feeding quietly, occasionally scratching himself, but being almost broadside on did not lessen the distance, and having quite recovered my breath I raised myself on my elbow to take aim.

He saw me instantly, and uttering the usual shrill neigh of alarm and challenge, half turned to where I lay; the movement was favourable, and the same instant my Express bullet crashed through his shoulder, smashing the bone completely, but not sufficiently high to pierce the body or cause instant death; and plunging madly forward, he galloped and stumbled some five hundred yards down the hill, where he lay down, and without a struggle permitted me to put him out of pain with my hunting-knife.

Sending Martin to the camp for help, I lighted my pipe and had a nice quiet smoke. Major, and the dead guanaco, formed a picture in the foreground, while far away in the distance stretched these grand unconfined plains, extending into boundless space, one great undulating meadow, inconceivable in extent and alive with game.

Shortly afterwards I had the good fortune to see H. and a couple of men in the distance. I fired a few shots in the air to attract them, and was exceedingly glad when they joined me, not being at all confident in "Mr. Martin's" powers of finding the spot again, and not relishing the idea of being left by myself half the night.

Having cleaned the guanaco, which proved to be a young buck about three years old, we set to work to drag him to the camp which was about four miles off, by a couple of dog-chains round the hind-legs; but afterwards getting more men, we slung him on an oar and eventually got him on board, where, minus head and interior, he weighed one hundred and eighty pounds.

In firing signals, one of my cartridges in the shotgun burst in the breech, and gave me a nasty burn in the wrist, driving in grains of unconsumed powder in a manner which has slightly tattooed me for life, and may in the event of a disputed identity help to prove me—myself.

Having abused the Express rifle as a weapon for guanaco-shooting at long ranges, I must now testify to its truly terrific powers when the bullet gets well home, as it did in the instance I have just narrated. On examining the guanaco next day, I was astonished at the terrible wound produced by so light a ball, the large bone of the shoulder just below the socket having not only been broken to bits, but the pieces themselves actually driven through the thick hide (thicker if anything than a bullock's) on the opposite side, where they came through with the ball in several small holes, covering a space a little larger than the palm of my hand.

CHAPTER IV.

Gregory Bay—Camp out—Duck-shooting in the Straits of Magellan—A quiet little lough—Hard work for Major—Contents of the bag—Elizabeth Island—Sold—Upland geese—Santa Magdalena—Laredo Bay—Black-necked swan—Punta Arenas—Don Enrique—Gold and Coal—Friendly relations with the natives—Ladies of Patagonia—Chus—Terra del Fuego—The Fuegans—A Chilian feed—Scenery in the Straits of Magellan—Williwaws—Extraordinary growth of moss—Ladies of Terra del Fuego—Seals.

Early in the morning of the 12th of January, we left Possession Bay, and after passing through the "first narrows,"—the country on the Patagonian side much resembling what we had already seen, while that of Terra del Fuego was more stony, barren, and cheerless,—we anchored the same afternoon in Gregory Bay, and shortly afterwards H. and myself, taking with us my tent and canteen (both of which I can recommend if portability be an object, though of course more comforts are obtained by more weight), set off to camp out on the banks of a small river some six miles from our anchorage, and where we hoped, on the principle of the early bird, to get good sport the next morning.

After pitching our tent and rigging up a sail for a couple of the boat's crew, and Martin and the steward who remained with us, we collected firewood and dried guanaco dung, the latter proving excellent fuel for the canteen stove; and, after a mess of guanaco hash for all hands, turned in and slept most comfortably, though it was blowing half a gale of wind all night. From the exposed position in which we were placed, which enabled an unusually strong breeze to act freely on the tent, I was most gratified at finding the next morning that it stood successfully so severe an ordeal.

Next morning, a little before daylight, I sounded the "rouse," and after a cup of hot cocoa, H. and I started along the banks of the little stream, which ran a few yards from our encampment. The country we shot over consisted chiefly of a line of small hills, making a well-watered valley between them and Gregory Range—a high and long line of mountains some seven miles distant, rather rugged and precipitous on the sides, but flat-topped, with apparently table-land on the summit.

A few stunted bushes grew along the coast line, but nowhere else, the country being either marsh or pampas, while the low hills were plentifully covered with califate berries (*Berberis axifolia*), and wild celery, which afford at this time of the year the principal food of the upland goose.

A bird so fed we discovered afterwards formed a dish well worthy of notice.

Little seemed to be stirring in the early dawn, and for the first half-hour a stray snipe, and a couple of crafty-looking foxes returning from their nocturnal rambles, were all we met. The ground was well-marked with guanaco paths, though we saw nothing of them. Shortly afterwards we entered a thick bed of long rank grass and water-weeds, covering some swampy ground, through the centre of which percolated a small sluggish stream. Here the fun commenced, and for about twenty minutes we got some of the prettiest duck-shooting imaginable, the birds rising singly and in pairs, and affording most excellent sport.

Major retrieved them very creditably, and after picking up a snipe, and getting a few very long shots at geese, we passed over a hill, from the brow of which we saw a small lagoon completely covered with wild fowl of all descriptions. Sea-gulls and wide-awakes hovered in hundreds over the water, on whose bosom floated in stately pride two magnificent black-necked swans; while numerous flocks of duck and teal disported and plumed themselves on its tranquil and sunlit depths.

A more beautiful sight I have seldom witnessed than this quiet little lough, so seldom disturbed by man in these unfrequented wilds of Southern Patagonia.

Being pressed for time, we were unable to contemplate its charms for many minutes, and, rapidly descending, soon altered its peaceful character by rapid discharges at the geese and duck who came flying round us. The edges of the lake were covered with floating lilies, and as the ground near it was soft mud, merely covered with a thick matting of aquatic plants, which were only strong enough to support a man's weight in certain parts, we were unable to get many of the birds that fell in the water, the thin lace-work of weeds preventing Major from swimming. We constantly went up to our waists through these plants, into the soft slush they covered, but had some exceedingly pretty shooting, which far more than compensated for our wetting.

Unfortunately we were obliged to be back at the camp by nine o'clock. Had we continued shooting all day, our list I am confident would have been something worth recording. As it was, our two men were quite satisfied with their load; and considering that we had some miles to march back to the camp, and that we packed up, struck tents, and embarked by 9 A.M., I think our bag, for a before-breakfast one—consisting of seventeen ducks, three geese, five snipes, five large water-hens (*Fulica chilensis*), one teal, and a grebe—was not a bad one. Could we have picked up all we knocked over, it would have been considerably larger; but at any rate it is sufficient to give an idea of what might have been done had we been enabled to remain for a whole day instead of only for a few hours. On our way back we crossed some plains quite covered with califate berries, and saw several large flocks of geese feeding on them; but they were much too wary to allow us to get within shot.

The ship having dropped down from her anchorage (close to a long isthmus at the head of the bay) to pick us up, we passed through the "second narrows," some nine miles long and from three to five broad, and went on to Elizabeth Island, where we expected to get the cream of Magellan shooting, but where we were doomed to be bitterly disappointed.

This island, named after our virgin queen by Sir Francis Drake, is about eight miles long, and seldom more than one broad. It is composed of ranges of heights extending in ridges in the direction of its length, the highest hill, on the north-east side, being one hundred and seventy feet above the sea. The sides are precipitous, and at the time we visited it, some half-dozen dried up lagoons constituted the only signs of fresh water. The hills were covered with berries of various kinds, and wild celery grew in profusion everywhere, affording excellent feeding for the swans and geese who visit it at various seasons for breeding purposes.

We heard such accounts of the number of geese killed here on different occasions by ships visiting the island, that we went on shore regularly prepared for slaughter. We brought several sacks which we expected to fill—the ship's company, some of whom had been here before in the *Nassau* and other surveying vessels, knowing the capabilities of the island, anticipated fresh rations for some days—and visions of *foi gras*, which was not only to last the entire commission, but to be given away wholesale, crossed our eager imagination.

"*L'homme propose*," etc.—the birds had all flown; and these grand anticipations ended in our only killing three geese. We were just a fortnight late; and the island, which appears to be inhabited in rotation during the summer months by these different birds for a nursery, was now occupied by immense flocks of tern (the wide-awake), whose eggs and young ones were in thousands at a point not far from where we landed. We got enough fresh eggs to keep us in omelettes, and to serve for other culinary purposes for some time, but it was a poor compensation for our disappointment concerning the wild geese.

These geese, commonly called "upland," to distinguish them from the "kelp," or coast goose, are the very handsomest of their species; and though I have shot many different kinds in China (which abounds with all sorts of wild fowl), as well as in other parts of the world, I never yet met any which could compare with them in personal appearance. Quite as large as the ordinary wild goose of Europe, they are distinguished by a more gamey look, and a far more brilliant plumage. The head and bill are smaller, the breast is covered with feathers very like those on a cock grouse, and exhibiting the same glossy sheen so noticeable in a healthy bird; the head and neck are of a delicate brown; the underneath part of the wing pure white; the upper, white and indigo black; the latter feathers in the sunshine taking the brilliant colouring seen in the plumage of a magpie or mallard.

Many other islands in the Straits of Magellan are during the breeding-season thus occupied, and to the innumerable foxes who frequent the mainland may be ascribed the reason that the birds wisely resort to those sea-protected abodes to escape their ravages.

Passing close to Santa Magdalena, an island covered with penguins, and having traces of the recent visit of some whaling or sealing vessels, whose old casks and useless spars were scattered about the beach, we anchored at Laredo Bay, where we entered on our first experience of wooding. A profusion of excellent drift wood for firing purposes was lying along the beach, and in a short time our decks were piled with huge stacks in every direction.

The country here began to change in appearance, and the first signs of wooded land showed themselves.

A large plain of high grass, with a few swampy places in it, lay opposite our anchorage, and in it we killed a few brace of wild duck and snipe. A mile across it was situated a large circular lagoon about two miles in diameter, on which were almost always eight or a dozen black-necked swans; they, however, carefully remained in or about the centre. The sides of the lake were partly wooded, and the scenery very pretty; clumps of timber being scattered on the hills resembling ornamental planting, so admirably were they placed by nature with regard to picturesque effect. The ground was covered with thick herbage well adapted for horse and cattle pastures, and the sheltered little valleys running towards the lake were covered with all kinds of flowers and berries, chiefly black and red currant.

Outside these wooded and wind protected spots, the country was bleak and desolate, and ran in one vast undulating pampa far away to some distant snow-capped mountains; dreary, uninteresting, covered with patches of tussac grass and clumps of moss, through which we sank above our knees, and utterly devoid of game.

A couple of Chilians had in charge a considerable number of horses belonging to the settlement at

Sandy Point which were being summered here, and we also saw two encampments or "toldos" of the Patagonians. They resembled gipsy huts in England in shape, only guanaco hides were substituted for the usual canvas covering used at home. *Àpropos* of guanaco, the one I shot at Possession Bay was excellent eating; it had dark flesh, like Highland mutton, and tasted something like veal. As fresh meat was utterly unprocurable, and owing to the steward getting drunk at Monte Video we had left harbour without any sheep (a great sell, as they only cost six shillings apiece there), the guanaco was a perfect god-send — soups, steaks, haunch, hashed, boiled and roast; in fact, in every conceivable form we consumed our friend, and the dogs came in for a share of meat and scraps which I have no doubt they considered a very favourable addition to their usual diet of ship's biscuits and chicken-bones.

A severe gale of wind delayed us a day longer at Laredo than we first intended, which quieted down towards evening. A short passage of a few hours enabled us to reach the Chilian Colony of Punta Arenas, named after a sandy point near which it is built, and by which name it also is not unfrequently known. A Chilian man-of-war, the *Chacabuca*, commanded by Captain Enrique Simpson, was lying at anchor, being on her way to place some pyramids for observation purposes on Cape Dungeness; and her captain kindly constituting himself master of the ceremonies, rendered our stay at the Settlement, through his exceeding kindness and hospitality, unusually jolly and pleasant.

Punta Arenas is a penal settlement, but has various colonists of different nationalities, all of whom are given grants of land by the Government on declaring their intention of fencing them in and undertaking their cultivation. This land becomes *bonâ fide* their own property on these conditions being complied with. The inhabitants, all told, muster about fifteen hundred, and live in small wooden houses with shingle roofs. The town is laid out on the principle of all Spanish-American ones, and has places marked out for future greatness, in squares and *plazás*, but which at present look somewhat straggling and unfinished. The military element consists of a small guard of soldiers; and as none of the convicts are very desperate characters, and are allowed almost perfect liberty under certain restrictions, and the natives who approach the settlement for purposes of barter are well disposed and friendly, their duties can hardly be termed onerous.

The settlement is ruled by a governor, his Excellency at present being Señor Don D., a shrewd, intelligent Chilian, who, though quite recently appointed, will, I feel certain, soon develop many resources at present lying dormant, having far less of the fatal *mañana* in his disposition than the generality of his countrymen. He was exceedingly good-natured, placed his house at our disposal, and kindly gave us the run of his stud.

Situated in the centre of the Straits of Magellan, and possessing a coal mine of considerable dimensions (though badly worked, and at present producing an inferior quality of coal) Punta Arenas may at any time make a sudden jump into prosperity. No shafts of any depth have as yet been sunk, and there is every reason to suppose that a stratum of superior quality exists, should they but take the trouble of working down on it.

Gold has been found in paying quantities in nearly all the small streams in the immediate vicinity of the town, and the Governor showed me a small portion, of great purity, which in a short time he had collected out of one of them himself. That other metals exist I have not the slightest doubt, and should coal, which is of course the first qualification towards success, only be properly worked, and prove of a superior quality to that already produced, all the other advantages to the colony will necessarily follow; and situated on the high seas between Europe and the west coast of South America, a prospector could hardly pitch upon a more favourable spot for an outlay of capital. With the Tehuelches the colonists do a very considerable trade, the former easily recognising the benefits of having a ready sale for their guanaco skins and ostrich feathers; and being quite alive to the advantages of breech-loaders and gunpowder, over the bolas and spear, are peaceable and well conducted. Both parties are amicable in their relations and willing to conciliate, so that each may obtain the benefit of trade, and a considerable amount of cordiality exists between them. Guanaco robes are made out of the skins of the young guanaco when they are only a few days old, the full-grown animal's hide being in every respect as tough and coarse as a bullock's.

A large tribe had left the day previous to our arrival, but a few remained either to complete their purchases or to finish a quantity of skin robes, at which we found some of their women employed when we visited them.

They were slightly above the average height of European females, but much broader across the shoulder and back, though without the slightest appearance of being fat. Their limbs were beautifully formed on massive proportions, their flesh hard and firm; but their features were quite as ugly as the Southern Chinese, to whose low-bridged noses, and ugly long eyes, their own had a remarkable similarity. Their hair was black and coarse, confined round the forehead by a fillet, which gave the skull a peculiar conical appearance; their teeth were beautifully white and regular; their skin a light brown; but they were all so filthily dirty that it might have been almost any colour beneath the mask of grime with which they were covered. The children were, if possible, more dirty than their parents, and more unprepossessing savages I have seldom come across. What their behaviour may be, away from the temptations of civilization and strong drink, I cannot pretend to say; but all the tribes who visit Punta Arenas, if they have any morality, invariably leave it behind them.

Having arranged a shooting-party, for which the Governor provided horses and a guide, H., myself, the Chilian captain, and Dr. P., a young Cornishman in the Chilian service, started for the day; but though we rode as far as the Rio Negro, with the exception of a few wild duck and some banduria, we killed nothing.

The country being thickly wooded near the settlement, we were obliged to keep for some miles to the sea coast, where, as little in the shape of game could be expected, our Chilian friends, who had lately seen some Indian hunting at Rio Santa Cruz, amused themselves in describing and illustrating the mysteries of the Tehuelches' circle formed for driving guanaco and ostrich. When completed and sufficiently narrow, the magic word *chus* is given, upon which, with loud yells, the warriors armed with the "bolas" rush upon their encircled prey. Our horses appeared perfectly acquainted with this familiar sound, as at each "chus" given they started off at full speed, which was anything but pleasant over the log-encumbered ground, as we were seated in high wooden saddles, with stirrups formed out of great balks of timber, each of them at least seven pounds in weight, and much larger than a quartern loaf. On emerging from the forest, we got to some pampas land, which was covered in many places with a very pretty evergreen, having a leaf something like a rhododendron, but bearing a bright red pendulous flower growing in clusters. Nothing could be more ornamental or more adapted for park growth at home; and as the weather here is infinitely severer than any experienced in England, there would be little fear of its not thriving in many exposed situations at home, where the more delicate rhododendron fails to flourish.

In conversing about Patagonia and Terra del

Fuego with Captain S., who having been lately on a government survey of both coasts was naturally well acquainted with the subject, he gave me a good deal of information about them.

The Chilians claim both lands, and point to the ancient maps drawn up by their early Spanish ancestors in proof of the country having been formally annexed by Spain many years ago. For similar reasons Buenos Ayres claims Patagonia, and both nations pay rations of cattle to native chiefs, whom they endow with honorary rank in their respective armies.

A Frenchman who commenced his career with Jules Gerrard, "The lion slayer," had lately been prospecting in Fuego and its neighbouring isles; and getting some people to join him, had appareled them in fantastic attire, and gone, after the bombastic manner of his countrymen, to conquer or to die; having obtained, by some means or another, immense grants of land from the Chilian Government.

The inducements he offered to his followers were of the most high-flown description, but the expedition proved a *fiasco*, and, neither dying nor conquering, returned to Punta Arenas, where I saw a couple of his men loafing about the settlement, their chief having returned to Europe with fresh schemes for further development.

The Fuegans are mostly cannibals, and looking upon Europeans not only in the light of enemies, but also as game, have a double object in their destruction: firstly, in self-preservation, and secondly as food. They are a miserable race, and inhabit a country which, if judged by the outline I saw of it, has but little to tempt the most greedy of promoters for annexation.

Captain S. gave me an arrow taken by one of the Frenchmen before alluded to. He had been attacked by five natives, and had (so he said) killed them all, but had been wounded by five arrows which had been discharged simultaneously by his foes. The arrow I had was beautifully finished, the barb being made of a piece of glass, evidently a bit of broken bottle picked up along the shore, and fitted so as to come out of the wood and remain in the wound on the arrow being withdrawn. The other arrows taken at the same time were almost all flint-headed, and from the extra care taken in the finish of the glass one, it was evidently looked upon as a great advance in the warlike art.

The settlers at Punta Arenas seemed industrious and contented, but even their little community had gone through certain state convulsions, and about twenty years ago had a revolution, in which they killed their governor and the chaplain, and, placing their dead bodies on a fire, danced hand-in-hand round the flames.

Having had many *chuses*, seen the lasso used by our guide, and experienced thoroughly the discomforts of a native saddle and wooden stirrups, Captain S. insisted on our finishing the day with what he termed the appropriate "wind up" of an entirely Chilian dinner, which he provided for us at Señor Ballester's, the most original of Bonifaces. Cazuela was our "*piéce de resistance.*" It is the national dish of Chili, and a more excellent one I have seldom tasted; and though Señor Ballester was more than slightly inebriated, and showed his adherence to liberty, equality, fraternity, and the rights of man, as became the citizen of a free and enlightened republic untrammeled by social distinctions, by insisting on embracing us all round, I must take off my hat and do homage to his pre-eminence as a cook. Cazuela is a kind of "cock a leeky," only far superior, highly seasoned, and eaten with its soup. Another dish was a pie, with a potato crust, of minced meat, chicken, olives, raisins, pepper and spices, uncommonly good also, and the whole was washed down by native wines, agreeable to the taste, and, leaving no ill effects the next morning, were I presume sound in quality also.

Early in the morning on the 20th of January we left Punta Arenas, and, by the time I found my way on deck, discovered that a complete change of scenery had taken place. It seemed as if the ship was on a lake, so surrounded were we on all sides by land. The shores were thickly wooded and mountainous, varying in height, from Mount Tarn, 2602 feet, to Mount Sarmiento, covered entirely with snow, 6800 feet above the level of the sea, lying some distance off in Terra del Fuego. The view was exquisite. The mountains, rugged and precipitous, took every conceivable form, and varied in aspect as each yard we steamed past them disclosed fresh beauties. They were covered with a variegated foliage which somewhat reminded me of the autumnal tints at Killarney; the trunks of the trees showing, in a white-thread-like and peculiar manner, where the biting winds had at some period checked the undergrowth and apparently nipped the lower branches. The summits were occasionally fringed with the brightest of very bright green verdure; and in the crevices, and on some of the highest peaks, the snow still remained unthawed, though the time of the year was midsummer. Nearly opposite Cape Froward, a bold promontory of 1200 feet, we saw an extensive glacier. Towards evening the wind freshening up prevented our proceeding; and as a succession of *williwaws* came on we anchored in San Nicolas Bay at the mouth of the De Gennes River.

San Nicolas is a picturesque and well-protected harbour, surrounded by high mountains whose rugged peaks were covered with snow. A dense and impenetrable forest ran close to the water's edge. A small islet lay in the centre of the bay, exactly opposite the river, and, nailed upon a tree growing in the middle, we saw several boards recording the times it had been visited by various vessels. We got a quantity of drift wood similar to that picked up at Laredo, and our seining party were particularly fortunate, bringing over two hundred salmon bass on board with them. We tried to pull up the river, but found it so full of old trees and snags that it could not be managed, and as it was impossible to penetrate through the entangled mass of undergrowth and moss skirting the forest, but little could be done with the guns. We got a few shots at duck on the river, the only birds worth mentioning that we came across, though we saw some green parrots also, which, for want of better, make a tolerable pie. We met quite fresh footmarks of Indians, but were unable to discover their wigwams.

Our next halt was under the lee of Cape Holland, in Woods Bay; rain and williwaws driving us there for shelter. "Williwaw" is the Magellan name for the sudden bursts of wind which come rushing down between the mountains. They vary much in degree of strength, but are at times so powerful that a ship is utterly unable to resist them, and for sailing vessels they are dangerous in the extreme. Fortunately the Straits abound in excellent and well-protected harbours, where safe anchorage and shelter can generally be obtained, and as those storms are seldom of long duration, common caution enables the mariner to avoid any very seri us damage, by taking refuge in time.

Inside a belt of trees encircling the harbour, lay about two miles of as likely looking snipe ground as I ever walked over; but though we worked it carefully, not a bird was to be seen. In some thick swampy undergrowth I put up a brace of woodcock. They were smaller than our English birds and much lighter in colour, but had the same kind of flight, and required very close beating to induce them to rise.

The depth of moss and luxuriousness of its growth exceeded anything I had ever seen. All the small shrubs were choked by it; fallen trees, so thickly covered that they lay completely screened, and often we went over our knees through the soft velvety covering.

Lichens were equally abundant, many of them

throwing out large leaves like brocoli. Quantities of parasites, more or less resembling mistletoe, hung from the various trees; and a profusion of edible berries of several varieties grew everywhere. Most of the shrubs were in flower, and several of them had delicious perfume, while the common fuchsia grew quite luxuriantly, and attained a size seldom met with in Europe. We left early next morning. The day was wet and misty, but what little could be seen of the coast was truly magnificent. Opposite Port Gallant, on both sides of the Strait, it was exquisite. Lofty and precipitous mountains, based with forests, and capped with snow—black-looking valleys and ravines—huge boulders of rock and precipices—glaciers—long, partly wooded islands, topped with plains of grass—rocky islets of different sizes, bare or wooded, jutting out of the sea—and the whole marked by a variety of different colourings, so rich and varied, that it would be almost impossible to even imagine a scene more full of beauty.

Off Rupert's Island, a ship's boat, with a crew of Fuegan women, came alongside, evidently with the intention of bartering their sealskin clothing. They were considerably smaller than the Patagonian ladies we met at Punta Arenas, of slighter make and different features; but, being in a hurry to get to our next anchorage before the tide turned, we could not stop to trade, and, as we took no notice of their solicitations, in a short time they shoved off. How they came by a ship's boat it would be hard to say; they looked in good condition, and had probably eaten the original proprietors. One woman had a terrible mouth; as she grinned it extended from ear to ear, disclosing a set of fangs capable of crunching anything; a more unprepossessing female I never saw.

During the day shoals of whales were seen spouting all round, and as from the winding nature of the passage we always appeared in a lake of not particularly extensive dimensions, it seemed odd how such big fish could inhabit such small waters. Occasionally we met seals and otters. A large rock near Whale Sand was so completely covered with the former animals, that it was only when they took to the water that we discovered what they were. Some hundreds must have been on it. The fish Indians wear no covering but seal skins, sewn together with threads of sinew, and, if we judge by the readiness of their owners to part with them for any rubbish offered in exchange, they must be easily enough procured; as a matter of choice, they will most likely prefer tobacco.

CHAPTER V.

Borja Bay—Coast scenery—Wild geese—Puerto Churruca—Terrible aspect of the country—The otter islands—Enormous bee—Mount Burney—First view of the Cordilleras—Trip for a yachtsman with a predilection for sport—Mayne Harbour—Puerto Buena—Alarm of Martin at strange sounds—Quarts *versus* Quartz—Guia Narrows—Chasm Reach—Quantities of seals—Grey Harbour—A tough old warrior—A tempting river—I air my rods—Halt Bay—Island Harbour—Fly-fishing in Patagonia a pitfall, a snare, and a delusion—Sombrero Island—We get on shore—Gulf of Peñas—Utter inefficiency of the *Rocket* and *Boxer* class of gun-boat—Remarkable kelp in Straits of Magellan—Massacre of the innocents.

On the 23rd of January we arrived at Borja Bay, the Island Bay of Byron. It is situated on the northern shore of Crooked Reach, two miles to the eastward of Cape Quod. At the entrance are some small islands—the Ortiz Islets, or Big and Little Borja—on the larger of which we found a wooden cross, but without any inscription to say what it meant. The shores are wooded with many different descriptions of trees, red and white cedar predominating; and a variety of shrubs, most of them covered with sweet-scented flowers, grow in wild profusion. A bright and sparkling stream runs into the bay near its centre, and a few hundred yards from its mouth, but concealed from the anchorage by a wooded hill, lies a small lake most exquisitely situated. The mountains on its distant side rise almost precipitously out of the water and are thickly covered with trees for about half-way up; at the head, a deep gorge led over the mountains towards the interior. The day was bright and sunny, and the reflection of the snow-clad mountains on the smooth mirror-like surface of the little tree-embowered lough, the perfume of the flowers, and the caroling of the birds, exulting in such unusual warmth and sunshine, combined to make a picture quite fairylike and charming.

In the afternoon we rowed along the coast, finding plenty to admire in the wonderful shades of moss and lichen which covered the rocks to the tide-mark. Every creek and corner formed a morsel varied and distinct, and some of these little pieces of colouring quite beggar description. The vegetation was of rank luxuriousness, but far more beautiful than anything tropical, which, though luxurious, undoubtedly wants that exquisite variety of colouring and depth of tone so perfect in Magellan.

The trees in places grew overhanging the water, which was deep enough close to the rocks, to have floated an "ironclad," and occasionally from some little precipice would project the gnarled remains of some old cedar of gigantic proportions, covered with mosses and mistletoe, and growing through them a profusion of long, pendulous, bright magenta-coloured blossoms, not unlike the foxglove in shape, flowers of the prevailing creeper.

I shot a couple of very handsome geese, one a pure white, and the other white body, black wings, and grouse-coloured breast. We killed some woodpeckers and several kinds of water-fowl, all of them afterwards eaten by the boat's crew and pronounced excellent, though I fancy a somewhat monotonous diet on ship's provisions must have assisted materially in disguising a fishy taste. Mussels were in abundance, but so full of small pearls as to be almost uneatable.

We made an early start from Borja Bay, leaving at daylight, *i.e.*, about 3 A.M.; our next anchorage being some distance off. The scenery grew wilder, and vegetation scarcer as we advanced, the mountains being only wooded at their bases, and all more or less covered with snow. We passed a magnificent glacier, running apparently into the sea; but the weather was too cloudy to discern very distinctly, and the mist occasionally enclosing the mountains prevented our obtaining a satisfactory view.

It was almost dark when we arrived at Puerto Churruca, our anchorage for the night. The entrance was exceedingly narrow, and we had almost to feel our way in with the lead, a matter of no small difficulty owing to the extreme depth of water so close to shore. Puerto Churruca is without exception the most weird spot I ever saw; and Desolation Island, which it is on, well deserves the name. We left "Nassau" anchorage at eleven next morning. The day was clear and bright; the scenery can only be described as being terrible; and as we steamed slowly through the narrow entrance, we had ample opportunity for looking about us. Such a combination of the horrid and the beautiful I feel utterly powerless to portray, and no one but a Doré could possibly imagine, or a Bierstadt paint.

Precipitous mountains, towering one above the other in indescribable confusion; the coast line, slightly wooded but steep and rocky; brilliant round its edges with the deep colourings of moss, lichen, and flowering shrubs so noticeable through Magellan where the coast touches the water, but they soon become lost in a mass of huge boulders, entirely bare, which continue for some thousand feet above the sea, until they reach the snow, which in its turn becomes buried in the clouds.

Deep and gloomy gorges, frightful precipices, black and unfathomable water, inlets and fiords, scooped as if with mighty power by a Vril-ya race out of the solid rock; glaciers, cataracts, and a scattering of wild fowl; group all these during some nightmare in their wildest and most terrible combination, and you may form a slight idea of Puerto Churruca. "Right in the jaws of hell rode the six hundred;" and a very slight attack of "the blues" might have led its possessor to imagine we were steaming out of the entrance to the same locality.

Sighting Cape Pillar, the south point of the western entrance to Magellan, and passing Westminster Hall and Los Evangelistos, four singular-looking rocky islets, rugged and barren, we bid adieu to the strait and entered Smyth's Channel, which separates a succession of islands of considerable magnitude—Wellington Island, one hundred and thirty-eight miles long, being the largest—from the western coast of Patagonia, ending at the entrance to the Gulf of Peñas.

The general features of the coast consist of innumerable peaks, bold headlands, and rock-covered mountains capped with snow when anything over a thousand feet high; all remarkably like in character, and desolate in the extreme. In the evening we anchored at a snug little billet among the Otter Islands, opposite Mount Burney, a lofty mountain, 5800 feet above the sea.

These islands—evidently well named, the ground being covered with the runs of the animal they are christened after—are a pretty little group, situated in the centre of Smyth's Channel. They afford an excellent harbour, the anchorage being well protected, and the holding-ground in six and seven fathoms of water, clean and good. They were full of sweet-scented flowering shrubs, the fuchsia attaining quite a tree-like size. Our wooding-party got some excellent fuel, chiefly cedar, and the seiners had a fair haul of fish. We killed some wild fowl, and saw besides a variety of singing birds, and several diminutive specimens of humming bird, some of them quite as small as many of the same species I had met in the West Indies. I also saw—and an extremely unpleasant object I considered it as it buzzed viciously in close proximity to my nose—an enormous bee, quite as large as a wren, and considerably bigger than most of the humming birds. I had not the slightest curiosity to examine it closer, and felt considerably relieved when it took itself off.

On the 27th of January, we left the Otter Islands

at daybreak, passing close to Vereker and Foley islands. The weather was quite altered, and, instead of the usual misty covering to the mountains, half obscuring their altitude, the atmosphere was dry and clear, and the view as we steamed along perfectly magnificent.

Mount Burney, covered with snow, was visible to its very summit—a somewhat unusual phenomenon in this cloudy locality; and as we progressed further, we saw for the first time the magnificent Cordilleras, standing in bold relief against the bright blue sky, some distance in the interior.

Pinnacle upon pinnacle, of the purest white, towered like clouds above the dark outline of the nearer mountains. The sea was smooth and land-locked; the numerous bays well wooded and bright with the exquisite varieties of colouring, for which the seaboard of southern Patagonia is so remarkable. Streamer-duck, a species peculiar to these latitudes (*Micropterеus cinereus*), and wild fowl, plumed their feathers, rejoicing in the unusual heat and sunshine; and enormous seagulls poised themselves, motionless, as they watched their prey. The sides of the mountains near us were rugged and torn, streaked with silvery cascades foaming and dashing over boulder and through glen; all these, with the snow-clad Cordilleras as a back-ground, formed a picture once seen not easily forgotten.

Columbine Cove was our next halt. We wooded, caught fish, and then went to Mayne Harbour on Owen Island, a most picturesque and lovely anchorage. The day was dreadfully wet, and we had reason to congratulate ourselves on the good fortune which enabled us to see the Cordillera, as had we passed it in weather like we experienced afterwards, one of the most magnificent views it is almost possible to conceive would have been lost. I cannot help feeling that in this very feeble description of the country we passed through there is a certain amount of sameness of expression, and that each place I attempt to describe has the never-failing characteristic of being lovely or beautiful. It would almost be a relief to have to write of something flat and uninteresting, but it cannot be helped. The entire scenery is so perfectly lovely everywhere. Each harbour visited, though possessing the same characteristics, differed so entirely in the grouping, that though descriptions of re-occurring scenes may pall on the reader, I can assure him that witnessing them would never satiate.

To any one with a predilection for yachting, a love of nature in its most charming garb, and a fondness for sport, I could not recommend any part of the world where the three combined can be had to such an extent as during a cruise between Monte Video and the western entrance to Magellan. From Cape Corrientes to Punta Arenas, a distance of over a thousand miles, there is not a single harbour in whose immediate vicinity a sportsman, using his yacht as a base for operations, might not obtain shooting to almost any extent.

From the Rio Negro to Cape Virgins the country absolutely swarms with guanaco and ostrich; while to a naturalist a land so little known, yet possessing such mines of hidden wealth, would be a positive Utopia. The climate is more than merely healthy; it is re-invigorating and salubrious. The natives are seldom seen, but when met with are friendly and predisposed towards Englishmen; and I only regret that circumstances prevent my again taking a cruise I can so strongly recommend to others.

After leaving Laredo Bay, the shooting becomes indifferent, but the scenery grander; still, taking the limits I have defined, no other part of the world affords such a combination to a yachtsman.

Mayne Harbour, which has an outer and an inner anchorage, is about a mile long, narrow in parts, and has several small islands scattered about it, on which were nailed the names of various vessels who had visited it for the same purpose as ourselves, *i.e.*, shelter for a night and fuel; indeed, at every place we touched, the wooding party provided sufficient to take us to our next anchorage with scarcely any consumption of coal. Among its recent visitors, H.M.S. *Albatross*'s card was conspicuous, a large board nailed to a tree on one of the rocky islets announcing that she had been there about a fortnight previous to our arrival.

From a small lough, "Lake William," a stream runs into the head of the bay, forming a picturesque cascade at its entrance. The rock scenery on the small islets and shores was perfect. Growing close to the water were many varieties of shrubs in blossom, or with bright red and purple berries. Twisted and crooked cedars, covered with moss and pretty bell-shaped flowers, overhung the banks. Massive boulders, with every conceivable shade of mossy green, from the lightest pale to the darkest olive, intermingled with various lichens and ferns, lined the coast; and to an amateur in artificial rockeries, such a lesson from nature would have been invaluable. Each creek was in itself a study, eack nook a perfect gem.

It rained in torrents while we remained here, and judging from the luxuriousness of moss, which over the fallen logs of timber nearly reached a man's shoulders, I should fancy that incessant rain was its abnormal state.

The mountains after we left Mayne Harbour became barren and rocky, streaked with deep fissures, but holding less snow. Some of the headlands were very grand, and one precipice in particular, rising like a wall for over a thousand feet, was extremely fine. The wind was against us all day, and though the distance we had to travel was only twenty miles, it was evening before we anchored in Puerto Buena, an excellent and well-sheltered harbour on the eastern shore of the channel; beautiful, of course, like every other anchorage we had visited.

Above the inner harbour a large fresh-water lake empties itself by a cascade into a little bight at its head. On ascending the mountains, I found that this lake was but the last of a series of four others, which, connected by a small stream running over a succession of falls between each of them, stretches a considerable distance into the interior of the country, hidden in a valley between the lofty mountains which spread away for miles from the seaboard.

Next morning, though the weather was anything

but promising, H., his factotum Martin, and myself, landed at the cascade. We worked the dogs over some good-looking ground round the border of the lake—(H. had a great, ugly, useless, long-legged brute, called "Joe," that he set great store by, and always took with him),—but without success; and finding nothing on the lowlands, I determined on climbing to the top of the range of hills to see if any game lay higher up.

The day was showery, and, disgusted with our bad luck, H. returned to the ship, sending Martin on to join me. The sides were steep and bare, and in places our only means of ascent lay in the water-courses, where the tangled scrub and small trees enabled us to crawl from plateau to plateau; though on gaining a couple of thousand feet, the walking became easy enough, and we were able to admire the magnificent view as it opened out more fully to our gaze.

Loughs, woods, snowy cascades, and rivers lay in a vast panorama at our feet. Miles and miles of unoccupied land, as far as the eye could reach, stretched away into misty indistinctness; not one human creature inhabited its vast space, and a couple of eagles, soaring high, even above the snowy ranges still above us, alone seemed monarchs of a land so uninhabited by man.

Our solitude was occasionally interrupted by strange sounds, which added to the weird aspect of all around; possibly wild cats, or wolves. On my asking Martin if he heard them, I was a good deal amused by his solemnly replying, "Aye, and I be thinking the captain must a heard them tew; they be wild beastesses, lions or bears most like, for he went on board uncommon quick, when he told me as how I was to go to you." H. had been chaffing him to such an extent about bears, pumas, and Indians, that though in an undeniable fright at the curious noises we both heard, he jumped at a chance of turning the tables on his master; firstly, for thinking so lightly of his personal courage; and, secondly, for leaving him in a moment, of what he evidently thought considerable peril. I remarked he kept unusually close to "heel" for the remainder of the day, though he constantly assured me he feared nothing.

We walked for three or four hours after gaining the first brow, over ranges of hills varying in height, and making for the highest peak, found that the same mountain formation continued as far as we could see. With the exception of some small birds like grey plover we met nothing, and sport being so very indifferent, I did a little prospecting for gold in the streams which flowed over masses of quartz rock, explaining to Martin at the same time that the precious metal was found in considerable quantities at Punta Arenas, where the river washed ground of similar formation, and that where he saw quartz he might possibly see gold also.

Shortly after, on looking back, I found him paddling about in a large splash of rain-water, which had accumulated in a slight hollow on the mountain side. "Hullo!" I shouted, "what are you doing there? It's getting too late for dawdling." "I be a-looking for gold," was the answer. "Why, you muff," I replied; "you are seeking in a splash of rain-water, that did not exist yesterday and may be dry to-morrow." "Well," he sung out, with a grunt of discontent; "you said as how I might find it when I seed quarts, and I be certain shure there be gallons here; but I never does nothink right;" and he shambled on, much disgusted with my evident want of appreciation for his talents as a prospector.

Leaving Porto Buena, we passed through the Guia Narrows, named after Sarmiento's boat. They lay between Hanover and Chatham islands; and are about six miles long, and from one to one and a half broad, except at the north end, where it is only two cables across. High precipices, of from two to nearly three thousand feet, were on either side; but the incessant rain prevented our seeing as well as we should have wished, though what we could make out was extremely grand. Off Innocents' Island we saw several large whales, and shortly afterwards anchored in Walker's Bay for the night. The weather was too wet and stormy to progress very far in such an infamous sailer and steamer as the *Rocket*, which, even in the smoothest water, was quite unable to steam against the slightest puff of wind; so our next halt was only four miles off, being at Molyneux Sound, which we left the morning after.

The scenery was fine on the Wellington Island side of the Channel; but on entering Chasm Reach, it became simply exquisite. The channel was the narrowest we had yet passed through, and, most fortunately, the sea was smooth and the day bright and clear.

The sides were precipitous masses of almost bare granite, trees only growing at the bottom, and along the clefts which occasionally cut into the surface. Cascades on each coast, like streaks of silver, came dashing with sullen roar into the sea. The spire-pointed summits of the distant mountains were draped in white. Occasional glaciers, sparkling in the sun, peeped from their snow-enshrouded beds. Quantities of otters and seals sported about in the dark, tranquil, o'ershadowed water, and a couple of small icebergs were seen floating slowly past the ship. To add extra picturesque effect to this romantic-looking spot, we went to "general quarters;" and the bright flashes from the guns, the reverberation after each shot or shell, as echo upon echo came ringing through the mountains, added considerably to the charm of all around.

Our destination for the night was Port Grappler, but, owing to extreme darkness by the time we got opposite it, we missed the entrance, and had to remain under steam until next morning, when we anchored in Eden Harbour—an anchorage formed by a group of thickly wooded islands on the western shore of Indian Reach, about five miles south of the English Narrows. The harbour was full of seals, who played and tumbled about in all directions, occasionally jumping several feet clean out of the water as they chased each other in the exciting game of "follow my leader," at which they evidently were proficients. We tried hard to find some game or wild fowl, but one wretched snipe was the sole reward of our industry. The seining party were fairly successful. They caught several fish beside the inevitable "bass," and among them a curious little pig-headed creature (*Agriopus Peruvianus*), which I kept alive in a bason of water for some hours before returning him to his native element.

After passing through the charming little archipelago of islands that form Eden Harbour, we came to the English Narrows, with its lofty, thickly wooded sides, and entered Messier Channel, a fine piece of water, extending for a distance of seventy-five miles, from the north end of the English Narrows to Tarn Bay in the Gulf of Peñas; free from all impediments, and containing safe and convenient anchorages throughout its length—an important consideration in these latitudes, where for ten minutes it is impossible ever to reckon on a continuance of fine weather.

On the 6th of February we anchored in Grey Harbour, two miles east of Halt Bay, at the head of Liberta Bay, and found it a well-protected anchorage surrounded by high, thickly wooded hills. At the head of the harbour, a channel affords easy boat passage at all times of the tide to a large fresh-water lough, about two miles in length, into the top of which flows a river of considerable size.

The lake was extremely beautiful; but though we rowed nearly all round it and hunted in various directions, saw no wild fowl except a streamer-goose, who, compassionating with us on our want of sport, kindly afforded us an hour's very fair shooting. The old story of the Jack-snipe, who lasted a man two years, and was eventually killed by a friend, to whom in a weak moment he offered a day's shooting, and *Punch's* "Frenchman," "whose woodcock remained to him for the season," rose vividly in my mind, as shot after shot was fired by H. and myself at this invincible old bird, who received our fusilade with the most extreme indifference. After each discharge he simply dived, swam a hundred yards or so under water before rising to the surface, and then, with the most *insouciant sang-froid*, flapped his wings in seeming derision of our efforts, before quietly settling down as if nothing unusual had happened. We fired at least twenty shots at this invulnerable abomination whose only value was to the boat's crew—men of "Jack Tar's" true definition for the word epicure: "kind of beggars as will eat anything,"—before a successful cartridge from the captain laid the tough old warrior low. A more unprepossessing goose I never saw. Its head was ugly and enormous, and the thick matting of down and feathers which protected its body accounted to some extent for its immunity from small shot.

Tempted by the similarity of the river to a fine salmon stream in Europe, we brought our rods next day, and diligently strove with small fish, which had been taken the previous evening in the seine, artificial minnow, and spoon-bait, to allure some of the finny monsters who, by all the rules of similitude, should have inhabited its waters.

The lake seemed formed for pike, or its opposite number south of the Equator, whatever they might happen to be, should our own fresh-water shark not exist *in propriâ personâ;* and the clear sparkling river dashing over its rock-strewn bed, with whirl and foam, or gliding—dark, swift and deep—by the black, tree-o'ershadowed, precipitous sides of the stream, appeared absolutely created for some Patagonian fish, answering in habits to the salmon. We trolled round the most likely parts of the lake, over spots that a fisherman would have expected every instant to have got a run, but without success; and H. at length, disgusted with our bad luck, landed to make a cazuela, and left me to try the river alone.

The forest grew so thick, and the under-cover was so dense, we were unable to go beyond the water commanded from the boat. The scenery was exquisite, and the day, for a wonder, almost tropical. The river, as far as we could see, ran in a torrent over crag and boulder, forming a succession of cascades and pools, until it became lost by a sudden bend in a forest of cedar-trees. The wooded hills ran up on either side to a great height, and in the distance a waterfall of nearly a thousand feet fell into the river from the higher mountains, whose summits were covered with perpetual snow.

After a few casts in the rapids I got a run, and before our luncheon was ready succeeded in landing a dozen and a half fish about herring size. They were shaped somewhat like a trout, but longer in proportion to their size, had no scales, and were a greenish colour, like the hue on a mackerel's back; not bad-looking fish, and turned out eventually to be pretty good eating also. They were all killed with a small fish caught by a seining party the previous evening, which I mounted on a flight of hooks with a spinner; but I was a good deal disappointed at not getting something heavier, as more likely-looking water I never threw a line across.

It was, however, a pleasant outing. The thin cloud of blue smoke from our wood fire, the perfume of flowers, the warbling of birds, the splashing of rapid water as it dashed over the rocks (sweet music to a fisherman), the knowledge that a *chef* was preparing food, that the drinks were cooling, and the magnificent scenery all around, unsurpassed I truly believe, in the world, all combined to make a "marked day," even in the eventful career of such wanderers as ourselves.

The weather, which for a couple of days had been quite delightful, next morning changed to wind and rain, and on our starting, compelled us to put into Halt Bay, only three miles from Grey Harbour; a short distance that took our "old tub" three hours' hard steaming to accomplish. The water here is deep, but space confined; and before anchoring in twenty-four fathoms, we were dodging about alternately from side to side of the little bay, and could have easily jumped on shore dry-shod. The coasts are lofty, precipitous, and wooded; and were marked by a line of trees, torn in a lane from about half-way up to the sea by some avalanche which had carried them away bodily, roots and all.

Our next anchorage was at Island Harbour, on the eastern shore, twenty miles from the Gulf of Peñas—a small but land-locked anchorage, well placed for vessels entering or leaving these channels, and possessing good holding-ground, with plenty of wood and water. Its position is marked by an island a short mile to the southward, and near the entrance are two small islets, called Brown and Phipps islands. A bank or bar of rocky ground stretches across from Phipps Island to the main on each side. Tempted by the appearance of a small river at the head of the harbour, I took my rod, and following the course of the stream, arrived at a picturesque little lake overhung with trees, but having on one side a gently shelving bank of pebbles and sand, which enabled me to wade well out of reach of the trees, and fish in comparatively deep water. A more propitious day for fishing one could hardly have wished for. It was cloudy, yet without any sign of rain, and sufficient wind to raise a gentle curl over the water; just, in fact, what a man would order were there any choice in the matter. The water looked most alluring. Sand and gravel on one side, and deep water with peat-like banks on the other; rushes and lilies to afford shelter, and a strong current of running water passing through the centre, carried food from the mountains to the fish who *ought* to have inhabited so fair a territory.

I worked for some hours with many kinds of fly, and tried both natural and artificial minnow without success. The streams also I searched diligently, and at last was reluctantly compelled to admit that the promising appearance of both lake and river was merely a pitfall, a snare, and a delusion, and that the angler has no place for his calling in the lovely but deceitful waters of Patagonia.

The country was very lovely, but the ground

lying in ridges about a hundred feet high, the valleys between them, being thickly timbered with the usual amount of undercover and fallen trees covered with moss, and which had to be got through somehow, we found it hard work getting along; and after beating several likely-looking covers without seeing anything except a few green parrots, we gave up all hopes of sport, by either land or water, and returned to our floating home.

Next morning we again attempted to get into the Gulf of Peñas. It had been our object to effect this without any stoppages ever since leaving Halt Bay; but again squalls of wind and blinding rain, shortly after starting, compelled a premature anchoring on the lee-side of Sombrero Island—a small thickly wooded spot, with one very high precipitous hill in the centre, which gives an outline, when seen from a distance, sufficiently resembling a man's hat to warrant the island receiving its name.

The gale continuing, we remained here a couple of days, amusing ourselves by catching some bright red perch-like fish, which were excellent eating, shooting a few small birds, and sending parties to cut wood; and on the 13th of February we again made an effort to cross the gulf.

Fate, however, as well as the wind, was dead against us, and no sooner had we cleared the island, than a succession of "williwaws" drove us back to our old quarters under Sombrero. As we were coming to an anchor, the wind suddenly shifted completely round; and the ship, as was constantly the case, not answering her helm, we tailed, before the anchor which we let go could prevent it, quietly on to the rocks. A kedge was immediately got out; another hawser was fastened to a convenient tree on shore; the ship was lightened where she struck, and in about five hours, with the help of a rising tide, we managed to hawl her off. Had there been a swell on we should have found it rather inconvenient; as most likely, in that case, we should have broken up and gone to pieces in about a quarter of an hour, and had to camp on Sombrero for perhaps months before anyone even heard of us. As it was, we only touched once very lightly, and succeeded in hauling off with but comparatively little trouble, and no apparent damage. Next day we again tried to cross this troublesome gulf, which was rapidly becoming to us what the Cape of Good Hope was to the "Flying Dutchman;" and again, after burning any quantity of coal and wood, we were driven into harbour at Port Ballinas, not more than ten miles from Sombrero Island, and not over two on our straight road. I never remember a continuance of more unpleasant weather—very cold and squally, with rain and hail; and this, too, in the height of summer, with flowers and fruit in profusion, and humming-birds fluttering over the open blossoms in every sheltered vale. I wonder what the winter can be like—cold, I expect, very.

On the 15th we left Port Ballinas, a swell, but no wind, being all we had against us; and at last got fairly into the Gulf of Peñas, after five separate attempts, and being six days doing fifty miles.

Of all the utterly useless, makeshift, waste-of-money

ships, we have in the British Navy, these double-screw composite gun-vessels of the *Rocket* and *Boxer* * class are the most so. They are badly built, can neither sail nor steam, and are at times utterly unmanageable, answering neither screw nor helm when wanted to go round, and are even unfitted for carrying the 7-inch 6½-ton gun they are armed with, the concussion, when fired with a battering charge, shaking them far more than they can properly bear. The few shots fired by way of practice once a quarter are all they can stand; but if required for a bombardment, half a day's incessant firing would completely knock them out of time.

As a matter of course, they were built for purposes of economy, *i.e.*, by way of utilizing the engines of a very small class of gun-boat no longer required after the Crimean War, by putting two of them together to do the work of one.

Had the brilliant originator studied the fifth chapter of St. Luke, and remembered the 36th and 37th verses, he never would have built new ships for his old engines. As it is, his neglected religious education has caused the country considerable expense, and given our Navy the disgrace of possessing a class of vessel like the *Rocket*, which took five weeks going through the Straits as far as Port Ballinas and the *Boxer*, who was ninety-six days going from Esquimault to Callao. That the constructor should be able to say "he never heard any complaints about them," is more than probable, and very easily accounted for. Notwithstanding their utter useless-

* See Appendix A.

ness, they are the best *commands* a lieutenant can have; and as it is far more pleasant to be captain of one's own ship, no matter what her defects may be, than subordinate in another, no growl is ever likely to reach their Lordships; and if the accommodation is pretty good, and the rate of speed only four knots, except in very exceptional cases, what does it matter? A commission can only last a certain time, and going four knots, or fourteen, will not shorten its duration, nor render the expected day of promotion or orders for England one moment the sooner.

Before bidding farewell to these regions, I must not omit to notice one of the most striking features of the Straits, and that is, the immense quantity of kelp, or sea-weed, which over the entire sea-board envelopes the coast. Through all the numerous bays and channels of Tierra del Fuego and Southern Patagonia are to be found enormous fields of *Macrocystis pyrifera;* many of the plants attaining a length of between three and four hundred feet. On shaking a bunch, which, as it is perpetually fouling boats, anchors, and fishing-lines, I had to do more than once, innumerable crustacea are discovered adhering to its leaves. Cuttle-fish, crabs, small fish, shells, sea-eggs, star-fish, holothuriæ, planariæ, and nereidous animals of a thousand forms, all tumble about together. The leaves below the surface of the water are so thickly encrusted with corallines, their natural dark olive is rendered entirely white with the delicate lace-like tracery.

Amid these vast aquatic forests are found quantities of fish who prey on the crustacea, and who are in their turn preyed upon by cormorants, kelp-geese, seals, and porpoises, so that each gigantic bed teams with life and animation.

Their advantage to the mariner can hardly be overrated. The sea inside these huge masses of *Macrocystis pyrifera*, in the roughest weather, is smooth as a mill-pond, no storm being capable of affecting their tough but yielding beds; so that a "kelp harbour" becomes a term synonymous with a safe one. As buoys they are even more useful, and no ship keeping the most ordinary look-out need fear sunken rocks, even in chartless and unsurveyed localities, every place of danger being distinctly marked by patches of kelp.

Off Cape Tres Montes, a bold and remarkable headland rising from the sea to a height of 2000 feet, at the southern extremity of the peninsula of the same name, which we wished to get round, the wind shifted, and for a short time we thought it possible that once more we should be driven back; but our ill-luck at length deserted us, and rounding the Cape we at last started fairly for Valparaiso, everybody in the ship except myself being heartily glad to get clear of the Straits, hard work and bad weather having completely extinguished all traces of their love (if it ever existed) of the picturesque. Off the Chonos Archipelago, we met with quantities of albatross, and one day, being nearly becalmed, caught eighteen in less than two hours.

The process of capture is simple. A stout line and hook, baited with pork and floated with pieces of wood, is dropped astern. Should the ship be moving, it is necessary to retain in hand a sufficient quantity of line to enable the fisher to play out enough to prevent the bait being dragged before the bird, after lighting in the water, has time to seize it. On the albatross taking the bait, the hook sticks in his strong horny beak, and after a good deal of hauling he is landed on deck.

The largest I caught measured ten feet six inches across the wings, and was as large and heavy in the body as a big swan. The long pinion bones make admirable pipe stems, the feet tobacco-pouches, the heads paper-weights, and the bodies were invariably skinned and eaten by the least particular of the ship's company, to whom nothing in the shape of fresh food ever seemed to come amiss.

The slaughter of these birds seemed to act on our fortunes in a manner very different from the fate which pursued the "Ancient Mariner," who "with his cross-bow did kill the albatross," as after their destruction we were blessed with strong favourable gales, which sending us one hundred and sixty-two, and one hundred and fifty miles in two succesive days, culminated in a run of one hundred and ninety-two on the third, and landed us on the 25th of February, 1875, at Valparaiso.

CHAPTER VI.

Valparaiso—Cleanliness of the streets—Powers of an Intendente—Union Club at Valparaiso—The mountain of Aconcagua—Trip to Santiago—A refreshment room *absolutely worse* than those in England—Good-natured Chilian—Muzzling the priests—Fruit—Santiago—Santa Lucie—The Alameda—Plaza Independencia—The park—The clubs—The fire brigade—The theatre—Chilian dinner—Pisco—A large herd of sea-lions—Coquimbo—The Guayacon copper works—Serana—The line to Ovalle—Mineral wealth of Chili—Gran Hotel de Francia—Limari—Chilian country-life—Farming—The lasso—Chilian mounted—A beggar on horseback—Compañia—Chili a well-governed and progressing country.

THE first view of Valparaiso on entering the harbour is disappointing in the extreme. A steep hill of bare red earth, on which are perched wooden shantics, apparently hanging to the sides of an almost perpendicular mountain by scaffolding and supports, are the first objects that catch the eye. Should the wind be blowing off-shore, clouds of blinding dust are whirled far beyond the shipping into the bay, covering everything it touches with a thick coating of red grit, which penetrates like coal-dust through the minutest openings, and fills one's mouth, nose, and eyes, most unpleasantly. The hill gives one the idea of a human rabbit-warren, the habitations being so burrowed into its sides; and the houses near the sea being half-hidden by the shipping, my first impressions were decidedly unfavourable of the most prosperous and important sea-port of all South America.

On landing I was agreeably surprised to find a street of fine houses, with shops which would be creditable in either London or Paris; while for scrupulous cleanliness it infinitely surpassed either of them. Two long streets, one of them extending nearly round the bay as far as the railway station, are the principal thoroughfares; and in them are the finest shops and most important houses of business. Street-cars run through their entire length on tramways, and are fairly horsed and numerous; but decidedly the most striking feature of the town is its extreme cleanliness. On remarking afterwards to one of its inhabitants how much I had been struck by this unusual feature in a foreign town, he informed me that it was entirely owing to the care and determination of the Intendente Echaurrin, who, on taking the reins of office, had found the place as notorious for its filth and dirt, as it was now celebrated for its cleanliness; but who, by establishing a system of fines, most vigorously enforced, aided by a keen personal supervision, had succeeded at length in making Valparaiso one of the cleanest towns I was ever in.

The powers of an Intendente appear to be almost absolute, and that such despotism should be accorded to an individual in a republic appears to me somewhat incongruous; not that personally I object to it, as, quite on the contrary, I think a little absolutism a most admirable tonic, which, if only applied at home,

H 2

where treason can be spouted unchecked in Trafalgar Square, or park railings torn down with impunity, would do an infinity of good; but it amused me, when I thought of the so-called "Liberalism" of Beales, M.A., Dilke and Odger; of a model Republic got up under their auspices; and what it would eventually lead to.

The "Intendente" is a kind of military Lord Mayor, who has not only the entire control of the municipality, but also command of the troops, and is answerable to the President alone for his actions.

A short time back, an inferior actor, an unappreciated play, or some other reason, caused a certain amount of hissing to take place at one of the theatres. The hissing was done by some young men of the best Chilian families, but was none the less a decided nuisance to the audience, from the persistent manner in which it was conducted. Señor Echaurrin immediately published a ukase prohibiting hissing at all. Next evening the young men applauded so vociferously that the play could not proceed, and Señor Echaurrin promptly ended the difficulty by sending in a party of soldiers, who cleared them all out and put them in prison.

He derives for the municipality, from fines alone, chiefly breaches of decency and cleanliness, over $80,000 a year. He fined a doctor $50 for not turning out one night when called upon to attend a sick person; and caused, or nearly caused, a strike among their learned fraternity. In fact, he is the Governor of Valparaiso, and he does govern it, and right well to. He has converted the dirtiest town in Chili into the cleanest, and has given monarchists a lesson they might well lay to heart.

The consul (at whose office we found a large mail waiting our arrival) was kind enough to get us made honorary members of the Union Club, an excellent and well-conducted establishment; and I accordingly deserted the *Rocket* during her stay in harbour.

One of the greatest drawbacks to Valparaiso is the plague of dust with which it is invariably afflicted. From the houses on the hill-side the shipping was at times hidden by clouds blown across the bay; and even Aconcagua, the second highest mountain in the world — 23,910 feet above the level of the sea—was seldom visible except through its murky colouring. The time of the year, unfortunately, was most ill-adapted for obtaining a good view, and though we could generally see Aconcagua every day, the atmosphere was so heavy and lurid with dust, that the view was never sufficiently satisfactory to be termed a good one, though the whole of the huge monster was constantly visible.

Santiago, the capital of Chili, is about a hundred miles from Valparaiso by rail. The morning H. and myself started to visit it, the train was so crowded with people returning from a course of sea-bathing —Valparaiso being one of their only fashionable watering-places—that we had difficulty in getting seats at all, and then only in different second-class compartments; the President—Don Frederico Errazuriz — travelling by the same train perhaps making it extra full. I was fortunate in getting in with pleasant people, agreeable and polite. H., less lucky, fell in with a lot of mothers and babies, and was half smothered by small children.

Shortly after leaving, a gentleman taking out his case of cigarettes offered them to a couple of good-looking ladies, and then commenced smoking without any further permission, though the ladies did not on this occasion join him. The journey was to a certain extent interesting, from the extremely high grade of the line where we crossed a mountain range, but lay through a perfectly hideous country. Bare hills of rock and red earth, with a few stunted bushes or prickly-pear, extended far as the eye could reach. Occasionally a patch of cultivated land was to be met with; but not until we reached Llaillai, where we remained twenty minutes to breakfast, was anything like farming to be seen.

Having been recommended to breakfast here, and having eaten nothing prior to starting, I was uncommonly sharp set on our arrival, and rushed with a crowd of others to the refreshment-rooms. Alas! infamously as our own refreshment-rooms are conducted, here was something worse; and, not speaking Spanish very fluently, I found I had not a chance with the ravenous Chilians, who pounced on everything eatable, like birds of prey.

At last I succeeded in getting hold of something, which on inspection appeared to be half-cooked hide with the hair scraped off and a little fat left adhering. I tried to cut it, but could not: in desperation, I adopted the national method I saw in use around me, of fingers and teeth, but failed most signally;

and before I could devise another plan, the engine whistled, and hungry as when I entered the rooms I regained my carriage. My expression of countenance was possibly so unamiable, that a Chilian gentleman remarked he feared I had not made a good breakfast; and entering into a general conversation, we had a long talk about the state of Chili, its government, and its resources. The President being in the train naturally became the subject of inquiries and remarks.

It seems that he owed his election mainly to the influence of the priests, whose nominee he apparently was. On obtaining office, however, his views underwent a sudden change, and he brought forward some admirable measures for curbing the sacerdotal power and obtaining freedom of religious worship for all sects, colours, and creeds in Chili. This in itself was a severe blow to the bigotry of the clerical party, who up to this period had been as intolerant as they were powerful: but when shortly afterwards, he brought forward a measure to subject the priesthood to common law, viz., that if a priest committed murder, theft, or any other misdemeanor, he was to be tried like any other Chilian, before the "judge of crime," their rage knew no bounds, and every effort was made to prevent the bill passing through Congress.

The warmest supporters of the priests were the ladies; and many a senator, though convinced in himself of the wisdom of the measure, had little peace in the domestic circle while the question still pended. One obdurate member, who persisted in his determination to vote against the priests, was rendered non-effective on the day that his presence in the house was most absolutely required, by the wife of his bosom administering a strong dose of croton oil; while another member was locked up in his own study by three strong-minded females, who assured him that they were quite determined to save his soul, and that go to the House he should not.

All these artifices were however insufficient to prevent the bill passing, and though there is no doubt but that the clericals worked to the utmost the Jesuitical doctrine of the end justifying the means, and used freely and with the usual unscrupulousness of Rome whatever methods they imagined would gain their ends, the measure was successfully carried, and the holy fathers became amenable to the common law of their country.

After leaving Llaillai the ascent became exceedingly steep, the grade in some places being one foot in forty. On the right-hand side we passed an immense tract of perfectly level land, lying in a valley almost entirely cultivated with wheat. Huge unthrashed heaps were lying on the plains waiting for mares to tread it out, such being still the primitive custom on their farms, though why a country, whose most important export next to copper is corn, should still resort to such a tedious and uneconomical habit is more than I can understand.

I observed one small herd of alpacas in a field near the rail, and occasionally herds of cattle and horses; but the country we were passing through was evidently but ill-adapted for cattle-breeding on

"MY NAME IS JIM DUFFIELD, AND THEM ERE IS MY VISITING CARDS.'

See page 312.

UNIV. OF MICH.

any very extended scale, the south of Chili, about Valdivia and Lota, being the chief seats of that particular branch of agriculture. Apples, pears, grapes, melons, and peaches were to be had in abundance; but though the latter attain a fair size, are perfect in appearance, and have a delicious perfume, I never tasted one worth eating in Chili.

Anything more dusty than railway travelling in this country it is hard to imagine. However, our journey was drawing to an end; my new acquaintance was a friend of the genial old Captain of the *Chacabuco* whom we had met at Punta Arenas. He gave me his card and insisted on our both dining with him, promising to get us made honorary members of the two best clubs in the town during our stay there; indeed, to my new friend Don C. R.'s hospitality and kindness I owed an extra-agreeable visit to the capital, and a considerable amount of useful information.

Santiago—perhaps best known in Europe as the scene of that terrible fire in a church, where over two thousand women of the first families in Chili were burned to death—is a town of about 130,000 inhabitants, and situated on a plain at the foot of the Cordillera Mountains. Admirably supplied with water, running streams of which flow through every house, it has a pleasant general aspect, from the trees and flowers which this plentiful supply enables people to grow in the *patio* attached to all the houses of the upper classes.

Santa Lucie, a curious rock, to the summit of which has been constructed a carriage-drive, is one of the remarkable objects of the town. From the top on a clear day a charming view is to be obtained. It reminded me a good deal of the one seen from the roof of Milan Cathedral, when looking at the distant Alps across the plains of Lombardy.

Though neither trouble nor expense has been spared to render Santa Lucie an attraction and a success, the execrably bad taste of the designer of the works has completely nullified the object in view. Tawdry statues, badly made paths, artificial rocks, with labels on them in badly printed characters informing the world in general that this is "The abode of bliss," "The home of love," or something equally absurd, are the prevailing features; and a general meretricious and intensely artificial appearance characterizes the whole affair. It really is a pity, as a tenth part of the money, expended with only average good taste, might have made the huge rock a very great ornament.

The Alameda, a promenade with rows of trees and streams of running water, is of considerable extent, and adorned with equestrian statues of the principal historical characters of the country. One of O'Higgins, a celebrated leader at the time of their war of independence, is noticeable for the extreme vivacity of the gentleman on horseback. He is depicted as having just ridden down a Spanish standard-bearer, who is lying under his horse's feet, still grasping the fallen banner; the reins are on the horse's neck, who is rearing madly, while the great O'Higgins, with hands and arms elevated in the air, one flourishing a sword towards Heaven, and the other pointing before him, is, with the widest possible stretch of open-mouth conceivable in an Irishman, calling on his comrades to follow.

The Plaza Independencia is another fashionable resort, being a large square, containing a frontage of the cathedral, post-office, some well-built shops, and a handsome arcade. In the centre is placed a fountain, surrounded by ornamental trees and beds of flowers. The cathedral is entirely without architectural beauty of exterior, and the inside is equally plain and uninteresting.

On the site of the great fire, which did not occur at the cathedral, as is sometimes erroneously stated, but at a church a few hundred yards behind it, a handsome statue has been erected to commemorate the catastrophe. Facing it are the new Houses of Congress. Nearly all the buildings are one-storied, the prevalence of earthquakes (there was a slight one the morning of our arrival) rendering it unsafe to erect any more pretentious structure, though the hotels and a few public buildings are exceptions to the rule.

Street-cars on the American system are in abundance; and owing to the roads being execrably kept and full of ruts, are a far more comfortable mode of progression than travelling in the two-horsed hackney-carriages, which jolt and throw one about most unpleasantly. The track through the town to the suburbs is between three and four miles long; the fashion of one-storied houses, all the better classes having a *patio*, naturally extends the city over a considerable space, which is otherwise out of all proportion to the number of its inhabitants.

Some of the dwelling-places of the poorer classes were very wretched, worse than the most miserable cabins in Ireland; still, on the whole, Santiago is a handsome, well kept town, and may be fairly compared with the generality of European ones. If, from their system of building all houses in one story, much of the poverty of the lower orders is exposed to the inquisitive gaze of strangers, we must not forget the filth, dirt, squalor, and wretchedness we have concealed in all the back slums of our own towns, which is probably greatly in excess of anything to be met with out here.

The Park was quite deserted when we visited it, but possessed nothing attractive. A flat badly turfed piece of ground, with a few scattered poplars, a *café*, and a pond of dirty-looking water, containing a steam-launch and a few pleasure-boats, were the prevailing features. In the season, however, it is different. Handsome equipages, with really pretty and well-dressed ladies, crowd the scene; and gazing at the attractive features of the Chilian fair ones, you forget the barrenness of their surroundings, their hideous poplars, and the dusty park.

There are two excellent Clubs, "The Union" and "The September," and each of them kindly made us honorary members. The Union, which faces the Alameda, is the most luxurious, and has a handsome billiard-room, with five tables in it. The *patio* is ornamented with statuary and trees; and a good-sized garden, with a few of the appliances of a gymnasium, stretches some distance in rear of the building. The cooking was good; but the constant succession of solids, and the quantity of substantial *entrées* which are handed round, is rather trying to the novice at a Chilian dinner. They certainly are very heavy feeders; and had the old Roman custom of serving out emetics at stated intervals during the banquet been adopted, it would not have surprised me. A few of their customs strike one at first as being a little singular. Large slices of melon are handed round immediately after soup; an occasional cigarette is taken between the courses, and no wine is drunk after dinner.

What volunteering is among us, the Fire Brigade is at Santiago; and nearly all the young men, no matter what their position in society may be, belong to some such corps. They elect their own officers, under whose orders they drill, wear an attractive uniform, and are ready to turn out on the faintest sound of the word "fire." The engines are either English or American, and are beautifully kept; in fact "fire duty" is the prevailing hobby, and all classes enter thoroughly into the spirit of the institution.

Of all the different features connected with this city, the Santiagans have more reason to be proud of their theatre than anything else. A little smaller than "Drury Lane," it is most beautifully proportioned, and exquisitely fitted up. The tiers of boxes, which are open, are supported on the outspread wings of angels; the decorations are in admirable good taste; and the furniture, such as chairs in the boxes, and fauteuil stalls, are most comfortable, and of the very finest workmanship. The stage is amply proportioned, and I certainly consider that without any exception the theatre at Santiago is one of the most beautiful I have ever seen. The exterior is quite simple and unattractive.

Existence at Valparaiso must be somewhat monotonous. In the morning we rode to Fisherman's Bay before breakfast and had a swim. Once we had a cricket-match, and once A. P. took me for a morning's partridge-shooting. We started fairly early, but the ground was so parched up that nowhere did we find the slightest particle of scent. I shot a bird, which Major saw fall on the off-side of a small ravine; and though he made a pretty good guess at the place, and went so near the partridge that at times it lay under his hind-feet, he could smell nothing, and at last only blundered upon it by accident.

Business even appeared stagnant. The town was slowly recovering from a commercial crisis, caused by over-speculation in the mining transactions which marked the time, and which had been carried to an extent bordering on extreme rashness. Numbers were ruined, and the others, either hard hit, or, rendered more prudent by the fate of their compatriots, viewed the most remunerative speculations with an eye of suspicion, so that enterprise and capital were equally hard to move.

We had brought an introduction to the Intendente Señor Don — Echaurrin, from Captain S., and shortly after presenting it were asked to fix any day it would be convenient for us to dine with him. A large party assembled on the appointed day, a good proportion of the fair sex being present, and, among others, Señor Echaurrin's sister, Madame Errazuriz, wife of the President. Several notabilities were among the men, all being either diplomatic or legal. The gentlemen wore frock-coats and coloured trousers; the ladies morning-dresses, which however they changed after dinner for the purpose of going to the opera.

The dinner was like the generality of Chilian feeds, namely, a great deal of solid food, commencing with cazuela and melon. Cazuela is rather a puzzler, as part of a young head of Indian corn, which is invariably in it, requires to be eaten with the fingers, it being utterly impossible to get off the grain in any other manner. I remember trying once to scrape them off with a fork, and found a very pretty Chilian lady watching me with a mixed expression of amusement and surprise. "Well, you *are* a 'Gringoe,'" she said, "to eat cazuela like that;" so for the future I ate like the natives while I was in their country. They are all very expert with their fingers, and can manage a knife for the purpose of picking up peas and gravy nearly as cleverly as the Germans, who are the best hands at the knife trick in Europe. I shall never forget an old German lady, with a face like a baboon, polishing off, by the help of a large dinner-knife, a soft-boiled egg one morning at a *table-d'hote* in Rome. However, we went through our dinner very comfortably, getting, besides European wines, two native beverages called *pisco* and *chicha*. The pisco was excellent. It is a kind of brandy, the finer qualities being made with great care from particular grapes, and has a delicious flavour about it of muscatel.

After dinner we adjourned to the opera, where we heard 'Trovatore' very fairly performed by an Italian company. To the Intendente's box a large retiring-room was attached, and between the acts we were given tea and refreshments. In fact, for a republic, I was astonished to see the prominent citizens going in for what in Europe we consider a privilege and exclusiveness only to be afforded to royalty. Señor Echaurrin walked back with us before the opera was quite over, and from the way he pitched into all the *vigillantes* we came across, and the life he put into what were at other periods a somewhat phlegmatic body, when they detected his approach, it was very evident that he constantly kept them up to the mark by personal supervision. I learned two things from my intercourse with his Excellency not quite patent to me before—that a republican is by no means necessarily a democrat, and that republican institutions are far more despotic than anything monarchial.

On the 11th of March we left Valparaiso, and after a somewhat rough time of it, during which we passed through a large herd of sea-lions, we arrived at Coquimbo. These curious animals (*Otaria jubata*) are to be met with in considerable numbers all over the Pacific ocean; and in Ferrol Bay enormous herds appear to reside all through the year. They vary in size from ten to eighteen feet, the males having large manes, which flowing round their neck and breast have probably caused the name of sea-lion to be given them. The females have no mane, and are rather darker coloured. Notwithstanding

their formidable appearance they are perfectly harmless and at a distance are not unlike the common seal.

Coquimbo is a most uninteresting-looking place, being merely a few rows of houses facing the bay, with a high background of rocks, sand, and brown earth. Not a vestige of vegetation is anywhere to be seen: indeed, nearly all the northern parts of Chili possess the same sterile features; but as the land is rich in mineral productions, and has such quantities of wealth buried beneath, it may be contented with its unattractive surface. Metals pay better than grain, and much of this wretched-looking country was more valuable than land covered with the finest crops.

A couple of miles from Coquimbo, in a little bay of sufficient depth to allow vessels to load alongside a wooden pier, are situated the celebrated Guayacon copper works. The manager, Mr. B., was kind enough to take us round and explain the process of smelting, and the qualities of the different piles of rough ore waiting for the furnace. Much of this ore differed in quality and character, so that a "charge" of the one differed very materially from a "charge" of the other. This term is applied to the mixture of ores when prepared for the furnace in the proper proportions, found, by previous experiments in the laboratory attached to the works, to be best adapted for producing pure metal. In all of them the mixture differs; and I noticed that among some were placed considerable quantities of slag, to assist in the development required. Some of the ores underwent quite a different treatment, and were, after a process of pounding, submitted to the action of sulphuric acid in a large bath; however, it is not my intention to enter on a critical dissertation on copper smelting, beyond saying that the process is interesting to a visitor, and particularly remunerative to the proprietors.

Two Chilian gentlemen, Messrs. Urmaneta and Errazuriz are the joint owners of these valuable works; and though they purchase considerable quantities of rough ore, by far the greater portion of copper smelted is produced from their own mines. They also possess coal, which, though of inferior quality for mercantile purposes (the stuff I saw at Guayacon being mere dust), is sufficiently inflammable to smelt their metal, and must of course be an enormous advantage in works like these.

Nearly opposite Coquimbo, and about seven miles across the bay, lies the town of Serana, to which indeed Coquimbo is but the seaport. After the latter wretched place, Serana looks lovely. It is a quiet little town, built entirely of *adobe*, and kept very clean. The *alameda* is more than a mile long and leads almost to the sea, having a greater portion of the way a row of poplars on each side. The *plaza* has a fountain, surrounded by a small garden in which were some very fine roses and carnations; a few trees grew round it, among which I noticed a fair-sized magnolia.

Having heard that pretty good partridge-shooting was to be had more in the interior of the country, H. and I procured a letter of introduction to a Chilian gentleman, Don R., and, taking Major, started by train to Ovalle, a town about sixty miles from the coast, and near which was the estate we were going to visit.

The line ran over the mountains, in the highest part two thousand feet above the sea, and the driver being an Englishman we availed ourselves of his offer of a seat on the engine to see better some of the steepest grades. The first five-and-twenty miles of our road ran through fairly level land, cultivated in the vicinity of the town wherever irrigation could be brought to bear; but as we got further tillage became less, and at last disappeared entirely. The characteristics of the country always maintained the same uniform appearance common to the north of Chili; namely ranges of hills in all directions, among which we seemed to wind in and out; parched-up plains, and bare red hills of earth, covered with rocks, cacti, and prickly pear.

The actual ascent of the mountains is by a zigzag road, in places having a grade of one foot in twenty-four. It was curious to watch from the engine the road we had travelled over lying beneath us; the one we had still to pass being close over our heads. The driver, a most intelligent man, pointed out all the places of interest we passed; showed us several copper mines just visible on the distant hills, and was in fact to his line the pleasant, communicative, well informed guide, that long ago was found in the driver and guard of the old mail coach. Coming to Chili originally as a fireman in one of the Pacific steamers, he soon gave it up for his present billet and has, I take it, as easy and pleasant a life as could well fall to the lot of a working man. About six hours' driving a day, no nightwork, no work on Sundays, and £20 a month pay.

One cannot help being struck by the apparent vastness of mineral wealth in Chili. Fresh copper and silver mines are daily being discovered, and as the network of railways which are gradually being pushed through the country open up and develop its resources, so will its immense mineral wealth expand and create for itself fresh outlets to the European market; and ere many years elapse, Chili will become the great copper emporium for the world. Several of the ores I saw contained eighty per cent. of pure metal; one specimen ran as high as ninety, and as most of these rich veins run close to the surface, and are to be got at with but little labour or expense, I fear the good times for the Cornish proprietors may be considered as having past.

The railway station at Ovalle is about three miles from the town. The road leading to it is steep and dusty. Carriages being in attendance, we hired a ricketty conveyance, with three horses harnessed abreast, to take us there. Some of the private carriages had four horses harnessed in the same manner. All small towns in Chili are so much alike, that describing them becomes mere repetition. All are built of adobe (large sun-dried mud bricks) constructed in blocks, have single-storied houses, the better class with a *patio;* a cathedral, a *plaza,* or large square with a fountain in the centre of it, and an *alameda* somewhere, and to this general description Ovalle was not dissimilar.

We put up at the "Gran Hotel de Francia," kept by Señor Juan Christian, a Frenchman of wandering disposition, who appeared to have been kicked all over the world in his search for gold. He had picked up English at the diggings in Australia, and further perfected his education in California by learning to swear; and as his conversation was freely interlarded with expletives more forceable than polite, the natives who could partly understand him must have had a queer idea of our national tongue.

A surveying party who had been prospecting for gold in the Andes, and were now going south to work a rich quartz deposit, were staying at the hotel. What their nationalities were it would be difficult to guess; but all spoke English, and had been much about the world. One of them informed us he had been a lieutenant in the Royal Navy; but he told us so many other curious things at the same time, it became utterly impossible to separate fact from fiction, so we took the whole as the workings of a somewhat heated imagination. In California he had grown beetroot, one plant of which four men were unable to lift from the ground after it had been dug up. In British Columbia he had chased deer with a steamboat among the numerous islands of the Gulf of Georgia; while, in Vancouver, he had hunted salmon up the small creeks in such numbers, that on arriving at the end they all jumped on shore to avoid capture.

We drove to Limari, and presented our letter to Don R., who most kindly pressed us to stay. Learning, however, that his house was overfull for the night, we determined on returning to the hotel, Don R. promising that early next morning we should be provided with horses and a guide to take us to the most likely parts of his estate for partridge, and that he would afterwards send for our luggage.

No Chilian has the slightest idea of the value of time, and it was nearly twelve o'clock before the guide and horses put in an appearance—quite too late for any shooting. Even had we been ardent enough to have ventured, the birds, more sensible, would have declined rising. During the heat of the day you may kick a partridge before he will take wing in this part of the world. Our guide took us a long ride in the evening, but not a partridge did we come across, nor any kind of game.

On our return to the house we found that Don R.'s friends had departed, that our traps had arrived, and that comfortable quarters had been found for us in a bedroom overlooking the farm, having a small sitting-room attached to it.

A large party assembled at mealtimes, the head farm-servants messing with the family. I was much amused one evening, when twelve of us were seated round the table, at number thirteen coming in rather late, and being laughingly packed off to find someone else to enter with him, or to eat his dinner elsewhere. I had often heard that thirteen was an unlucky number, but this was the first time I had ever seen summary justice dealt out to the individual that made it.

Next morning, with a fresh guide, an old French gardener devoted to "la chasse," we again tried our luck, but only killed a brace of banduria and a couple of dozen tortolita, not having even seen a partridge. The tortolita-shooting was rather good, as they were very numerous and are a quick-flying bird, not easily to be hit. They belong to the dove tribe, and are excellent eating; much better than the partridge, which are dry and tasteless. The immense number of hawks and kites we saw everywhere, fully accounted for the scarcity of game, and I only wondered how any birds could exist where these latter pests were in such abundance.

Giving up all idea of shooting, we devoted the remainder of our time to riding about the property, and indulging in the *dolce far niente* which forms no inconsiderable portion of life in Chili.

The farm, which was of considerable size, having a large proportion of acres under actual cultivation, chiefly produced wheat and cattle. Charmingly situated on a level plain between two high mountains, through which ran a sparkling little river, it was also supplied by the hills on each side of it with an extra quantity of water, thus enabling the owner to completely irrigate every foot of his land. The great scarcity of moisture, and the entire absence of rain except at certain seasons, is what makes the country at this time of the year so arid and bare of natural vegetation. In the winter, and after the rains, these apparent deserts are clad with wild flowers and a redundancy of verdure, and even the barren hills of Coquimbo are carpeted with nature's loveliest garb.

Where an ample supply of water can be commanded, everything will grow that is simply put into the ground. Manuring land is a thing unheard of, the natural richness of the soil being so great, that such a process would be merely time lost. Farm labour is from eighteen pence to two shillings a day. The most ancient methods are still retained for treating grain, the ears of which being merely collected, it is then trodden out by mares, and winnowed by hand. The system of irrigation is wasteful and laborious, no wooden sluices or floodgates being constructed in the waterways. When the water requires turning, a cumbersome process of digging a dam on the spot has to be resorted to; yet, notwithstanding all these drawbacks, Don R. assured me that, after deducting all expenses connected with the farm and house, it returned him ten per cent. clear money. The cattle-breeding farm was a day's ride from Limari, the beasts being generally brought in when required for sale, so as to undergo a fattening process on the vast fields of long stubble and lucern, prior to appearing for sale. Lucern thrives in a remarkable manner, as many as five crops being frequently taken from the same ground in the course of a twelvemonth.

The Chilians are very expert in the use of the lasso, which forms part of the equipment of every mounted man. Don R. showed me what is considered their neatest feat, namely taking the two fore-legs of a horse at the gallop. In doing this the lasso is not swung in the usual manner above the head, but trailed, and cast underhand. We went into the "corral," where some hundred horses were running about, and, making me select an animal out of the crowd, we drove all past where he was standing as hard as they could gallop. In a moment the lasso flew, and sure enough there was the victim I had pointed out, with the rope round each fore-leg. The swinging cast is comparatively easy, and I soon managed after a few lessons to get it out pretty straight, but the *peons* can place it unfailingly on the horns of the wildest bull going at the top of his speed across the country.

The natives may almost be said to live on horseback, and their costume is exceedingly picturesque; high-peaked wooden saddle padded with skins, boot-shaped stirrups of solid wood, elaborately carved, and weighing about ten pounds the pair, knee-boots, with solid silver spurs weighing frequently over three pounds, the rowels being sometimes much larger than a Mexican dollar; and a gaily-coloured poncho and straw hat complete the attire. The bits are terribly severe, the very slightest touch being sufficient to bring a horse on his haunches. Ladies dress much the same as everywhere else; but the black manto, covering the upper part of head and body, is common to all classes, though generally worn during Divine service.

No one could have been kinder or more hospitable than our friend, Don R., and though we were disappointed about the shooting, we had a very pleasant time and enjoyed our visit immensely. On our way back we met a veritable beggar on horseback. He was old and dilapidated, but his mount was by no means a "screw," and looked in very good condition. I thought of the old saying, "Put a beggar on horseback," etc., which I certainly never expected to have seen so literally realised; and thought that if our old ancient undertook the journey mentioned in the proverb, his gallop would be a very quiet one, as he certainly looked, poor old man, quite unable to travel fast.

Going through the town poor stupid old Major, getting bewildered by some carts that were passing, ran under the wheels of our carriage, and got one of the small bones of his fore-paw broken. It did not appear to pain him very much, and it might have been worse.

The only pretty place near Coquimbo is Compañia, a property belonging to Mr. L., a name well-known on the Pacific station from his excessive kindness and hospitality. Plentifully supplied with water, he is enabled to keep the land in the immediate vicinity of his house well irrigated; and large green fields of lucern, and quantities of flowers and trees, make the place a veritable oasis in the desert. His copper works, though not so extensive as those of Guayacon, were very interesting; and we saw there the process of moulding bars or ingots from the molten metal, which we had missed at the other establishment. He has gone in largely for planting the Australian *Eucalyptus*, which appears suited to the climate and grows well. It is to be hoped he may succeed, and that, prompted by his example, it may soon be extensively cultivated, and banish in time the hideous poplars which at present disfigure the country.

Since going on shore at Sombrero Island the ship's

bottom had not been looked at. A diving-dress being available in the *Nereus* (the store-ship for the station), her gunner went down (old D., our own diver, was too big and fat to get into it), and after examination reported a small portion of the false keel knocked off some eight feet from the stern-post, and two or three sheets of copper—not very serious damages, and easily repaired when occasion offered. On the 20th of March we left Coquimbo, which was the last port in Chili we touched at.

From Lat. 24° S. to Punta Arenas, the coast-line on the Pacific belongs to this Republic. Every kind of climate can be had in their country, from burning heat on the northern deserts to the icy cold of their southern glaciers. Almost everything that grows can be produced. Though still in its infancy, property is respected and life cared for in a manner very unusual among South American Republics. Her leading men have expanded ideas, encourage emigration, and protect the foreigner who casts his lot among them, offering in many parts of the country considerable inducements to settle. Notwithstanding the diplomacy of England (who treated her exactly as she did Denmark at her moment of trial), the individual Englishman is rather liked, and his good opinion courted. Bigoted and intolerant as is the opposition of the Roman Catholic priest, freedom of religious worship and general education of all classes is becoming common. Railways are being pushed into the interior, and the vast mineral and agricultural wealth of the country is being rapidly developed. The people are proud of their country, which is always a good sign in these new lands; and they have reason to be so, which is perhaps better. Her statesmen are patriotic and incorruptible—another novelty in Southern and Central American Republics; and on the whole, Chili is a rapidly progressing country, and may, with every prospect of its hopes being realised, look forward to a brilliant future.

CHAPTER VII.

Callao—Lima—Hotels—Ladies—The manto — Cathedral — Pizarro's bones—Midnight funeral—Priestcraft in Peru—Frequency of murders —Fate of the brothers Gutierrez—Earthquakes—A bull-fight—Bull-baiting—The Oroya railway—Highest point on the line 15,645 feet above the sea—Aztec cultivation—Distances from Callao and height above the sea of the various stations on the Oroya railway—Chorrillos—Corruption of all classes of government officials in Peru —Death of Major—Payta—Cross the equator—The Cocos Islands—Sharks—Turtle-turning *au naturel.*

On the 30th of March we anchored in Callao Bay, formed by Callao Point and a long spit that stretches off from it towards San Lorenzo Island. A part of this spit, termed the "Whale's Back," just shows at the water's edge, the sea breaking violently along its ridge. Callao Point is low, and consists of a bank of small round stones. The roadstead, assisted by the climate and prevalent southerly winds, becomes a fine harbour; the island of San Lorenzo protecting it from the long swell from the ocean. Before sighting the harbour we passed through a large herd of sea-lions, who did not appear in the least alarmed at our presence. They reared their huge bodies half out of the water to gaze on us, and then continued their gambols with the most perfect unconcern.

Passing Horradada, a curious rocky islet with a

hole quite through it, we saw clouds of birds. Pelicans, wide-awakes, and sea-gulls of every description were in myriads. The rocks were white with their droppings, and without seeing the "Chinchas" one was able to form a tolerable idea of what a guano island would be like.

The town of Callao extends about a mile along the beach that fronts the bay. Some of the houses are fairly built, and it has an excellent mole with a well protected inner harbour for boats. The railway station connecting it with Lima is close to the landing-place, but on the whole the town is dirty-looking and dilapidated, its streets ill-paved, and a general neglected and seedy appearance prevails everywhere. Such should not be the case. Hundreds of large vessels engaged in the guano trade are constantly here. The Pacific Steam Navigation Company make it the head-quarters for their magnificent fleet of vessels. A large export trade in nitre and metals necessitates much shipping, so that the harbour dues must be enormous, and the money spent in the town by merchant seamen alone very considerable.

Nothing about Callao rendered a stay there desirable; and as Lima, the capital of Peru, was only six miles off by rail, we soon took our departure. Any person having read Prescott's charming book of the history of the conquest of Peru, and the fate of the unfortunate Incas who governed it, will naturally take an interest in the town of Lima, which was founded by Pizarro in 1535. It stands on a plain at the foot of a lofty range of mountains, and through it runs the river Rimac, a turbulent, rapid stream, subject at seasons to considerable floods. The houses are mostly one-storied, flat-roofed, and, in fact, of precisely the same style of architecture as at Santiago or Valparaiso. The Plaza Mayor, Cathedral of San Francisco, and the Alameda del Acho, on the banks of the Rimac, are among the sights; but the streets are ill-paved and dirty, and in no way can Lima be compared to either of the Chilian cities.

We put up at the Gran Hôtel, in the Plaza, first of all; but shifted afterwards to Hôtel Maury, where Mr. R. B. N., one of the lieutenants of the *Tenedos*, was also staying. He had been there some time waiting for his ship (to which he had recently been appointed) to come into harbour. He knew most of the Lima people worth knowing, and was very good-natured to H. and myself, introducing us to his friends and rendering our stay up there an exceedingly pleasant one. With regard to the hotels, there is little to choose between any of them; all alike being dirty, exceedingly expensive, and cooking execrable.

The quantity of solid meat got through by a Peruvian in one sitting is simply marvellous. No sort of an attempt at delicacy of cooking is required to tempt his ravenous appetite: solid after solid disappears with extraordinary celerity, until one marvels how such a miserable under-sized little animal, as nine-tenths of them are, should possess such Gargantuan appetites and be able to stow away so much. The working classes and lower orders among the Peruvians are generally a mixed breed called *Mestizos*, and are as ugly a race as can well be met with. The pure bred Indians are not bad-looking, but the Lima ladies are exceedingly pretty, and, as a rule, particularly well dressed also. All classes of females wear the manto. The middle and poorer habitually, and the higher when they go to church or wish to be unrecognized. No feminine costume is more charming than the black dress and manto. It is becoming to all classes, whether rich or poor. A Peruvian servant is as gracefully dressed as her mistress, and looks some hundreds of degrees better than any of our own female domestics, got up in their mistresses' cast-off finery or in the cheap tawdry imitation they delight to stick on themselves.

This wearing of the manto gives the women a certain amount of licence not accorded in any other country, and as all classes usually dress in black devoid of ornament, when wearing it to recognize one's most intimate acquaintance becomes almost an impossibility. Sometimes half the face is exposed, at others but one eye. One eye is often quite sufficient to do much execution, for I doubt if anywhere are they softer or more expressive than in Lima.

Byron, in one of his poems, makes a very pertinent allusion to the peculiar effects of a sultry climate. Lima is only 12° from the equator; and absolution, where almost every other man you meet in the streets is a priest, is neither difficult to obtain nor costly to purchase.

I was disappointed on visiting the cathedral to find the interior so tawdry and filthy. A few paintings, concealed under a coating of dirt, adorned its principal altars; some revolting images of our Saviour, covered in blood, were scattered about the building; and even poor Pizarro's bones, which are exhibited to the curious for a trifling *douceur*, seemed to have caught the general infection and looked more dirty than bones have any right to do. The stalls were handsome carvings in walnut wood, the subjects—saints, prophets, and patriarchs; but so covered with dirt, that all the delicate arabesque traceries by which they were surrounded were completely hidden. Considering the enormous wealth the Spaniards got out of Peru, they certainly might have left some more lasting monument of their occupation than the miserable cathedral at Lima. The other churches, if not absolutely so dirty as the cathedral, were far from being clean. Funerals constantly take place after dark. I followed one I met in the streets at about eleven o'clock at night, into a neighbouring church, and watched the ceremony. The effect was theatrical, still impressive. The coffin lay on a raised marble slab; the lofty arched roof, the dim light, the solemn music, and the long rows of white-clothed priests, each holding a lighted taper, made me feel quite creepy, so that I was glad to get out of the holy precincts.

The priesthood in Peru are omnipotent: for which reason it is probably the worst governed and most miserable country in America; except perhaps Mexico, where the priests having been allowed their own way until quite recently, things are much in the same state. In exchange for this power, they amuse the populace with religious spectacles. On Good Friday, an image of our Saviour is placed on an ass, and lead about the streets, accompanied by a begging-box of course. The Last Supper is acted in the cathedral, a table being spread with all the luxuries in season. Images to represent Christ and the twelve Apostles are seated round it, each figure having a cigarette placed in its mouth, except our Saviour's, who gets a capital cigar. Judas is dressed as a soldier. The populace gaze with holy fervour on the pious scene, after which they are turned out and the priests devour the banquet.

Life and property are equally unsafe, and no one dreams of going out after dark unarmed, or riding in the country alone. Shortly before our arrival, an Englishman's house was attacked while the family were at dinner; several were wounded, but in the end they managed to beat off their assailants, one of whom was badly hit. His comrades carried him some distance; but finding themselves pursued, stabbed the miserable wretch, cut his head off, and took it away with them. One murder a day is about the regular allowance for the town, and it is very rare indeed to hear of the assassin being discovered and brought to justice. One man, José Chacamago, or some such name, whose photograph was exposed for sale among other notorieties and celebrities of Peru, was known to have committed fourteen murders; and how many more the miscreant polished off without detection, it would be hard to guess. Affairs being in such a condition, the country lives in a state of chronic insurrection. The mob, as a rule (cowardly, and brutal as mobs always are), generally allow the parties most interested to fight it out among themselves, after which they join in and finish off the vanquished. In July 1872, three brothers Gutierrez were implicated in a rebellion which they appear to have made a complete hash of. The mob waited very quietly until there was no doubt that the Gutierrez had lost the day, and then murdered them with every description of barbarity.

One brother was shot at Callao while walking on the platform of the railway station. The other two brothers were seized while endeavouring to escape from Lima, dragged to the cathedral, and hung upon one of the turrets over a hundred feet from the ground. They were then cut down, their bodies being dashed on the pavement, after which they were burned in the Plaza, and portions of them I believe actually eaten by the rabble. When the Lima people heard that a Gutierrez had been shot at Callao and was buried there, they went down, dug him out of his grave, and with every species of indignity dragged him along the road to the capital, just in time to join his brothers for their *auto da fé*.

The Zoological Gardens are worth a visit, being exceedingly well kept and very ornamental. The collection of beasts is poor, but the grounds being more botanical than zoological, the deficiency of animal life is made up for by a profusion of everything beautiful in the vegetable. A magnificent hall for dancing—it would make a grand skating-rink—is at the entrance, opening on the gardens, and a handsome building, sometimes used as an hotel, contains a fine picture of the death of the last of the Incas; a scene which, with most questionable taste, is occasionally engraved on some of their bank-notes.

Perpetual revolutions, corruption among all classes of government officials from the President downwards, and an uncertainty of life quite bewildering, are the chief characteristics of the people. An absence of thunder and lightning, and a prevalence of earthquakes are the most striking features of the country.

A slight earthquake took place early one morning while I was at Lima; but though it awoke most of the people, I did not feel it. I got so accustomed to shaking in the *Rocket*, that it would require a very rude shock to awake me now. Of course the shocks vary considerably in severity; but one curious fact about them is, that instead of people getting accustomed to these unpleasant visitations, the more they feel the less they like them, and the oldest inhabitants are invariably the greatest cowards.

In October 1746, Lima was visited with a most destructive earthquake, on which occasion Callao was suddenly submerged by a huge wave and completely destroyed. Out of 4000 people only 200 are said to have escaped.

The bull-ring at Lima is a very large one, and during the season a fight takes place nearly every Sunday. The operations are conducted in a manner very similar to those I have witnessed in Spain, but are not quite so brutal, their horses being very rarely killed; whereas, in Spain, the chief delight of the audience consists in seeing the wretched blindfolded screws they send to the arena gored to death. I remember seeing one bull at Algesiras kill six horses in less than five minutes, amid the frantic plaudits of a crowded house, among whom were many ladies, whose shrill voices screamed "bravo toro" with the loudest of them. The bull-fight we went to at Lima was given in honour of General Prado, a candidate for the presidency; and shortly after the time announced for the sports to commence, the judges having taken their seats, a flourish of trumpets announced that operations were about to begin.

The performers first promenaded the arena and made their bow to the judges; the parts of Picador, Banderilléro, Toreadór, and Matadór, being similar to those in the mother country. They were equally beautifully dressed, their jackets being one mass of gold embroidery. The gaily decked team of mules for carrying out the defunct bulls was similar, but there were only two Toreadórs, instead of a dozen. Instead of being on wretched screws, blindfolded for the attack, they were beautifully mounted, and their horses permitted to see; and instead of being armed with lances, they only carried a bright-coloured cloak over their arm. Another feature in the procession not met with in Spain, were twelve bull-dogs, fantastically clothed, and led by niggers in rear of the procession.

The cavalcade having retired, the doors were once more opened, and the two Toreadórs again making their appearance, waited calmly in the centre of the ring for the rush of the bull, who, mid a flourish of trumpets, shortly afterwards dashed towards them. The mastery these men had over their horses was simply wonderful. Wheeling round, as the animal was in the act of charging, the man attacked dropped his cloak over his horse's quarter, holding it about six inches from him; and then just keeping it, not certainly more than two inches in front of the bull's horns, galloped round the ring, the bull all the time tossing at the flag, and almost touching the horse; who, though snorting with alarm, was kept at this exact distance, until in disgust master Toro ceased the pursuit. These men were not padded like the Spanish Toreadórs, whose legs are cased in steel and leather (something like a cricketer's pads), and bandaged up to the waist, and every instant the bull's horns appeared on the point of striking them; but during the entire day, though several bulls were brought forward, not once did any of the horses receive the slightest scratch. This much of their bull-fighting is without any cruelty; the bull up to this period had not been tormented or received a single dart; and the man's sole defence lay in his matchless horsemanship and three yards of coloured cloth.

The rest of the performance was similar to those of Spain, and it is needless to recapitulate so well-known and oft-repeated a story. The most brutal part of the exhibition was reserved for the last. A bull having undergone sufficient tormenting to make him wicked, was left in possession of the ring. His human assailants having withdrawn, from all sides of the arena came racing up to the wretched animal the dogs we had seen in the procession, who stuck literally all over him. The bull appeared perfectly paralyzed, and after the first dog had seized him did not offer the slightest resistance. The bull-dogs held on with their usual tenacity to every part of his body) amid the frantic plaudits of the crowd), till at length, overcome with pain and exhaustion, the wretched beast fell to the ground, where for some minutes he lay, being eaten alive, until at last he was happily "pithed" by some of the attendants and put out of his misery.

A more cruel and brutal sight I never witnessed. There was nothing in it but sheer wanton barbarity, as the wretched bull never made the slightest resistance, or even attempted to shake the dogs off, who for some minutes after he had fallen were simply eating him alive. Before the dogs had succeeded in pulling the bull down, one of the brutes in the ring passed a sword twice through the wretched animal's body, avoiding a vital spot, but causing sufficient hemorrhage to render the dogs' task of pulling him down the more easy.

I am happy to say that no ladies were present, and but a small sprinkling of women belonging to the lower classes.

During our visit to Lima, I got an opportunity of seeing the celebrated Oroya Railway, which, running over a pass in the Cordillera, 15,645 feet above the sea, connects the rich and fertile valley of the river Amazon with the seaboard of Peru. It was constructed by a Mr. M., sometime a banker at San

Francisco, where he failed for a very large sum of money. He is now a kind of "Hudson," or "Railway King," of Peru, and I believe made several million of dollars through the Oroya contract. As luck would have it, N. heard that he was taking a party up the line, and succeeded through one of his friends in getting us asked to join them.

A regiment of red-breeched warriors were washing their clothes by the river-bank as we left at eight o'clock in the morning by a special train, and passing up the valley of the Rimac, cultivated on each bank with fields of maize and sugar-cane, soon got to the foot of the Cordillera. All along this valley lay the deserted towns and villages of the Aztecs, the extraordinary dry climate still preserving their walls intact. We halted for about an hour at one of the stations, where we found provided for us an excellent breakfast; and after leaving this, the zigzag ascent up the mountains commenced.

The difficulty of laying down a line of rails across the Cordillera can hardly be over-estimated, and as a great feat of engineering skill it is undoubtedly one of the most wonderful in the world. As a commercial speculation it is as absurd as it well can be, the traffic being utterly insufficient even to keep the line in repair. Landslips constantly carry away great portions of the track; people, owing to the extreme rarefaction of the air at the summit, are unable to remain there beyond a very limited time; and a few years will probably see the entire line deserted, it being an exceedingly expensive one to keep in repair. Its construction was a government job, started for the purpose of robbery, and by all accounts it has answered the purpose to perfection, enabling the various ministries to plunder their wretched country to the tune of millions.

As we travelled up the mountains, traces of the ancient Aztec cultivation became more apparent. To the highest brow of many of the hills, and for miles along the mountain, lay the distinctly marked terraces which Prescott alludes to in his interesting account of the Conquest. In layer above layer, like huge steps, they covered entire mountains; and the labour necessary for such gigantic farming must have been fabulous.

In parts of southern China, where the population is greater to the square acre than in any other country in the world, and where every inch of ground is brought under cultivation, I had seen similar means adopted for planting and irrigating the sides of steep hills; and from the knowledge I possessed of the amount of labour requisite for such an undertaking out there, could form an approximate idea of what the population must have been here, to have produced the stupendous works I saw in all directions around me.

As the ancient Aztec cultivation of these mountains by means of terraces, greatly exceeded in extent, owing to their altitude, the similar method in use among the Chinese who are the most thickly populated people in the world, so is it only reasonable to suppose that, in the same proportion, the Aztek population must have exceeded that of the Chinese; in which case, the enormous number of two hundred millions, supposed by some authors to be about the population of Peru at the time of Cortez, would not be greatly out of reason. The Indian population now is under two millions. When one remembers that Peru was only discovered in 1524, and conquered in 1536, it is simply fearful to think of the cruelty and oppression the Spaniards must necessarily have been guilty of, to have reduced so populous a country to its present state.

These terraces are the chief, I may almost say the only, traces left of the original possessors of the soil, and they had for me a sad and mournful interest, as looking on them I thought of the many millions of happy, peaceful, and industrious Indians they helped to support under the mild rule of their Incas princes, before Pizarro and his successors, aided by the Jesuits, caused their extermination. With all its benefits, Christianity has much to answer for; and as foul crimes have been perpetrated in its name, and by its ministers, as ever disgraced Mahometanism or idolatry; but in all its history, never was our Saviour's name more prostituted than it was among these unfortunate Aztecs, who, under the plea of conversion, their Christian conquerors barbarously annihilated.

Shortly after starting, Mr. M. presented us with a railway ticket, to keep as a souvenir of our trip, having on it the names of the different stations, their distances from Callao, and the height of each above the level of the sea. The carriage we travelled in was quite gorgeous, but exceedingly comfortable, and as we pursued our tortuous course, it was strange to see the line we had to travel on just over our heads, while that we had just left lay equally plain below us. The entrance to two tunnels, one exactly over the other, looked very curious; but it was undoubtedly the most extraordinary line I ever travelled on, or am ever likely to see again. The Americans talk a great deal of theirs over the Rocky Mountains, which at Sherman, their highest point, is eight thousand two hundred and forty-two feet above the sea; a very considerable altitude certainly, but one which sinks into insignificance when compared with the highest point on the Oroya, namely the Túnel en la Cima, fifteen thousand six hundred and forty-five feet above the ocean, and only a distance of one hundred and four miles and a half from Callao, which is at its edge.

From time to time, as we approached particularly interesting portions of the line, the train would stop, and the passengers get out and examine them. We walked over a high and spider-like bridge, spanning a ravine about two hundred feet below us, which was of a construction far more delicate in appearance than anything I had ever seen in Europe. During our journey, servants were constantly handing round ices and cunning drinks, and a pleasanter railway trip, or a more interesting one, I have never taken.

Chorrillos, a small town on the coast, and the Brighton of Peru, was well worth a visit. During the summer months nearly all the better classes from Lima go there for sea-bathing and promenade each night, most wonderfully attired, until past twelve o'clock. I went with N. one evening after dinner. The band was playing, and hundreds of well-dressed ladies were strolling up and down listening to its strains. In the verandahs, ladies might be seen swinging in grass hammocks, occasionally smoking cigarettes. The rooms were brilliantly lighted, and their occupants appeared to court observation, everything evidently being done for effect. The effect was however very pretty, and as the Peruvian ladies are really good-looking, one can only feel grateful to them for being so fond of showing themselves.

With the exception of Havannah, Lima is the most expensive town I was ever in. Everything is extravagant, and generally bad. The commonest necessaries of life are terribly exorbitant; and as everyone knows that the country is on the verge of bankruptcy, where all the money comes from to support this wilful waste it is hard to say.

The Government, and every official connected with it, are corrupt to a degree almost inconceivable. Always hard up for money, they resort to any means to obtain it, and it is not unusual for merchants to get from Government as much as thirty per cent. on money advanced by them, through taking advantage of the customs, and passing goods to the amount of their high rate of interest.

If anything could thoroughly disenchant some of our Radicals in England with their ultra-republican proclivities, it would be a visit to Peru; and I doubt if even Mr. Odger, or Sir Charles Dilke, would stand the ordeal. Our visit was drawing to a close, and after a couple of days' dawdling about Callao, a wretched place to stay in, on the 8th of April we started for Payta.

The day after leaving, we passed through many patches of discoloured water of various sizes, at times only a few hundred yards in diameter, and at others extending for several miles, but invariably marked by the deep blue which immediately surrounded them. There was no toning down or blending of these blood-like-coloured patches round their edges, though occasionally a bright blue streak of clear water would be seen distinctly passing through them. We brought some on board, and on examining it in a tumbler saw particles of apparently red dust floating through it. We had no microscope, but I believe they were animalculæ. A merchant skipper told me afterwards that whales were supposed to feed on them. The effect of sailing through this ensanguined sea was very peculiar, and I should fancy that it must have astonished the early and somewhat superstitious mariners considerably, as it really seemed as though we were steaming through blood.

We passed close to Ferrol Bay, celebrated as being a haunt and breeding-place for sea-lions. We saw two or three outside the harbour, but it was getting dusk, and H. would not go in.

N. visited it once, and told me they lay in thousands along the beach, and were perfectly indifferent to his party, who walked about among them without causing the slightest alarm.

Several were eighteen feet long, and had great manes like a lion; from his description the sight must have been one of extreme interest, and I was sorry we missed going into the bay.

Poor old Major, who had quite recovered from his accident at Ovalle, about this time began to show symptoms of strange excitability.

From being the greatest possible friends with the other dog on board, he became cross and snappish, and thrashed him whenever they met. At first we thought it was merely jealously, owing to Joe having gone on shore by himself while Major's foot was in bandages; but the poor fellow got from bad to worse, and the morning after we reached Payta died raving mad, and was buried in the harbour.

Poor dog! he was a general favourite on board and had served us well in the Straits.

Without him we should not have picked up a quarter of the birds we shot, the other animal being utterly useless, and he deserved a better fate than to perish thus miserably at the most wretched hole of a place in Peru.

Payta is situated on the slope at the foot of a hill on the south-east side of the bay. At a distance it is scarcely visible, the houses built of mud and bamboo being the same colour as the surrounding cliffs. It is the sea-port for the province of Puira, and does a considerable export trade in salt. Petroleum has recently been found there. The necessaries of life, such as meat, poultry, fruit, vegetables, and eggs, are reasonable in price and fairly good. The mangoes rival the celebrated kind at Bombay, and the alligator pears were excellent, both coming from a well-watered valley sixteen miles from the port. Even on the east coast of Africa, or in Madagascar, I have never seen a more miserable or more dirty town than Payta. Not a vestige of grass is to be seen, and not a single tree, or even bush, is to be met within miles. Many people living in the town have positively never seen a tree, if we except some wretched daubs that are painted on the walls of the cemetery. Tradition says they were once painted green, but the colour being so attractive to the donkeys, they soon eat it all off the walls; so they are now exhibited with bright blue foliage, and red trunks, in hopes that the more unnatural colour may preserve them. Over the door is a picture of our Saviour lying on a bench after the Crucifixion; and at each side are figures of Adam and Eve, the former with a battle-axe over his shoulder, and the latter carrying a sickle and bundle of corn.

The population is chiefly Indian, and on going to market early one morning, I was surprised at the number of pretty girls I saw, several of whom had ridden in on mules from the country. Their complexion was light bronze, features regular, with nose slightly inclined to be aquiline; eyes large and soft; and figure, slight, well formed, and graceful.

Considering Payta is only five degrees south of the equator, the climate is wonderfully cool. A light blanket is requisite in the early morning, and the temperature of the sea is delicious. Sharks seldom visit the harbour, and the bathing is the nearest approach to perfection I have ever had; indeed, there was nothing else to do but swim about. We had a tremendous haul of the seine one night, catching several thousands of fish about the size of herring. The Indians who assisted in pulling the net on shore were given as many as they could carry; we supplied every vessel in the harbour; fed the ship's company until they were tired, and afterwards had to throw overboard a couple of cartloads which we could not use. Their flavour was not bad, but they were too full of bones for any person to eat them with comfort. On the 20th of April we crossed the Line, Long. 84° 15′, and I felt a certain species of satisfaction at once more being in my own hemisphere.

Going through the "doldrums" we saw quantities of turtle, and lowered a boat to try and pick some up. They allowed the boat to come right on them; but the clever individual who took on himself their capture, merely poked the slumbering reptile about with his boat-hook, and Master Turtle went away.

On the 24th we anchored in Chatham Bay, Cocos Islands, an uninhabited but beautifully wooded and picturesque little spot, Lat. 5° 32′ 57″ N., and Long. 86° 58′ 22″ W. The shores appear to be composed of broken perpendicular rocky precipices, beyond which the surface rises unevenly to the summit of the island. Near the shore the jungle is composed of small trees, thick undergrowth, and a profusion of vine or supple-jack; but in the interior, large spreading trees and cocoa-nuts are numerous. Bright sparkling streams of deliciously cool water dash down the mountain sides, and a profusion of ferns and exotic leaves line its banks. Wild goats and pigs are on the island, but the cover is too thick to get at them, the only apparent way into the interior lying in the bed of a watercourse. Off the coast are several pretty little detached rocks and islets, particularly on the south-west side of the island, where they run off fully two miles. Colnett, who visited it in 1794, compares it in beauty of scenery to Tahiti, but without the advantages of its climate or hospitality of its inhabitants. Quantities of sea-birds were flying about, many of them pitching on the rigging as we came in. Pretty little birds the size of pigeons and perfectly white were flying in pairs through the woods; and far above all, floated stately frigate birds, sailing in majestic circles, many of them so high up as to resemble mere specks in the firmament.

With the exception of parts of the Mozambique Channel and Port Royal, Jamaica, I never saw a harbour so full of sharks as Chatham Bay. We caught two very large ones with hooks, and shot several others, but still the brutes kept swimming round the ship, constantly cutting the lines which the men were trying to catch small fish with. Every variety seemed to have a representative: the dreaded ground-shark were the most numerous; but several of their hammer-headed brethren (*Squalus zygæna*) honoured us with a visit also.

We left Cocos Island the same afternoon, passing through quantities of floating and sleeping turtle. On many of their backs were perched birds, and almost invariably, when a boat approached them, the bird would give three or four sharp pecks on the turtle's back, to apprise him of his danger, before flying off themselves. The temperature, which up to the equator had been quite cool and pleasant, at about

5° north became disagreeably warm, the thermometer constantly showing as much as 90° in the shade. The sea was smooth as a mill-pond, and as considerable quantities of turtle still floated on the surface, I determined to try my hand at catching one.

Getting a boat one afternoon, and arming the crew with boarding-pikes to keep off sharks, a large one having been seen swimming round the ship in the morning, I took a log-line with a running noose, and set off; my intention being to swim up gently to the sleeping turtle, fasten the line round one of his back fins, and allow the boat's crew to haul him in. A turtle was soon sighted from the ship, and pulling in the direction pointed out to us, we saw his shell shining above the water as the long gentle ocean swell caused him slowly to rise and fall. When within fifty yards of where he lay, the boat stopped rowing, and taking the end of the line between my teeth I swam silently towards him, one of the boat's crew paying out rope to me as I wanted it. When, however, within a few strokes of my still sleeping friend, he put his head out of water, looked at me, and was off before I could reach him. It was rather discouraging; however, I determined to try again, and another and larger one being soon discovered, we pulled very quietly up, and I resumed the same tactics. This time I slipped extra noiselessly into the water and swam with the utmost caution, but just as I was getting the noose ready, up ame the head and down went the turtle. This time, however, I was not to be done. Turtle, though they swim at a fair pace when they once get "way on," are slow starters; and never under any circumstances, no matter how greatly alarmed, do they dive perpendicularly. Knowing this, the instant I saw his head rise I threw away the log-line, and gave way all I knew after the alarmed and fast disappearing chase. It was pretty hard swimming to collar him, but knowing that unless I got level in less than thirty strokes I might shut up, I did all I knew, and coming up before he got steam on, I seized him by a hind-flipper and held on like grim death. It was a regular case of "pull devil, pull baker," the turtle doing his best to get down, and I trying equally hard to prevent him. He was uncommonly lively and kicked like mad, cutting my hands a good deal with the sharp nails on his fins. Once he got my head under water; however, when he did so I managed to get hold of his other flipper with my left hand, and succeeded in getting him over on his back, where I held him, until the boat coming up, hauled us both in together. I caught a smaller one by fair swimming, as from some reason best known to himself he did not dive more than three feet below the surface. Starting at about ten yards behind him, I got level and had his fin in about a minute's spin, judging from the time he detected the presence of an enemy, and succeeded in taking him to the boat. It was capital fun, and had it not been for the dread of sharks I might have got any number of them. Nothing can be simpler or more easy, and any moderate swimmer, when he once learns the way, will have no difficulty in catching them. The great object is to get them on their backs, and this once accomplished, holding them until the boat's crew come to the rescue is easy enough. Occasionally these turtle (*Testudo caretta*) are very heavy, weighing sometimes as much as nine hundred pounds. These were very much smaller; but the buoyancy of the animal causes it to float, and the slightest exertion prevents it sinking when once turned over. Until this is done the fight is pretty equal, and the sole art lies in quickly doing the trick.

CHAPTER VIII.

Acupulco — Massacre of the Protestant inhabitants by the fanatic Roman Catholics—Intolerance of the priests—Pira de la Questa—Tickle an alligator with small shot—Mexican cusine —Wild-fowl shooting on the lagoon—A ride in the dark—Manzanilla—A wild-goose chase—Kill an alligator—Fight between sharks and alligators—St. Blas—Cigars—Magnificent duck-shooting on the river Santiago—Alligators and dogs—Disagreeable encounter—Mazatlan—Freight for H.M. ships.

On the 6th of May, we anchored in the much-abused harbour of Acupulco, in Mexico. From the different accounts I had read, as well as from what had been told me, I expected to find a perfect oven, and was most agreeably surprised at discovering by experience that it was far cooler than it had been anywhere since leaving the equator: the thermometer one morning before sun-rise being as low as 75°, while outside, it had run as high as 94°.

For safe anchorage, the harbour is unsurpassed in the world, and the lofty ranges of densely wooded high volcanic mountains render it as beautiful as it is secure. The bay is a mile and a half deep, having an extent from east to west of about three miles, and is perfectly land-locked, the town lying on the west side of the port.

Acupulco, though once of some importance, has

gradually been going down hill. Prior to its occupation by the French, during their late war with Mexico, it almost enjoyed the privilege of a free port, paying a reduction so considerable on the imports, that the resident merchants were enabled to do a brisk trade with the interior, as well as with the capital. After the French left, the custom-house duties were again enforced, and shortly afterwards, the railway being completed between Vera Cruz and Mexico, all commerce went round to the other coast, and the final death-blow was given to Acupulco. Everything in connection with the government of this republic is managed by bribery. The salaries of the officials are small, and it is distinctly understood on both sides, that any appointment conferred carries with it the privilege of extorting as much money from the public as ever they can possibly screw out of them, and whoever can bribe the highest gets served the best. The Vera Cruz merchants manage this so well, that they are able to land their goods, and not only undersell the towns on the west coast up at the city of Mexico, but can also take away all their trade with the small villages and towns in their immediate neighbourhood. The town of Acupulco is clean, and the country, particularly after the arid hills and sandy plains of northern Chili and Peru, appeared a veritable garden of Eden. Once more we saw the graceful feathery palm-trees waving in the breeze; the verdant mango laden with its golden fruit, and the broad-leafed banana glistening in the sun. Alligator pears, oranges, limes, and pine-apples were abundant and inexpensive, and quantities of fish could be had by hauling the net.

Shortly before our arrival, Acupulco had been the scene of a shocking massacre of Protestants by the Roman Catholic inhabitants of the place, while the former were engaged in Divine worship; and the ruined remains of the little chapel were pointed out as we passed them on our way to the old fortress of San Diego castle.

It appears that a Protestant mission, being successful at the capital, had determined on pushing its way through the country: and there being some eighty converts and believers at Acupulco, it was determined, at their request, to establish among them a small place of worship. Unfortunately for the success of the undertaking, the local priest, one Padre Justo Pastor Nava, a bigoted and most intolerant papist, had in this particular district his cure of souls. His notoriety in this respect, as being a dangerous fanatic, was so generally known, that in 1859 on being taken prisoner at a battle fought against the Liberals at Casta Chica, he was tried by General Alvarez and sentenced to be shot. As ill-luck would have it, some influential friends succeeded in getting his sentence of death commuted into one of banishment: the temporary establishment of Maximilian's empire brought him back to Mexico, and the ordinary course of events took him here.

On the 26th of January, while the Protestants were at church, the building was surrounded by a mob armed with guns, and their deadly machetes, the doors were forced, and men and women promiscuously butchered. Fortunately some of the congregation had pistols; and others, rendered desperate by their terrible emergency, with arms wrested from the murderers, and stools, forms, or anything they could lay their hands on, drove the assassins through the doors, which they succeeded in barricading until help arrived, but not before seven men and women killed, and ten others severely wounded, had fallen victims to religious fanaticism.

The intolerance of what is termed the priest party in Mexico is beyond belief in these days of enlightenment and freedom of religious opinion. Very many, indeed almost the majority, of the better classes of Mexicans are in favour of liberty of conscience for all persuasions; but the unscrupulousness and vindictiveness of the priests and their more immediate followers, nullify the efforts of the enlightened few. Until these bigoted and fanatic gentry get thoroughly well trodden down, no peace, prosperity, or happiness, will be possible for the country.

I had a long talk on the subject with a Protestant Mexican. He was armed to the teeth, and told me that he considered it almost certain that some day he would be assassinated, and that his chief consolation lay in a knowledge that with the weapons he carried about him, unless completely surprised, he would at any rate send some half-dozen of his assailants to travel the unknown path before him. I commended his truly Christian spirit; advised him to emulate Joshua, David, Samuel, and the rest of the hard-smiting holy ones given to us for an example, to read his Bible, and burn powder freely whenever he got the chance.

The day after our arrival, H. and myself, getting mules and a guide, started for Pira de la Questa, a small Indian village about twelve miles from Acupulco, and situated near the extremity of a large lagoon, some thirty miles in circumference, which we were informed was full of wild fowl.

Over many a rough road, and in many lands have I ridden, but never did I travel a highway like unto this. The path ran over the mountains through a thick forest, and more resembled the bed of a water-course than an actually connected route. Nothing but mules, whose cat-like propensities enable them to overcome apparently insurmountable difficulties, could possibly have done the journey. In places the path was so narrow that two of these animals were unable to pass abreast, so that one would be obliged to back into a convenient corner, or scramble up a bank, to permit the other to go by. The forest was dense, but, as it was just prior to the rains, almost leafless, everything being burned and parched up except in the valleys and bottoms of ravines, where running water rendered the vegetation luxuriant and flourishing. This absence of foliage, though detracting considerably from the beauty of the forest, permitted us to view all the better its feathered denizens, and in few tropical countries have I seen such lovely birds, or in such numbers, as out here. To classify or name them would require a man to be a perambulating encyclopædia of natural history; but among them all, I was most struck with the number of specimens of the woodpecker class, several of which were very beautiful. One in particular with a blood-red top-knot, which glittered vividly in the sun, I envied much for my fishing-book, and regretted the guide had my gun in his possession nearly a mile behind.

As the sun was setting we entered the village, which consisted of a few mud huts with sideless roofs, and, halting before one of them, were informed by the guide that it was to be our quarters for the night. It was simply a roof of palm-leaves over a mud floor, there being no kind of wall or even screen, and it formed the universal dormitory of men, women, and children, pigs and poultry, at the principal hotel—the Claridge's, in fact—of Pira la Questa. Leaving the proprietress and her numerous progeny engaged in hunting down an active-looking fowl for our evening repast, we rode to the lagoon, and giving the guide our mules to hold, shot a few of the curious-looking aquatic birds, which he pronounced to be "buéno," or good for eating, that were feeding round the banks. It was rapidly getting dark, and seeing at a distance some birds that I took to be duck, I noiselessly crept down on them. To do so I had to pass over a small spot of white sand, concealed, until I was on it, by a clump of bushes. While still silently watching the birds I saw something move a little to my right, and on turning round discovered a huge alligator, whom I had almost cut off from the lake. The bushes had hidden us until absolutely face to face, and he came by me with his teeth grinning, and tail half cocked, in the most unamiable frame of mind I ever saw in one of his tribe.

Without intending it, I had very nearly cut him off from his native element; and though naturally a cowardly brute, feeling himself to a certain degree cornered, he had evidently made up his mind to fight. Not being prepared, with only small shot in my gun, for a duel with the reptile, I stopped short and gave him right of way, and, as he cleared me at about two yards, let him have both barrels behind the shoulder to expedite his movements, and had the satisfaction of seeing him give a jump into the water that would have done credit to a performer for the "Grand National." They are cowardly brutes, and, though I have been frequently in parts of the world they inhabit, I have never yet heard of an instance of a man being attacked by one on land. In the water it is different. A boy had, while bathing, been taken down some months since close to this very spot, and from what I saw of the lagoon next morning, I would not have ventured a swim there for untold gold. Had I been a little quicker, and unintentionally barred this fellow's way to the lake, I am quite certain he would have attacked me, as he must have passed somehow. These creatures never take to the jungle, and, like a rat driven into a corner, he would have been obliged to fight.

On returning to the village we found our dinner nearly ready; bread and liquor we had brought with us; but the hunted fowl, new-laid eggs, and hot tortillas, formed no bad meal for travellers sharp set by a mountain ride. After feeding, we visited some of the principal houses in the village, chaffed some of the good-humoured and pretty little Indian girls, and arranged about a canoe for the following morning. We then slung our grass hammocks among the miscellaneous company, and wooed the drowsy god of slumber, our guide slinging his hammock up between us, and sleeping with his machete buckled round him, ready for attack or defence at a moment's notice. The machete is the invariable companion of the poorer and middle classes of Mexicans, and the multiplicity of uses to which it is dedicated are something wonderful to the uninitiated. With it he clears the tangled paths in the forest; it helps to build his hut, to cut his firewood, and eat his dinner; he uses it for purposes of warfare, and too frequently also for purposes of assassination. The blade is broad, slightly curved, a little shorter than an infantry officer's regulation sword, and about twice as heavy. The handle is generally made of wood, the scabbard leather, and the edge invariably as keen as a razor. Occasionally the blades are ornamented with gold or silver, but the ordinary machete is perfectly plain.

Next morning we were up before daylight, and hastened to the banks of the lagoon, where according to agreement we should have found our canoe; none was forthcoming, however, and not until the sun broke fiercely on our heads, and our patience was completely exhausted, did the guide prevail on the man who was to have provided it, to go in search of another. After a still further considerable delay, at last he arrived, but with a rickety conveyance that would only hold one gun beside the paddler; and H. taking the canoe, I walked along the edge, and our shooting commenced.

The place was full of all kinds of odd-looking water-fowl. Geese, duck, teal, pelicans, flamingo, and spoon-bills were in hundreds, and many kinds of waders unknown to me; in fact, such an extraordinary variety of fresh-water birds I had never seen together before. The ducks were particularly handsome, having bright bronze breasts, which shone like burnished metal in the sun. Of teal I shot several varieties, many of them with exceedingly beautiful and brilliant plumage; but I think among the "queer ones" I killed, there was none more beautiful in plumage than the spoon-bill; for though his singular and uncouth beak did not improve his countenance, he had the most lovely and delicate tinge of rose-colour through his white feathers it is possible to conceive. We had him for dinner two days afterwards, and found him excellent. Not knowing a quarter of the birds that got up, and many of them being fishy and unfit for food, whenever one rose, the guide would cry either "buéno," or "no buéno," as it happened to be fit or unfit for culinary purposes; and so on for nine miles along the banks, sometimes through mud, at others through sand, and at others through jungle or water, did I plod along, taking whatever was termed "buéno," and occasionally peppering an obtrusive alligator when he came anything inside twelve yards.

The heat was intense, and to add to the discomfort of walking the paths through the jungle and mangrove swamps occasionally bordered the edges of the lake, and were so thickly crossed by cobwebs, that they were perpetually knocking off my hat, getting in my mouth and eyes, and at times almost impeded my progress. I never saw anything like them. Occasionally large forest-trees were entirely covered from top to bottom, and so thickly shrouded, that not a leaf or twig could be seen through its unnatural-looking winding-sheet. The lagoon seemed full of fish, who were jumping in shoals all over it; but not once during the entire day did we see a single bird settle on its surface, and from the number of alligators swimming about, I think they showed their wisdom.

It was capital sport, but precious hard work also, and I was just about "played out," when we reached a "ranche," where, after a pull of cold water that must have somewhat alarmed my constitution, I tumbled into a grass hammock, uncommonly glad to get out of the burning sun.

A pleasant-featured young Mexican woman, with a dark-eyed good-looking sister, soon dispatched between them one of the many chickens running about the house; and while the cazuela was preparing, they very good naturedly washed out my shirt, lending me, *ad interim*, some embroidered garment of their own. The rest of my clothes were hung up to dry, every stitch on me being thoroughly saturated. H. and the canoe soon after arrived; and how we did enjoy the homely but excellent fare our hostess put before us! Then came pipes and a siesta, and a couple of hours' rest saw us fit to return. H. had got enough of it, and borrowing a horse rode back to the village; I returned in the canoe, and got a good many shots *en route*. Our bag was a mixed one, and consisted of the birds I have already mentioned, with several others whose names we did not know, and four rabbits. Wild duck and teal predominated; and the guides could hardly stagger from the canoe to the houses with our united bag.

The sun was fast setting as we left Pira la Questa on our return journey, and ere we reached the mountain-top it was quite dark. Unable to see a yard before us, but knowing that we must go on, I threw the reins on my mule's neck, and, lighting a pipe, resigned myself implicitly to his sagacity, not only to find the path, but to avoid the obstacles which at every step lay before him. My confidence was not misplaced. With nose almost touching the ground, he seemed to smell his way along, and not once during our long ride did he deviate for a second from the proper track, or make a single false step or stumble. The sounds and strange cries during the dark stillness of the night were very remarkable. Whether caused by bird or insect I could not tell; but one in particular, resembling the prolonged whistle of a locomotive steam-engine, was frequently of more than a minute's duration without ceasing, and of such volume and intensity, that unless I had been aware of the utter impossibility of a train being within hundreds of miles, I would have almost sworn to so familiar a sound. The lights of Acupulco at last came in sight, and our animals soon after deposited us safely, after a somewhat trying but very agreeable trip.

The chief amusement of the Acupulcites appears to be cock-fighting. On Sundays and feast-days the pit is crowded all the afternoon, and the noise of crowing from the warriors in waiting all round the building is quite deafening. I observed that the men never carried their machetes in the cockpit—a very wise precautionary measure. No women were ever present. The population of the town is about four thousand inhabitants, chiefly mixed breeds, with an occasional dash of the nigger. Very few of its people showed any pure Spanish descent; but on the whole they were fairly good-looking and were certainly very civil.

On the 10th of May, we left Acupulco and steamed quietly along the Mexican coast in sight of land until we reached Manzanilla Bay, on the south-east part of which are situated the few wretched huts that constitute the village. The harbour is well protected from southerly winds but not from those directly from the westward. Behind the village, and only a few hundred yards from the sea-beach, is a large shallow lagoon which runs nearly forty miles into the interior, and at the end of the dry season becomes almost empty. The exhalations at this time rising from the mud and stagnant water are most dreadful, and even at our anchorage the stench during the night was almost unbearable. How anything can exist in such a fœtid atmosphere is in itself a puzzle; but being the port of Colima, a large city of forty thousand inhabitants, lying some ninety miles inland, persons connected with the customs, and merchants doing business with the interior, are compelled to keep it open. Colima is, I believe, healthy enough, and near it is an active volcano a little over 12,000 feet high, bearing the same name, and occasionally visible from the anchorage.

About three miles north-west from the harbour, across the bay, a small brook is marked on the charts as a watering-place. Immediately after anchoring I started for it, the sailing directions having stated that duck, geese, snipe, and alligators, abounded there. The only one of the four mentioned that we came across, was the latter, and on inquiring from the natives, they assured us that none of the others ever frequented the stream. There were, however, several kinds of water-fowl, which we knew from experience were tolerably good eating, and plenty of parrots and brilliant-plumaged birds, whose feathers were valuable for salmon-flies, so that we managed to get plenty of shots at something, though we were considerably disappointed in our expectations concerning the duck and geese.

While thus innocently amusing ourselves, we little knew the excitement we were creating among the harbour authorities at Manzanilla. That people should deliberately go out shooting in the heat of the sun, or move in it at all without some particularly strong inducement, was more than Mexican Custom-house officials could possibly conceive; and seeing our boat put off from the ship for a distant part of the bay, as soon as we had anchored, they at once fancied some grave offence against the state was about to be perpetrated, and despatched a boat after us in hot haste; at the same time sending eight mounted men (armed to the teeth) by the coast, to intercept us in that direction also. We were quietly paddling about in the stream, intent on discovering the whereabouts of the game mentioned by Mr. Imray in his book of coast directions (a very wild-goose chase we found it), while the excitement was going on; and before our return to where we left our boat, the Mexicans, by talking with the crew, became aware of the interesting fact that they had found a mare's nest, and of course when we arrived concealed from us the fact that they suspected smuggling, and had actually planned our arrest.

On returning after the day's shooting, we saw a strange boat lying near our cutter; her crew were very civil and gave us some water-melons. On the way down we had met a couple of men with two revolvers each, holding horses with holsters on their saddles, but they said nothing to us; and only when we returned on board did we find out, through the American Consul, Mr. J. H. D., the excitement we had been creating in the quiet little village of Manzanilla.

Next morning, before daylight, we started with Mr. D. across the lagoon, to a place about an hour's row from the village, where he was in the habit of getting wild duck. The lake was so shallow that our boat often grounded, and the oars at each stroke disturbed the black ink-like mud that constituted the bottom. The sides were beautifully wooded, and surrounded by ranges of hills extending far into the interior, the edges of the water being fringed by a belt of mangrove-trees, whose peculiarly bright green foliage contrasted pleasingly with the sombre colouring of the leafless trees behind them. The perfectly stagnant water was of a light yellow tint, and as full of alligators as it could well be. On reaching the shooting-ground, large patches of reeds, scattered along the edges of the lake, with fields of water-lilies and aquatic plants growing around them, we saw several flocks of duck, as well as spoon-bills, flamingo, pelicans, jackana, and water-fowl innumerable. Any number of small alligators were basking on the thick matting of weeds, through which the native boatmen, bare-legged and wading with the utmost indifference pushed our canoe. They did not seem to care three straws about even the largest of them; and at last, familiarity breeding contempt, we also got over our knees in water, and waded about among them perfectly unconcerned, intent only on the ducks.

Several eagles and hawks were hunting the ground as well as ourselves, and once on winging a jackana—a very beautiful bird, with a spur on each wing and large spider-like claws peculiarly adapted for enabling their possessor to run over the floating leaves of the water-lilies—a large and handsome eagle swooped down to where I was standing, and seizing on the wounded bird who lay not fifteen yards from me, carried him off, until a dose of No. 1 shot, properly administered, reminded him somewhat forcibly of the laws of "meum and tuum," and he paid the penalty of petty larceny with his life. The boldness of all the eagle, hawk, kite, and vulture tribe in these climates is quite remarkable; and as they are never molested by the natives, they are not only numerous, but so bold that they will sit on a tree without attempting to fly, though a man passes within ten yards of them. After firing a good many shots, and gathering a somewhat miscellaneous bag, (H. knocked over five ducks with one barrel), Mr. D.

saw a large alligator asleep on some mud, lying half in and half out of the water, and as I was the only one of the party who had brought any bullets, he sent one of the guides to show me where it lay, in hope that I might get a shot.

Slowly and with the greatest caution, I waded through the water until I got within twelve yards of where the brute lay, and aiming about an inch behind the eye, drove a bullet clean into his brain. He gave a convulsive kind of shudder and lash with his tail, and was, I believe, dead; but to make certain I gave him the second barrel at about four yards' distance behind the shoulder, and then felt quite confident that I had indeed "wound him up." It was some time before we could induce the natives to assist in pulling him on dry land. Though they do not mind them living and swimming about, they are particularly careful of a wounded one, a single sweep of its powerful tail, even when mortally stricken, being known to break both legs of a man, like a pipe stem. Though dead enough to all intents and purposes, an alligator, like either a shark or a turtle, will continue possessed of a certain amount of vitality and motion for a long period after life is really extinct. This fellow was still gently swaying his tail about while we bent on a rope to it, and, all five of us clapping on, soon hauled him to the dry mud on the bank, where we took his length, opened his jaws, and generally examined the formidable-looking reptile at our leisure. He was about fifteen feet long and inconceivably hideous. The first bullet had smashed a large hole exactly where I aimed, namely about one inch behind the eye; the skull seemed comparatively thin there, was unprotected by any thick skin, and a large lump of his brain was oozing through the wound. The second bullet went through his heart; but I am convinced that it was unnecessary, as the first shot had done all that was needful. Much as people have written to the contrary, I am quite satisfied now that an alligator is as easily slain as a rabbit, if only hit in the right place; and that place is *not* in the eye, as is generally stated; but on the same level, and from an inch to an inch and a half behind it. The brain in all reptiles lies rather far back in the head, joining almost to the neck. By striking one in the eye from many positions it is quite possible that the brain may not be touched at all; while, if the ball hits the slightest degree in front of it on the creature's long ugly snout, the bullet might as well be chucked in the river for all the harm it will do the alligator. Unsightly as these gentry are the Indians occasionally eat them. The skins are sometimes tanned; but they smell so strong, it is an awkward job to handle them. During dry seasons they collect in vast quantities in the small pools still left unevaporated, and are then killed in large numbers for their hides, which when tanned are found serviceable for many purposes. They are tougher than ordinary leather, and resist water better. Only the belly pieces are used.

Some few years ago, during a very heavy rain, a number of alligators got taken out of the lake by a small river running into the sea, which was greatly flooded. They were immediately attacked by the sharks, and a strange battle ensued between these equally voracious monsters, which all the people of the village flocked out to witness. The battle lasted all day, and the noise of the combat could be heard half a mile off. John Shark was, however, more at home in his native element than his scaly antagonist, and eventually the alligators were all eaten up or killed.

The chief exports of Manzanilla are cedar and ornamental woods, any quantity of which grow in the forests. Many of these woods are rare, one in particular, "rainbow-wood," being particularly valuable. Rose-wood, mahogany, and ebony, are quite common; but the country is so little opened up, and the inhabitants are so lethargic, that hardly any trade exists. Colima coffee is celebrated, but very little is grown, and the whole country is gradually going from bad to worse.

The seining party had a pretty good haul, getting quite a mixed bag—a fish, not unlike a salmon, weighing about thirty pounds, and a very fine well-conditioned turtle, being among the number.

We left Manzanilla on the 15th of May, continuing our course close to the shore up to Cape Corrientes. The scenery was picturesque and diversified, consisting of ranges of wooded mountains, extending as far as the eye could reach into the interior. Not one single tract of flat or table-land appeared anywhere, and the whole of Mexico seemed nothing but a succession of mountains all over the country; at any rate, for sixty miles or more bordering the Pacific.

On the 17th we anchored at St. Blas, a small village built near the mouths of the River Santiago. It consists of one street, a custom-house, and a quantity of huts rather picturesquely situated among cocoa-nut, palm, and banana trees. St. Blas is the port of Tepec, a town of some importance, with a population of 20,000 inhabitants, about sixty miles inland, and does a small export trade in ebony, mahogany, rose-wood, cedar, india-rubber, and tortoise-shell; it also has a cigar manufactory belonging to a Señor Mardrasso, which turns out a very smokeable weed. They are superior to those made at Tepec, and although only $2 a hundred, are certainly better than any cigars I have bought at Manilla, Brazil, or Gibraltar, all of which places manufacture largely. In fact, the only cigar that is superior to them is the genuine Havannah, and *that* luxury few people ever get hold of, though they have Julian Alvarez, Cabanna, or Partegas stamped on the boxes they smoke them from. Some years ago I visited Havannah, and smoked on the premises of the above-mentioned celebrated firms many of their different brands. I can only say that they were very unlike the same cigar as sold by most of the tobacconists and at half the clubs in London; and I do not believe one man in twenty in England has ever had a genuine Cabanna or Partegas even in his mouth.

We were fortunate in meeting here a very nice fellow, an American, who, having gone somewhat through the *rôle* of the Prodigal Son, was doing his husk-feeding among the swine at St. Blas, prior to the execution of the fatted calf by his relations in the States, who will, I believe, come to the front when they consider his penance sufficient. He was very fond of shooting, and offered to show us the ground if we liked to come with him; so taking our guns, in the afternoon we did a little pottering about the settlement, prior to a longer expedition next morning, for which we had to make arrangements. We met during our stroll a few rabbits, crested quail, doves, and parrots; but owing to the cover being very thick, and the sand-flies after sunset as active and fierce as tigers, we did not make much of a hand at them. The rabbits were well-sized and heavy, and the quail remarkably handsome birds, about the size of young partridges, and carrying a small Prince-of-Wales-like plume on the top of their heads.

Mr. F. having provided horses and a guide, we started next morning at four o'clock for the shooting-ground, which we imagined, from our guide Fokia's description the previous evening, to be about five or six miles off. We rode along at a brisk pace for about an hour, and then asked: "How far had we to go?" "Some way!" was the reply. In another hour we again ventured to inquire, and again received the like answer; and at the end of the third hour could only elicit the same information to our cross-questioning. Our horses, who were wretched screws, were about this period unmistakably pumped, owing to our having, in ignorance of the distance, pressed them somewhat at the commencement of our journey, and we were uncommonly glad at hearing from a cottager, whom we found looking after a lot of bee-hives, that a cigarette, *i.e.*, the time taken to smoke one, would bring us to our destination, which eventually proved to be about a mile off. The entire distance, we afterwards learned, was twenty-four miles. The village which we stopped at was called Autan; and consisted of merely a few detached huts built near a ford across the River Santiago; a mud-coloured stream about the size of the Thames at Richmond. At the best-looking and cleanest of the shanties we took up our quarters, stabled our tired nags, prepared food, and made ourselves generally at home. It is the custom of the country, and in Mexico a man must do everything for himself. After watering and feeding the nags, and getting some breakfast, we set off, but lost much time in finding the proper place, having been directed first of all to a lagoon at least a mile out of our road. On getting there, a peasant told us that though there were lots of duck, they were hard to get at, as no canoes were to be had, and the sides of the lake were thickly coated with mangroves, in many places impenetrable. He strongly recommended us to try the river, where he declared them to be in thousands; but all through the village, and wherever else we inquired, the same pleasing intelligence greeted us, namely, that "mocho patíco" abounded. With some difficulty we secured a couple of canoes, and at last got fairly off on our way down the river; and within ten minutes of the time of starting saw wild duck pluming themselves on the bank, and had opened the ball by knocking over a brace. The further we went the more we saw of them, and at last we came to a kind of shallow spit in the centre of the river, where they literally were in clouds. Even in China—one of the finest countries for duck-shooting in the world—I never saw them in such quantities. They rose in thousands, and though repeatedly fired at, constantly returned to the same spot.

There were many varieties, some of them being larger than Muscovys, and of almost black plumage. The teal tribe were well represented by several beautiful species; but by far the majority were widgeon, like those we had shot at Manzanilla, whose prevailing colour was an exquisite light bronze.

That we were to have come in for such sport, never for a moment entered our wildest imagination; and though we both brought some No. 1 shot, it soon became expended, and No. 5, our other kind, was too small. We lost a number of wounded birds, the alligators took a few more, but we carried home twenty-nine couple and a half, which was pretty good work for one afternoon, firing chiefly with No. 5, which was not half large enough for the heaviest kind of duck, or for some of the ranges we often had to take them at. I am quite certain that, had we known our ground, had proper ammunition, and been on it by daylight, we would have killed at least a hundred ducks each. Had we gone at them with duck-guns we might have loaded a waggon.

The country for a considerable extent on each bank consisted of large fields of Indian corn, in which the birds feed every night, and on which they get fat as butter, well-flavoured, and deliciously tender, losing all fishy taste completely. Their crops when opened were full of this grain, and the damage and loss they cause the farmer must be very considerable. The river was full of alligators, whose ugly heads were to be seen in all directions. Coming back, we saw three large ones sleeping on a bank of sand, about fifty yards off. I gave the largest a bullet, but as it evidently was not properly applied, it merely caused him to hop into the river with extraordinary agility and quickness, and his slumbering comrades followed suit.

Alligators are desperately fond of dogs, not with the same kind of love that we bear for the constant companion of our wanderings, but with a carnivorous affection, particularly unpleasant for the recipient. *Apropos* of it, I heard a story, to the truth of which several people vouched, but which is still so marvellous, that, although I believe it myself, I will not ask anybody else to believe it unless they please.

Along the banks of the Santiago, on each side, are numerous little villages, and in each village are any quantity of dogs. Now, on certain occasions, even the most moral dogs become particularly amorous, and when the fit is on them, naturally feel desirous of visiting their kindred on the opposite bank. But how to cross the river? Long acquaintance with its dangers, and possibly experience handed down from a long line of canine ancestors, have made them so dread these yellow waters, that on ordinary occasions they dare hardly drink, and swimming they never think of. Behold now the cunning, as well as the power of love. Half-a-dozen go to the water's edge and commence howling. In a few minutes some twenty fearful heads gently protrude themselves from the turbid depths, in eager expectation of their prey. The curs slowly retire down the river, followed by the heads; fresh slimy figures join the procession; and occasionally going so near the water as to tempt their enemies, and still keeping up their music, they lead the alligators a mile from home. At this point the dogs redouble their barking, and for an hour render night hideous by their constant and incessant cries. All the alligators within reach of the noise are irresistibly attracted by its (to them) seductive sounds. The river, opposite this nocturnal concert, is alive with excited *caimen;* and having thus succeeded in obtaining an immense audience, the cunning dogs turn tail, and race like mad up the river, dash across the now deserted ford, and from the midst of their expectant companions chuckle over the alligators, who are left to crawl up the stream again as best they may, labouring under the pleasant conviction of having been sold.

One of our boatmen was very clever at bringing the canoe on birds, but was equally talented at getting our brandy-bottle, which he seized and emptied in the most barefaced manner whenever he could claw hold of it, without so much as saying "By your leave."

On our way out we shot some *chichilaca*, which we had cooked, and found excellent. They are noisy, chattering birds, about the size of an English water-hen, but with bright brown plumage, and long tail, like a pheasant. They inhabit the dense forests in considerable numbers, and are considered by the

Mexicans a great delicacy. We had a charming moonlight night for our return ride, and reached St. Blas about four o'clock in the morning, after a good solid twenty-four hours' work; all day in the sun, and all night in the saddle, but certainly after the best day's duck-shooting I ever had.

On arriving at the town, sounds of revelry and music proceeded from a house we were passing, before which a number of men were lounging about; one of them gesticulating frantically drew his revolver, and stopped before my horse, which happened to be leading. It was rather startling, particularly with the knowledge that, of all places in the world, the cut-throat ruffian exists to greater perfection in Mexico than in any other part of it. Having a pistol handy, I instantly drew it, and was on the point of shooting the fellow down (which I would have been perfectly justified in doing—nineteen out of twenty Americans would not have hesitated), when, fortunately for the Mexican, Mr. F., who was behind, cried out that he was drunk, so keeping my revolver cocked I waited quietly, resolving to shoot him as quickly as possible should he point his pistol at me, trusting to luck to get first fire.

The man, however, was not drunk, though he might have been drinking; he walked steadily enough, and his speech, though loud and vociferous, was perfectly distinct. To me it mattered little which he was, it being quite as unpleasant being killed by a drunken Mexican as a sober one; and though wishing much to avoid bloodshed, and quite satisfied with my bag of duck, I kept my finger on the trigger, and watched his every movement as I never watched man (but once) before.

For about half a minute we thus stood facing each other, and at last, much to my satisfaction, the brute turned on his heel and walked off.

It seems that the ruffian was a captain of cavalry, who had that evening come in on escort duty, and had been on the drink ever since. During the night he had been firing off his revolver, much to everybody's alarm; no one dare go near or prevent him, and virtually he had taken charge of the town. The fright every one appeared to be in of this exceedingly disagreeable person was almost amusing, as one of the authorities, who came up shortly after this little episode had taken place, devoutly exclaimed, when I told him I was on the point of firing, that "he wished to God I had, as shooting would have done him good."

The amount of brigandage, robbery, and murder that goes on in the immediate neighbourhood of St. Blas is simply dreadful, and life in Mexico seems quite a drug on the market. I may, for all I know, have had a close shave of mine; but I can answer for it, that my friend was as close to death that night as he had ever been. We were not three paces apart; I felt as cool as a cucumber; and had the muzzle of his pistol for one second covered my body, I should have let drive at him like lightning before he could have drawn the trigger, and H., who was a few yards off, would have let him have it also. These brutes are like vermin, and are generally treated as such, being killed without any mercy when they show their teeth; but my little adventure ending as it did, I cannot help feeling sincerely thankful that, much as he deserved shooting, I did not fire.

Being somewhat short of fuel, and no coal being obtainable in the place, we bought twenty tons of coquito, or palm-nuts, from a German Jew, who considerately charged us, we afterwards discovered, five times its market price. This fellow proved himself an exceedingly sharp practitioner, as just when we were leaving harbour,—indeed, we were under weigh at the time,—he came alongside with a log of rosewood, which the first lieutenant had ordered for ship adornments, but which turned out on examination by the carpenter to be only mahogany, and of course not a quarter of the value of the money paid for it. We left St. Blas on the 19th of May, and reached Mazatlan the following day.

Mazatlan is by far the most important, as well as the largest, town on this side of the Mexican coast-line. Some of the houses are well built; it has a considerable population, and is the outlet for the products of the valuable mining district of St. Sebastian. The town is fairly healthy, being built on the crest of some heights clear of mangrove and swamp. It is comparatively clean, and has a good hotel, where we managed to get a decently cooked dinner.

On Sunday and Thursday evenings a military band plays in the square, and until eleven at night the fair damsels of the period promenade to its enlivening strains. The river, bearing the same name, is about a third of a mile wide at the entrance, and about twenty miles from its mouth lies old Mazatlan, well known to ancient navigators as far back as 1587, when "Master Thomas Cavendish in the talle shippe *Desire*, refreshed his gallant company before cruizing off Cape Lucas for a Spanish galleon." There was no shooting to be had, the wild fowl having all migrated, and I felt the five days we remained here, waiting for a chance of "freight," hang very heavy on my hands, having nothing whatever to do.

Apropos of freight, I cannot help feeling that the action taken by England in this matter is both cowardly and disgraceful. With the laws of Mexico, whether they be right or wrong, just or unjust, we have nothing whatever to do; and permitting H.M. vessels to engage even surreptitiously in smuggling, is certainly not acting up to the high tone of moral policy which, in public, our statesmen are so fond of vaunting as the leading characteristic of English diplomacy.

With a view to prohibit the enormous and continual drain of bullion from the country, the Mexicans have placed the crushing impost of nine per cent. on all silver leaving their shores; to avoid this the people having dollars or bars which they wish shipped, smuggle them on board our men-of-war, which—our diplomatic relations with the country having long ceased—seem to cruise in Mexican waters for no other purpose than that of aiding and abetting the subjects and residents in the country to break her laws.

That nine per cent. is an arbitrary and unjust tax, I do not for a minute attempt to deny; but that her Majesty's ships should be mixed up with smuggling, the officer in command having a direct monetary interest in the transaction, I consider still more arbitrary, unjust, and disgraceful on the part of England.

What should we say, if German or French vessels-of-war systematically engaged in traffic in contraband on our own coasts? Or dare we attempt the same game with any nation as powerful as ourselves? We certainly have a kind of precedent for our conduct in encouraging the people of foreign countries to break their excise laws, inasmuch as for many years we protected opium smuggling in China; but I am unaware of any instance in which we have so acted with regard to any country able to hold her own, or defend her constitution.

No people in the world are more apt to brag of their national character for honesty and justice than ourselves. We thrash the Chinese, Japanese, and Abyssinians, on the smallest provocation; we go frantic with delight at the great military achievement of a well-armed and disciplined force licking a few miserable niggers in Ashantee; yet we let our councils pass unheeded in Europe, sneak out of our defensive treaties with Demark—(how bitterly *now* must France regret her conduct in that affair),—and submit to many a cousinly kick from America. Truly we have a deal to be proud of; but, I take it, more so of the past than the present. Our foreign policy for nearly the last twenty years is enough to make any person with the slightest spark of honour in his composition, who takes the trouble to think on the matter at all, perfectly sick with disgust.

On the 24th of May we left Mazatlan, and next

morning saw a most remarkable and interesting sight. On going on deck I found the ship in the midst of a huge shoal of porpoises, who were performing the most extraordinary antics I had ever yet seen that agile but otherwise sedate animal go through. Not content with taking unusual and terrific bounds out of the water, they varied the entertainment by occasionally turning complete somersaults; while, at other times, they leaed perpendicularly from the ocean, their entire bodies shivering like a fresh-hooked spring salmon, or a lively sea-trout on first feeling steel. Occasionally some thousands of them would form line, wheel, and change front, with military precision, charging occasionally in perfect order. The cause of all this commotion was an immense school of small fish who had the misfortune to fall in the way of the porpoises, and who were now having a particularly hot time of it. While these relentless enemies pursued them in the depths and pushed them towards the surface, thousands of birds had congregated over the animated scene, and were swooping down on the luckless fish, who in avoiding Scylla perished on Charybdis. All manner of birds seemed present; and, above all, soared the graceful frigate-bird, a predatory and rapacious gull, whose stretch of wing almost equals that of an albatross; but who, disdaining to work for himself, chiefly exists by plundering others. This game lasted for hours; and as we passed away in the distance, the occasional plunges just faintly visible on the horizon showed that the work of death was still continued.

Next day we sighted Cape St. Lucas. We here met a stiffish head-wind, and from this point commenced the only miserable period of our long cruise from England; for I honestly confess that the next five weeks were the most irksome I ever passed on board ship. We ran out of coal, and had to beat up under sail, making occasionally twenty miles on our course in one day, only to find ourselves the next thirty farther off. The coast-line was uninteresting and desolate. Barren, rugged, arid mountains of volcanic formation, devoid of the smallest particle of verdure, was the character of the only land we ever saw, and my cruising off Lower California will long be remembered only as a species of hideous nightmare. The coast was misplaced on the chart, and as our chronometers were several miles out also, our track occasionally showed us as being from ten to twenty miles inland. Shortly we ran out of beer and all fresh provisions, and the ship's company had to go on half-allowance of bread, with every prospect of its being still further reduced; so, what with one thing and another, everyone felt thoroughly disgusted.

On the 9th of June we passed the islands of Cerros and Natividad. The former is twenty miles long, and consists of a succession of high and abrupt mountain peaks, ranging up to 2500 feet. A few pine-trees are on some of the highest of these sharp ridges, but not a blade of grass or other sign of vegetation is visible. Indications of quartz rock and copper abounded, and many of the southern slopes presented a dark red hue, interspersed with high variegated cliffs, perfectly devoid of the smallest particle of green. About this locality we saw numerous whales, and indeed for several days we seemed to be passed by incessant schools of them. Many rose within a few feet of the ship, and watching these huge monsters—for they were of the very largest size I ever saw—sport about, gambol and blow, helped to relieve our monotony, and gave us something besides our own bad luck to talk about.

On the 16th we passed Guadaloupe, an island about fifteen miles long by five broad, and containing a range of mountains varying from 2000 to 3412 feet in elevation. On the south side of the island are two rocky islets at some distance from the shore, the outermost of which presents a bare face of cliff 500 feet high. On the northern extremity there is, in comparison to the rest of the coast in the immediate vicinity, a considerable growth of timber. The island is uninhabited. I noticed two very perfect craters of an extinct volcano. The cones were still marked by streaks of lava, and deep indentations at the apex showed that at some not very remote period it must have been in a state of action. The slopes of the mountains were gradual and very different from the abrupt formations on Cerros.

A day or so after leaving Guadaloupe we were followed for many miles by a very beautiful little seal, who was quite alone. At night he made several efforts to come into the ship, and often rose to smell the hands that were extended towards him. We lowered a grating and made several efforts to assist our little friend on board, but without success; and at last, though evidently reluctantly, he left us, but I cannot help thinking he must have been some tame seal got adrift, as such perfect confidence I never witnessed before. About this time we were really hard up. Biscuit all gone, except two days' half-rations; water allowanced; coal only sufficient to anchor by; and everything else equally short; so on the 28th we sent the cutter to beat and pull up to San Diego (a distance of a hundred miles) and get us assistance. After she left we had a slice of luck, and succeeded in making port on the last day of June (just as the boat was coming out of harbour again to meet us), after having been over five weeks doing the wretched little distance of one thousand miles.

This brings my wanderings by sea to a close. Owing to the incredible time of eight months which the *Rocket* had taken in reaching San Diego, my object in going to Vancouver had been entirely frustrated. Knowing something about ships and average passages, in talking the matter over at my club with H., prior to leaving England, we both allowed, with every possible margin for delays, and taking into due consideration the character of craft she belonged to, that six months was the very longest time we could possibly be in reaching Esquimault. Had our deductions been right, our arrival would have been on the 4th of April—almost a pity it was not the 1st, as it would have rendered the sell more complete; but even then we both expected to have arrived sooner, and only allowed six months as being the extreme limit.

My intention was to have fished during the summer months in the various rivers of Vancouver, British Columbia, and Alaska; however, "*L'homme propose et Dieu dispose*," and to attempt doing all I had intended, particularly as I wished to penetrate as far north as possible in the new possessions of the United States, would have been, so late in the season, simple folly.

To pretend indifference would be absurd. Passionately fond of salmon-fishing, it was at the time a bitter disappointment; and if I mentally blessed the designer of such a piece of rubbish as the *Rocket*, it is only what he deserves.

His answer, I know, would be, "She is only intended for river work, not ocean passages."

I have been in her in river work, and she is not fit for it. In the river La Plata, H. lost his handkerchief overboard, and she took half an hour cruising about the harbour, on a perfectly fine day, in her endeavours to get round to pick up a boat which had looked for it. The scene was somewhat ludicrous. H., in taking off his cap, dropped overboard a handkerchief which was in it, and a merchant-skipper's boat happening to be near at the time, he hailed her to drop astern and pick it up, promising in return to give him a tow. Down went the helm—scrunch, scrunch, went the starboard screw to get the old beast round — and away goes the good-natured skipper to look for the lost rag. After a short search, the handkerchief, which has been floating tranquilly astern, goes down, and the skipper again turns his boat's head towards his own ship. Scrunch,

scrunch, still go the *Rocket's* screws, as H. again sings out, "I am coming to pick you up!" So apparently was Christmas. The skipper held up his hand, the recognised sign among seafaring men of having heard and understood, but continues at a slow leisurely stroke on his way to his own ship. Away we go all over the harbour wildly endeavouring to get round, a very slight wind and a two-knot tide completely humbugging us. Perseverance is however ultimately crowned with success; but as we pass the skipper's ship, we see him on the quarter-deck, and his boat already at the davits. "I was coming to tow you up," shouts H. The silent skipper smiles, and again raises his hand. "D——n it," says H. turning to me, "if the fellow had *only waited*, I'd have towed him up."

All through the Straits of Magellan and Smyth's Channel, where the sea, owing to its tortuous course, narrow passages, and high protecting mountains, is far smoother than three-fourths of the navigable rivers in the world, she behaved equally badly, and took five weeks in doing a distance performed by th ordinary mail steamers in five days. In a dead calm but with a little swell against her, she could never go beyond three knots. Under sail, her leeway was something incredible, and nothing but a perfect gale on her quarter ever induced her to go over five knots. A battering charge from the 7-inch gun invariably tore up everything about it, nor do I consider it possible that any number of shots in the event of bombardment could be fired from her in rapid succession. Looking, therefore, at her in every possible light, her class is a rank failure; and it is much to be regretted that a class of vessel which almost above all others is most necessary to the service in time of war, should be merely represented by the miserable failures which are at present the only kind we possess.

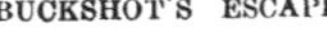

BUCKSHOT'S ESCAPE.

See page 323.

UNIV. OF MICH.

CHAPTER IX.

Deductions concerning "universal suffrage" in South America and Mexico—How they apply to England—Deductions concerning priestcraft in South America and Mexico—How it applies to England—San Diego—Los Angeles—Californian wine—Quail—Ground-squirrels—Californian driving—Sold—San Francisco—Expectoration—Peculiarities—of dress—The 4th of July—Soda Springs, Siskiyou Co.—Headwaters of the Sacramento—Salmon-fishing extraordinary—Headwaters of the McLeod—Dolly Varden trout—Watching a deer-lick—Night-watch for a bear—A game salmon—Railway companies and guns.

INDEPENDENT of the mere interest inseparably attached to visiting strange countries, much is to be learned from observing their manners and customs, and, I take it, few lessons are more beneficial than the one gained by travel.

Shooting, fishing, and becoming acquainted with nature in its grandest and most exquisite features, are strong inducements to most men; but to enjoy these the traveller has to sojourn in many lands, peopled by strange races, and living under laws widely different from his own. By mixing freely with these people, putting all narrow prejudices entirely aside, and by endeavouring as far as possible to blend and amalgamate with those around, a stranger invites confidence, and learns their civil and religious state, as well as renders himself more welcome by the delicate and judicious flattery imperceptibly conveyed by endeavouring to adopt their habits.

By these means I picked up a good deal of information in South America and Mexico, which, added to what I actually saw, enabled me to arrive at satisfactory deductions concerning many things not quite patent to me on leaving England; and, at the risk of being considered a bore, I shall endeavour, in as few words as possible, to put these conclusions before my reader.

For some years past there has been a steady growth of what I call "Republican," and others term "Liberal," ideas in England; and many advocates have sprung up who have freely given vent in public, with an exuberance somewhat contagious, to certain wild fantasies which have been eagerly grasped at by the uneducated or idle. Of all these partisan cries, I know of none more mischievous than the one for "universal suffrage," or, in still plainer English, the government of the ignorant upon the principle of being the most numerous.

The extension of the franchise has done mischief enough, and is rendered none the less obnoxious for having been helped through Parliament by a Conservative ministry; but "universal suffrage" is an evil which at any rate may be prevented, and having lately observed its workings in all the principal Republics of South America, the chief countries in the world where it is most in vogue, I think I may be permitted to state what I have seen in connexion with its many and most notorious evils.

I commence with Uruguay, it being the first of these so-called "free countries" I went to. The result of universal suffrage there may be summed up very shortly. Everyone was discontented. The men selected for holding the reins of office were invariably those who bribed highest, and, when once chosen, as invariably repaid themselves out of the public treasury for the expenses of their election, with a considerable bonus to boot. The country was in a state of bankruptcy, and revolutions were incessant. No foreigner had the slightest guarantee for the safety of either his life or his property, and the government for the time being was almost despotic. A few months after I left it, Monte Video was in a state of siege, and such, without entering into a lengthy dissertation, are a few of the chief characteristics of "universal suffrage" in Uruguay. In Buenos Ayres, the neighbouring state, things are equally bad, and they were, at the time I am speaking of, in an active state of absolute revolution, and busily engaged in cutting one another's throats.

In Chili affairs are managed better, but chiefly owing to the accident which has placed efficient men at the head of the government. Were incapables, armed with the powers conveyed to the rulers of this republic, in possession of the reins of office, instant revolution would be the result; and I much doubt if the most ardent admirer of republican institutions in England would approve of some of the arbitrary acts of government alluded to by me already, in giving an account of Valparaiso and its surroundings.

This strength of government, judiciously exercised, is the one only thing among republican institutions that I at all admire—the power as well as the will to curb sedition and check a mob. Strange as it may appear, all the republican governments that I have ever seen have invariably held the people in control by a firmness of administration, mingled occasionally with a little judicious (or injudicious) blood-letting, that too plainly shows of itself the necessity for there being strong measures always in immediate readiness for the "universal suffrage" gentry when they overstep the bounds of prudence, and which my reader may be quite certain would be equally necessary at home if such a measure ever became law.

The republic of Peru is in a worse state than either Uruguay or the Argentine confederation. Misappropriation of the public funds, corruptness of the ministry and all classes of government officials, and a fearful prevalence of unpunished assassination, are its chief characteristics — none of them very favourable as exponents of the benefits to be derived from an extended franchise.

Bolivia, Ecuador, and Central America, present pretty nearly the same features; but the entire system culminates in Mexico, where universal corruptness of government, combined with individual dishonesty and lack of all honourable feelings, again points out the miserable effects of a "universal suffrage," terminating in universal misery.

What good, I should like to know, has the already

extended franchise done our country. I could point to many counties and boroughs in England and Scotland which would certainly be better represented without it, while in Ireland it has ended in a perfect *fiasco*.

The absurdity of giving a man a thing he does not want, and has no use for, ought to be patent to the meanest comprehension; yet the great bulk of voters brought in by the Reform Bill neither wanted a vote, or (bribery being pretty well checked) had any use for it. A lot of unscrupulous agitators make the "great unwashed" inflammatory speeches, endeavouring to persuade them that the country is going to the dogs, because they do not take an active part in the elections, and endeavour to show them, according to their own lights, the difference between Conservative and Liberal.

This political education of the masses is, however, not quite disinterested. The first object of a man who has a thing he does not want, is to get rid of it; but with these newly created voters, the difficulty is how. Of course they would prefer selling; but not always finding a market, they naturally say, "So-and-so got us this thing; it is of no use, as we cannot make an honest penny by it, so we'll just vote as he tells us." But as for using any personal discretion in the exercise of their newly acquired rights, they care far too little about the matter to do so, unless indeed some person comes forward who promises them impossible and outrageous concessions, when they generally vote for him.

This latter case in a country where the government of the ignorant upon the principle of being the most numerous, is the law, is the great danger to be feared, and is the one creative of so many evils in the South American republics already alluded to. So also in England, the masses of the people, being in numerical preponderance, and comprising the least-educated or entirely ignorant of the population, are always liable, like their prototype in South America, to be influenced by false and seductive promises; and in giving such people a vote, one is arming them with a dangerous weapon, which, like a loaded firearm in the hands of an inexperienced child, is liable at any moment to explode, and possibly injure their truest friend.

In a country where universal suffrage obtains, a candidate for election must be prepared to flatter and laud the fools he intends gulling. Accommodating himself to his audience, he appeals to their vanity and not their judgment, their passions and not their reason; and he who can lie most freely as to the transcendent abilities of the "great unwashed," has the strongest chance of being selected for their representative. With ministers taken from such an elected Parliament, what has a country to look for, save dishonour and disgrace? Their sole object in the first place being to obtain office for the emoluments it confers, they eventually become subservient to their tools to retain it; and the masses, instead of being elevated in the scale of intelligence by the exercise of political power, are lowered by the delusion and craft to which they become the willing victims.

As a rule, the Irish uneducated voter is in favour of some avowed rebel disguised in the flimsy garniture of "Home Rule," but in case of doubt generally goes to his priest for advice, and a very particularly nice lot *they* usually return; so, on the whole, I don't think the country has gained much by an extended franchise.

How very few people who advocate extreme Liberal views know anything about the working of their ideas except in theory! Half of them have never been out of England, and nine-tenths never beyond Europe; and yet they talk as confidently, and lay down the law as plainly, in support of their principles, as if they had from personal supervision made themselves acquainted with the interior economy of every republic that exists.

With the exception of the United States (who have, after all, very little to brag about) and Switzerland, those governments based on the principle of universal suffrage have been proved an utter failure, and, having so very lately travelled in most of them, I consider myself justified in pointing out a few of the evils that exist, with a distant hope of inducing people holding these views to inquire for themselves how the countries where they are actually in play get on, and to learn also how far republican institutions, or what some more modestly term "extreme liberal" ones, would add to the happiness, prosperity, and freedom of England.

Next to the decided failure of universal suffrage in the countries I visited, I was most struck with the rapid decline of the sacerdotal power of the Romish priesthood. In Peru they still manage to hold their ground, chiefly owing to the influence they possess over women and Indians. A strong feeling is however growing against them, and a very few years will see their position alter. Chili, while preserving its religion, has entirely freed itself from priestly trammels.

Uruguay and most of the other republics have followed suit, and even Mexico, degraded and corrupt as she is, makes at any rate from time to time spasmodic efforts to shake off the yoke of bigotry and superstition that for so many years has sapped and undermined her energies, and now neither monasteries nor nunneries are to be found throughout the country.

It is impossible for anyone reading the early history of these republics, and visiting them afterwards, to avoid attributing their present deplorable condition to the government and teaching of the priests, who for so many years held unbridled sway and were quite omnipotent.

In making these statements, I wish it to be distinctly understood that I am not urging a crusade against their religion, and that I would not willingly say one single disrespectful word that could wound any person belonging to it. All the South American republics are as much Catholic now, and as likely to continue so, as they ever were; so are the Italians and other Catholic nations in Europe; but, after long experience, they have determined to check the palpable evil influences of its teachers with regard to their perpetual interference in secular matters, to suppress both monasteries and nunneries in every part of their kingdom, and prevent an undue monopoly by the sacerdotal power. That is all I would wish done at home.

Prior to the Reformation we suffered under the curse of priestcraft, and very wisely made a clean sweep, such as all sensible nations are doing now; but why we should let things get quietly back to their old standing—and they very quietly are,—is more than I can understand. At the present moment I firmly believe there are more monasteries and nunneries in Great Britain and Ireland, than in every other Roman Catholic country in Europe put together. Surely the present condition of Ireland, the most utterly priest-ridden country in the world, is sufficient warning to us of the danger of such a policy. Yet notwithstanding all this, and in spite of the example we have set us by every Roman Catholic country on the face of the globe, a man in England holding my views on the subject, is, by the greater number of its inhabitants, either looked upon as a bigot or ridiculed as a fool.

Having sufficiently bored my reader, and relieved my own feelings, by abusing universal suffrage and priestcraft in South America and Mexico, I can now start fairly on my travels over new ground. Independent of slow progression, I had enjoyed my trip in the *Rocket* up to this date well enough: time had rarely hung heavily on my hands; but nothing to eat and nothing to drink for the last month, with every prospect of just such another fate continually overtaking one, was too much for the delicate state of my nervous system, so, soon after anchoring, I cleared out, and, wishing my late companions "*Bon voyage*," performed the rest of my wanderings by land alone.

San Diego was originally an old mission settled by the Jesuits as far back as 1769. As a harbour it is almost perfection. The climate is exceedingly fine, the thermometer never falling below 45° in the winter, or rising above 85° in the summer. Should it ever become the western terminus of the Southern Pacific Railroad, its rise in importance will be rapid and certain; at present it is merely a sanitary resort for the delicate and consumptive, and its inhabitants can merely speculate on what may result when the all-hoped-for railroad meets them. It is only fourteen miles from the Mexican frontier; and from the Horton House, a most comfortable and well-conducted hotel, stage lines run in all directions.

The lions of San Diego were soon visited, and the same evening witnessed my departure for Los Angeles, the chief town of the county of the same name, and the principal seat for all branches of the wine trade in California.

We left San Diego at seven in the evening, and travelled during the night over as bad a road as it is almost possible to imagine. Deep fissures on each side, caused by the sudden and heavy rains in wet weather acting on a kiln-dried and friable soil, sometimes became perfect ravines. Occasionally we drove along the edge of a *cañon* some thousand feet deep, with the road so constructed that the off-wheels must pass within six inches of certain death. At others, we descended places where the horses were almost on their haunches the whole way, and the severe drag on the wheels almost powerless to hold us. However, it was nothing particularly out of the way for California, and after a time I got sufficiently reconciled to my situation to be able to look about me, and rather enjoyed hanging from my outside seat over the brink of a *cañon*, and gazing on the diminished objects right beneath me.

At about eleven the next morning we got to San Juan, another of the old Jesuit mission-towns, where portions of the stone and adobe church were still visible. On our way we passed some magnificent "ranches"—one I remember in particular as belonging to an Englishman called F., which was over eighty thousand acres in extent, fully stocked with cattle, and beautifully situated on a level plain at the foot of the coast range of mountains facing the sea. At 6.30 P.M. we reached Anaheim, a small town, from which a two hours' railway trip brought us to Los Angeles, after twenty-four hours' driving over the most dangerous roads I ever saw. The coachman, like most other far-western Americans, was well informed, and had gone through the usual amount of hair-breadth escapes from Indians that all these early settlers are so fond of talking about. The day was fine, the weather warm, the atmosphere clear, and I enjoyed greatly my long drive, the complete pleasure of which was only marred by a blackguard at the principal hotel in Anaheim stealing my favourite umbrella, after having in vain endeavoured to make me late for the train.

The country in the immediate vicinity of Los

Angeles is highly cultivated and productive. Corn, grapes, olives, oranges, castor-oil beans, and I know not how many more fruits or vegetables are to be had in the greatest abundance. The population of the town is about thirteen thousand, and it is situated on the Los Angeles river, twenty-three miles from the port of San Piedro. Los Angeles is the chief seat of the wine trade, and as most Californians are exceedingly proud of their supposed ability to produce a marketable vintage, and as they talk a great deal about wines, and know almost nothing, I may as well warn my reader against forming pleasing anticipations of good or cheap drinking when he visits their country. Having heard Californians speak so rapturously of their wines, and having from experience discovered the excellent quality of many cheap and unmarketable vintages in France, Spain, and Italy, as well as Madeira and the Cape of Good Hope, which are never seen in England, I was quite prepared to be delighted with the native wines here, and was doomed to be disappointed. During my journey through California, (which afterwards extended from the Mexican frontier to within a few miles of Oregon), I never once tasted a commonly decent glass of wine. Hardly anything was ever sold under a dollar a bottle, and though I martyred myself in tasting it on every possible occasion in hopes of something wonderful at last turning up, I never once came across even a moderately good specimen throughout the entire State.

Several enormous vineyards are in this district, but none of the grapes being ripe, and the season of the year being unfavourable for witnessing anything connected with the working of this particular branch of industry, I determined to push on for San Francisco, so as to arrive there in time to witness the patriotism invariably displayed by our American cousins on the 4th of July, the anniversary of their independence.

The beginning of the journey having to be performed by rail, it necessitated a start at 3 A.M.; a most inconvenient, and I am happy to say unusual, hour for commencing a trip, but one which was in this instance quite unavoidable, no other way being available during the day. At 4.30 A.M. we met the stage, and after an excellent breakfast we were packed inside and outside as close as herrings in a box, and commenced our journey.

The first portion of our drive was quite delightful. The morning air was keen enough to render an overcoat desirable; the scenery up the mountain-pass—Turner's, I think, they call it — was very beautiful; and the team, consisting of six horses in admirable condition and full of go, rendered the whole thing exhilarating and delightful. From the time of starting until past one in the afternoon, we were occupied in reaching the summit of the hills, after which, for several hours, we passed through a perfect desert. On leaving Lake Elizabeth, the dust became unbearable. Huge whirlwinds, over a hundred feet high, traversed the parched and sandy plain, and clouds of red dirt obscured all things from our vision, and penetrated to the inmost recesses of our wearing apparel. After passing the desert, a complete change came over the aspect of the country, and the hills, which since leaving San Diego had been quite devoid of trees, now became covered with handsome forests, the pine, oak, fir, and ilex predominating.

The country seemed alive with quail (*Ortyx Californica, Audubon*), and I constantly saw at least a couple of hundred birds in one bevy. These birds are about twice the size of the European quail, have a darker plumage, and are crested. A worse bird for the table I have seldom tasted, as they are dry and flavourless to a degree; but they afford very fair sport, and are certainly a pretty bird to look at. Cotton-tail and jackass rabbits abounded, and on the plains we saw the coyote (*Canis latrans*), a kind of prairie wolf, thousands of ground-squirrels, and a few deer. The ground-squirrel, or chipmunk (*Tamias striatus*), is a curious, lively little animal, found in great quantities over the western parts of the States. From San Diego to Oregon they abound. I was often amused by their quick, singular movements, and the extraordinary curiosity, which, quite overcoming their natural timidity, frequently induced them to jump upon a log or again leave their holes after having been thoroughly frightened. They are about ten inches from end of tail to snout, of a light yellowish brown, darker anteriorly, and on the thighs toning into chestnut. The under-parts are white, and on the body are five distinct black stripes, one dorsal and two on each side. Grizzly bears I heard of. The old Vaqueros, or Californian gaucho, constantly lassoed them; but there are not many left, and what few there are have it pretty much their own way, everyone treating them with much respect.

The latter portion of our drive into Caliente was

down hill, and the way we raced along was wonderful. And now for a few words on coachmen. I have had a good deal of coaching during my life in various places — in Ireland and Wales before the days of railroads, and in many foreign lands since then, but I can honestly say that I never saw any men handle their ribbons like these Californian drivers. Their teams, nearly always consisting of six horses, are as well turned out, with regard to size, pace, and condition, as any four-in-hand one sees in the Park during the London season; of course I do not allude to appointments or harness, or even grooming—these are rough and homely enough. The roads as a rule are simply frightful; often hanging over the edge of a precipice, constantly crossing at this time of the year the dried-up bed of a river, paved with huge round boulders, or going down a declivity that many fellows would funk out hunting. They have no guard or anyone to assist them, but work the brake themselves, go full spin round corners almost sharp enough to hide the leaders, avoid bad ruts (chuck-holes they call them here) in the most extraordinary manner, have less accidents, and get more out of their horses, keeping them at the same time in perfect condition, than any other men in the world. I am fond of driving, and nothing gives me greater pleasure than to see good driving. These men I consider the finest "whips" in creation, and it is worth coming all the way to California if only to learn what coaching really is. Plenty of the members of our "Four-in-hand Club" look very workmanlike in their tight-fitting trousers, white box-coats, and curly brimmed hats. Their teams are perfectly matched, and a long purse, or long credit, procures them pace, size, blood, and bone. They carry their legs straight, their reins are properly arranged in the orthodox fashion, and if the two grooms they generally take behind, elaborately attired in buckskin and tops, are moderately active, they can get round a tolerably sharp corner, or succeed in doing Hyde Park much to the admiration of griffins or women, and to their own entire satisfaction; but as to driving, in the real sense of the word—well, ignorance is bliss, though in their case it would not be folly to be wise. Our old coachmen *could* drive. Between Cork and Dublin and Limerick and Galway; and before those days between London and York, there were many real workmen. French, German, and continental coachmen generally, are nearly all tailors. Like most Englishmen, I always fancied that driving was our speciality; but after going about a thousand miles over Californian roads and with Californian drivers, I confess that we cannot so much as touch them.

It was quite dark when we drove into Caliente, and much as I appreciated the coachmanship of the Far-West, I was delighted at the opportunity of testing the convenience and (to me) novelty of a palace sleeping-car, being pretty well exhausted from my long day.

About ten miles before reaching Caliente, while going quietly up a small hill, we were somewhat startled by hearing a man's voice, in the most distressed tone begging for help. The accents were piteous, and the sounds seemed to come from a little wood, a short distance off the road. We sung out, "What's the matter?" but could get no other answer save, "Help! help!" and at last had to pull up and consider what was to be done. Several people suggested that "some one" should go and see what was the matter, but no one seemed inclined to move. One good-natured man offered to lend his pistol to anyone that liked to go, but did not stir himself; and for my own part, looking on the affair, whatever it might be, as a purely American transaction, of which nationality all but myself were citizens, I quietly determined to let them settle their own affairs their own way, having however a shrewd suspicion that there was a "plant" somewhere, though I could not tell what form it might assume. My impression was, that it was a dodge to separate our party, and then attack the coach, while some of us were looking for the individual requiring assistance. A naturalized Dutchman from the inside was evidently of the same opinion, as, leaning his head out of the carriage, he lustily bawled to our "coachy," "Mein gott, man, why for you not drive? Drive, drive, drive like h—ll!" and fell back exhausted with contending emotion and excitement. I never saw men in such a fix. No one liked to go into the dark wood from whence the sounds proceeded, yet no one liked to drive on and possibly leave a fellow-creature in mortal distress. Again the voice besought help, and much to our relief a gentleman from behind, immediately exclaimed, "By thunder! It's a ventriloquist on the coach." So indeed it was. He knew the Dutchman had money on his person for the purpose of buying some property he was going up to purchase, and he merely did it to get a rise out of our fat friend, who was notorious for his timidity and wealth.

I found the sleeping-cars delightful; but unfortunately had the Dutchman in the opposite bunk, and as he trumpeted variations through his nose with an amount of power and vigour I have seldom heard equalled, the best part of my night was occupied in stealing his boots and throwing them at his head, it being perfectly impossible to sleep through his fearful snoring. In the morning we stopped at Lathrop for breakfast. Not a hurried, scrambling, badly-served meal, like we get in England on similar occasions, but a good wholesome repast, consisting of fish, fruit, three or four meats, and a dozen kinds of bread, and all for little over two shillings. On each side of the line the country was perfectly flat, and every inch of it cultivated. Corn-fields of from one hundred to a thousand acres, without either break or fence, seemed common enough. The carriages led from one to another, so that passengers could walk the entire length of the cars, and at last arriving at Oaklands we crossed the ferry to San Francisco; and, tired and dusty from my almost incessant journeying by rail and coach for three days, I drove up to the Lick House Hotel.

I was a good deal disappointed about San Francisco, having been led to expect too much. The harbour is a very fine one, undoubtedly, and well sheltered. Some of the streets are well built; the houses are large; and property is valuable; but the chief thing about San Francisco is said in announcing that five-and-twenty years ago it was merely a sand heap, and that probably in another five-and-twenty it will again have doubled itself. The climate, when I was there in July, was simply detestable—cold, raw mornings and evenings, occasional fogs, burning hot noons, and a running accompaniment of dust and sand at all times. I was struck by the number of extremely pretty faces I met in the streets, and nearly all their owners were well dressed and graceful. The predominating cast of countenance among the men is Irish.

California Street is as busy and seems as much crowded as any of our own thoroughfares in the City. People jostle each other, expectorating profusely, and as trade prospers, so in proportion does saliva seem to flow. This shocking habit is not, however, confined to one locality. All the pavements in the best streets and vestibules in the hotels are similarly befouled; but nobody seems to mind it, and well-dressed ladies trail their dresses through it all with perfect unconcern. Habit, I suppose, accustoms them to what Englishmen view with disgust; but a stranger cannot help noticing a custom at once so repulsive and notorious. I do not think, however, any person giving his views of the town and its inhabitants will find any other fault, and as spitting is looked on by them as being quite legitimate, their *amour propre* cannot be wounded by its being mentioned. The mere fact of being an Englishman—and somehow they seem to know it instinctively—seems to predispose everyone to be kind and civil. Everyone I met appeared willing to go out of his way to do me a kindness. I invariably met with the greatest courtesy when brought in contact with perfect strangers; and I think it almost impossible for any foreigner to leave San Francisco otherwise than favourably impressed with the natives he may have been thrown among.

They are a little given to brag about the wonderful resources of their State, but as what they are so fond of talking about is, after all, only the common truth, one can hardly find fault with their very natural pride on such a subject. The markets are most interesting, indeed about the best-worth-seeing thing in the town. The Chinese quarter, to a person who has never been in China, is of course extremely singular; but having wandered all over the Celestial kingdom, from Canton to Pekin, many years ago, it possessed but few charms for me. Woodward's Gardens, the Park, and the Cliff House, should be visited; after which very little else remains to be seen that one has not already habituated oneself to looking at in every other decent-sized town all over the world.

The Cliff House is an hotel and restaurant facing the sea, a short distance from the "Golden Gate;" its great attraction a couple of rocks a short distance from it, which are covered with seals and sea-lions. The sight is an extremely singular one, and as very excellent feeding is combined with this curious spectacle, and a charming view obtainable of all the vessels entering and leaving one of the most thriving seaports in the world, it naturally becomes a favourite resort for all holiday seekers. The Palace Hotel one of the *employés* was kind enough to take me all over, and I need only say that at present it is the largest in the world, and seems well planned and comfortable. The "Lick House" was quite the reverse, and I heard several complaints as to the "go-a-head" nature of the visitors' bills on leaving. There are two clubs, "The Union" and "The Pacific," both of which were kind enough to extend their hospitalities to me during my stay in their town.

Some of the restaurants are admirable, and at one, "The Poodle Dog," an American gentleman gave a dinner to which he was kind enough to invite me, which equalled in every respect any I ever saw in similar establishments in either London or Paris. The gentlemen's customs with regard to costume are at times somewhat bewildering, and an Englishman unwittingly may occasionally give offence through not knowing exactly how, on their festive occasions, he should apparel himself. Our ordinary dress-coat seems to be reserved for very great occasions, and a kind of *demi toilette*, consisting of an open waistcoat, black frock-coat and black trousers, seems to be *de rigueur*—the kind of "get up," in fact, one occasionally sees a respectable mechanic wearing in England on a Sunday. Of course one would be safe in adopting ordinary evening-dress, but still most of us dislike being singular, and, being unaware of the happy medium, Englishmen are apt to plunge into extremes.

A certain nobleman visiting the West fell into such a trap, and I suppose for the next fifty years one of the first things an Englishman will hear will be that the Duke of—— went to a party in a coloured shirt. San Francisco is however so well known, and described so fully in hundreds of works, that I will not say any more about it. It is interesting chiefly on account of the immense strides it has taken towards prosperity in so short a time, but I do not think any stranger having seen it once will ever care to do so again, and certainly not if his first visit, like mine was, should be in July.

The celebration of American Independence unfortunately happened, when I was there, to fall on a Sunday; and anxious as I naturally was to view one of their characteristic and most popular fêtes, I must warn my readers against undergoing a similar infliction.

From early on Saturday until the following Tuesday morning, the town appeared to be handed over to the tender mercies of hordes of children of both sexes, who for three entire days kept up an incessant and terrible discharge of fireworks. Their chief amusement appeared to consist in dropping crackers in the most crowded and principal thoroughfares, with rather long pieces of touch-paper attached to them, so that they might explode under the dresses or feet of pedestrians who did not diligently avoid walking over the smallest spark. For carriages and horses they had another and far more dangerous description of weapon. It was a large bomb,—I think in the trade they are called maroons or some such name, but often in a pyrotechnical display have I seen a discharge of them usher in the more refined novelties about to follow. The noise they produce is as loud as a small field-piece, and when scientifically exploded beneath an unwary street-car, the result is occasionally extremely gratifying to all parties, and must add considerably to the patriotic feelings which no doubt animate them. The fourth, falling on a Sunday, the following Monday was selected by the Municipality for the national holiday, and on Monday came the usual procession. Most civic processions unaided by military display are ponderous and stupid, and this was certainly no exception. All kinds of guilds, crafts and interests, straggled loosely in semi-martial array for a couple of hours past the windows of the Union Club, where I perched myself to watch them. Among the most numerous were a band of "The Ancient Order of Hibernians," carrying a green flag with a harp on it, and so large that the unfortunate standard-bearer could hardly stagger.

I do not think at this period there is a single man in England, unless he happens to be a lunatic, who begrudges the Americans their independence, or who would have them otherwise than what they are —prosperous and powerful; but why, in the name of goodness, they should turn one of their chief towns into a pandemonium for three days, and suffer the inconvenience of crackers being fired at their legs, and squibs at their faces, in honour of an event that ought to be a source of pleasure, is more than I can quite understand.

Disappointed through the lateness of the season about getting up to Alaska, I cast about for information respecting salmon-fishing nearer San Francisco, and hearing favourable accounts of the sport obtainable in the head-waters of the Sacramento and McLeod rivers, away in the heart of the Sierra Nevada mountains, I determined on joining an American gentleman who was going up there, and trying my luck on these little-known and certainly imperfectly-fished streams.

Fortune was more than kind when she sent Joe G. to be my companion. Particularly well read, a first-class fisherman, brought up from childhood to a life requiring a capability of roughing it, and accustomed to all the shifts and expedients of a backwood life, had I secured a comrade made to order I could not have got a better one, and to his companionship I certainly owe three-fourths of the pleasures of the trip.

As far as Redding we were able to travel by rail, passing through the San Joaquim valley, two hundred and fifty miles in length by about thirty miles broad, and celebrated as being the great grain-producing farm of California. The size of the fields is astonishing, and twenty miles of standing wheat without a single break or enclosure is neither extraordinary nor uncommon.

At Redding we took the stage, and travelling all night, with the usual team of six horses, arrived next afternoon at the Soda Springs, Siskiyou County, which was to be head-quarters during our campaign against the scaly monster.

The drive from Redding lay through a forest of pine, fir, and cedar; and as morning broke we found ourselves well into the Sierras, whose high peaks ranged for many miles on all sides. The size of the timber was very remarkable, particularly some of the sugar-pines, whose broad, clear trunks rose like huge giants to incredible heights above the ground before the smallest branch broke the exquisite symmetry of their appearance. I never saw more magnificent timber; but at present its growth is more ornamental than useful, there being no means of carrying it from its native spot.

The road more or less ran the whole way near the banks of the Sacramento, which at times lay many hundred feet directly below us, and amid whose clear waters, even at these great heights, we could see the salmon swimming about distinctly, some of the pools being black with them. The further we advanced among the Sierras the grander the scenery became. Castle rocks, rugged and fantastic of outline, a sudden turn revealed to our astonished gaze, and Mount Shasta, nearly 15,000 feet above the sea, covered with perpetual snow, reared its majestic head far above the neighbouring "butes," towering like a huge bully towards the sky—monarch of all around it.

The hotel at the "Soda Springs" is kept by two backwoodsmen—George Campbell and Uncle Dick; who have for many years been settled in the Far-West. The house was scrupulously clean and comfortable, the charges exceedingly moderate, and the two hosts, not only thorough sportsmen, but well informed intellectual men, not too conceited to work hard themselves, and only happy when they were making their guests comfortable.

A good many visitors come here from Yreka and other places, merely to drink the water, which from a small well opposite the house comes bubbling and effervescing from the earth. It has a strong pungent taste which grows rapidly in favour with its habitual drinker, and is supposed by many to be a sovereign remedy for all the ills the flesh is heir to. Strange to say, it has not been analysed, but people coming here with a multiplicity of complaints invariably declare themselves benefited by its waters; though I think myself that it is quite probable that regular living, good air, and total abstinence from all intoxicating beverages (and I never saw a drop of wine, beer, or spirits for the month I was up here) may have had much to do with their rapid recovery. For my own part, I got to like it immensely, and as I left the Soda Springs in the same excellent state of preservation I arrived in, I can at any rate guarantee that it will not make any one ill.

The river is about a hundred yards from the house, one of the best pools being the nearest spot. We found it full of fish. They would not rise at fly, but took bait greedily, and were so easy to catch and so little sought after, that having all the river at our sole command we took it very easily, never commencing before breakfast and invariably returning to dinner. The proof of the pudding is in the eating, and without entering into any lengthy dissertation on a sport so well known and frequently described as salmon-fishing, I give the result of a week's work to my own rod, the record for the remaining period I stayed here being very similar.

23rd of July,	4	salmon,	weighing,	12, 12½, 7½, 8½ lbs., each.
24th „	7	„	„	12, 9, 7, 17, 12, 15½, 17 lbs. each.
26th „	7	„	„	13, 15, 6½, 23½, 11, 21, 10 lbs. each.
27th „	15	„	„	3, 8, 14, 10, 4, 15½, 7, 9½, 17½, 18½, 12, 2½, 6½, 16, 16 lbs. each.
29th „	27	„	„	7, 19½, 9, 15, 14, 13, 13, 9½, 15, 10, 11, 15, 14½, 15½, 21, 15, 2, 6½, 15, 13, 9½, 15, 2½, 12½, 7½, 13, 15 lbs. each.

The 29th was the only day I really worked hard, and then did not commence fishing until 7 A.M., and, having allowed myself an hour for luncheon and a meditative pipe, ceased operations at 6.30 P.M. Nearly half these fish I gaffed and landed without assistance, and I very much doubt if there is any record of any one person having killed a greater number in a shorter time, in any other river in the world.

For eleven hours and a half, excepting luncheon, which is only a polite name for a rest much needed, I was in salmon, as hardly a minute elapsed after one was captured before another was on, and back and arms bore testimony the next day to the severity of the contest.

This fishing, gentle reader, is yours if you like to come for it. Without one penny of cost, all the rivers of the West are at your disposal; and when I remember the prices charged on the Lochy, the Thurso, Castle Connell, and a host of other places, where the sport obtainable is not one quarter as good, I am surprised ingenuous youth does not occasionally find its way out here, where deer, bear, and salmon are only waiting their disposal.

To my idea, one of the greatest luxuries connected with salmon-fishing lies in not being hurried. At Lough Tay I was always bustled off before I had half finished my breakfast; and how distinctly I remember, at a well-known river not a hundred miles from Connemara, the rush, and bad feeling engendered by the perpetual anxiety daily displayed to get first on the best throws. To keep a favourite pool, a man would either remain all night or start long before daylight the next morning.

Once I was tempted by the enthusiastic "gossoon" who constituted himself my attendant, to attempt to cut out a Manchester tradesman, who, more energetic than skilful, invariably got the best water to make the worst use of. At an hour, horrible to contemplate, some small pebbles struck against my window, and as I opened it, a subdued voice from without—"Whist! Whist! yer honour; kape quiet what iver you do, and don't be after waking thim blackguards below yer. Bedad! we'll do them this turn any how." With the utmost caution and carrying my boots in my hand, I proceeded to arouse my comrade, a Scotch Baronet, invariably eager for the "fishy fray," and in the shortest possible space of time we were wending our way to the favourite pool with the delighted Pat, who was exuberant at having, as he thought, done the tradesman.

Imagine our horror when, a few minutes afterwards, we found "Manchester" hard at work thrashing the river in the very place we were going to, and all our trouble taken for nothing. Our *bête noir*, though an unskilful fisher, was a keen man of business, and having paid his £3 for the week's sport, was determined to get his pound of fish if possible.

Here one rarely finds the slightest competition, and as salmon are quite at a discount, the only anglers one ever meets are those who confine their attention entirely to trout. The trout-fishing is as first-class proportionately as the salmon, and Mr. G., who generally devoted himself to that branch of the gentle art, usually brought back from nine to eighteen dozen, the largest running to about three pounds.

The fishing was so good, I paid little attention to the shooting; but deer must have been round the locality in very large numbers, as the ground in places was quite cut up by their trails, and I do not remember Campbell ever having a blank day when he went out to provide venison for the table. There were a few coveys of mountain-quail about the house; but for bear and deer, at certain seasons, a man could not get a much better starting-point.

From the Soda Springs I went to Sissons, a prettily situated ranche at the foot of Mount Shasta, intending to climb to the crater for the view, it being one of the highest "butes," as they are called, of the Sierra Nevada, and with a chance also of getting a shot at a mountain-sheep on the way there. When, however, I arrived, the country was so overwhelmed with the smoke of burning forests, that the view part of the undertaking was at once demolished, and as a crack at the mountain-sheep seemed somewhat problematical, I retraced my steps and got ready for camping out with Mr. G. on the banks of the McLeod.

The McLeod river lay by a rough trail through the forest about twenty miles from the Soda Springs, and having chartered a light waggon and pair of horses for the job, we started one morning with rods, tent, &c., and all the necessary paraphernalia for an outing. Sam McNeil, our driver, was the slowest and most careful "whip" I met in California, and gave us ampler time than was perhaps quite requisite to admire the magnificence of the forests of stately timber through which our road lay; however, all things have an ending, and after making a trail for the last couple of miles through some scrub and brushwood, we at length halted in a beautiful grove of trees on the banks of the river, and set to work pitching our camp. This done, we caught a large basket of trout, the best of which we had for dinner:

and piling heaps of wood as it grew dark on our fire, until the flames illuminated the tall pine-trees to their highest points, we smoked and chatted by its cheerful light. Voting that the tent, though an ornamental addition to the picturesque effect of the surroundings, was utterly unneedful in such a charming climate, we cast ourselves on a luxuriant couch of fragrant boughs; and canopied only by the blue vault of heaven, and soothed by the music of the rushing stream whose murmuring waters acted as a sweet lullaby to our wearied frames, tired and worn out with prolonged slaughter, we slept as sound as the proverbial "top" of innocence and childhood.

The McLeod is, without any exception, the "gamest" river I ever fished on, and in no other water in the world have I ever seen trout so perfectly conditioned or so well-fed. Though but ten miles from its source, it possessed a body of water almost equal to the Shannon at Castle Connell, and of so clear and transparent a quality, that in pools of from twenty to thirty feet deep the smallest object could be discerned on the bottom, and the movement of every fish watched as he darted at the hook.

Daily we killed large baskets of trout, among whom were many "Dolly Vardens," but unfortunately the salmon had all either spawned or were spawning. The river was absolutely full of them, and while fishing for trout we were perpetually hooking the huge brutes, who played the mischief with our tackle, and were utterly useless when banked. Spoon or bait, it was all the same; they would take anything, and I seldom managed to get through a day without killing at least six or seven, though I did all I could to avoid them, constantly lifting my rod when I saw them coming. The average weight of these ill-conditioned gentry was about 18 lbs. I saw some dead ones—(the mortality that prevails among them after spawning is inconceivable; so much so, that many of the inhabitants firmly believe they all die)—that weighed at least 40 lbs., and hooked several that were even larger. I am quite convinced that at the right season the salmon-fishing in this river must be simply wonderful, and as they take a fly in the Shasta, which is but a few miles distant, it is more than probable they would rise to it here also.

The "Dolly Varden" is looked upon by the natives as, if not a *lusus naturæ*, at any rate a fish peculiar to the waters of the McLeod, and they are consequently proud of possessing what they believe to be a singularity. Nothing annoys a Welchman more than to tell him his cherished "sewin" is a sea-trout. For my part, though I have killed many of the former, and several hundredweights of the latter, I am unable to distinguish the difference, and for a like reason am equally convinced that the "Dolly Varden" is a genuine trout. The ordinary trout inhabiting the waters of all rivers west of the Rocky Mountains, bears no specks of red like his English prototype; instead of which, he carries a bright vermilion lateral line, extending from the gills to the tail on each side of his body. The trout in the McLeod are beautifully shaped, and indeed possess the most perfect forms of symmetrical excellence I have ever seen exhibited in any other of their species. Their bodies are deeper, their heads smaller, and their general colouring more brilliant, than the trout (*salmo fario*) of our native land; but above all those attributes, they have a gameness and determination when hooked which is only equalled by our sea-trout (*salmo trutta*), a totally different fish. We killed none above 3½ lbs., and from what I could gather from old fishermen on the river, they seldom exceed that size.

The "Dolly Varden" (and not having, I regret to say, the slightest claim to be considered a naturalist, I shall not attempt to classify, but merely allude to it by the local name) possesses far more of the attributes of the *salmo fario* than the ordinary trout of the Pacific rivers. Its markings are similar to our lake-trout, except that the red spots are brighter and more distinctly perceivable above the lateral line than in any home species I have ever observed. Their weight varies considerably. I have heard of them running as heavy as 10 lbs., but our largest was 4½ lbs. Its head is large and coarse, and stretch of jaw prodigious, enabling it to swallow with little difficulty fish of certainly a quarter its own size. Its body is thickset and round, but unduly long in proportion to its depth; and though undoubtedly rapacious, taking freely spoon, phantom bait, or minnow, it is when hooked a sluggish, cowardly fish, affording but little sport, and is not particularly good eating either. Its shape is, in fact, as like a pike's as it well can be, or, describing by trout analogy, it would look like an ill-conditioned cross between the *salmo ferox* and *gillaroo*. To my unscientific eye it is only a badly conditioned species of the *salmo ferox*, whose ungainly proportions are more prominently brought to notice through being unusually placed in juxtaposition with the ordinary trout of the McLeod, the most symmetrical and beautiful in existence.

In the neighbourhood of our camp, and along the banks of the river, were situated several deer-licks, and, tempted by the number of beaten tracks leading to and from them, I determined one night to experimentalise on this very ordinary method of shooting them out here.

A deer-lick is generally a small spring of saline or sulphur-impregnated water, to which, should it be a tasty one and not too frequently disturbed, all the deer in the country for miles and miles will come to "liquor up." The *modus operandi* is simplicity itself, and consists merely in concealment and waiting for a shot,—not particularly sportsman-like, or as good fun as stalking, still in the backwoods sport is not *always* the only object; occasionally one wants food, and it requires a little endurance to lie entirely alone all night amid the profound stillness of a primæval forest, with no fire, no pipe, no companion, and not even a dog. One afternoon, shouldering my blankets and food, I started for a neighbouring lick, which at some distance from our camp lay close to the river's bank, and, concealing myself on the opposite side, commenced the vigil.

Reader,—have you ever been alone all night? I do not mean in your bedroom, or even riding or driving on a beaten road; but absolutely companionless in the heart of a great forest, extending with but little intermission for hundreds of miles, without either fire or pipe, and entirely occupied with watching, while vision lasted, a small opposing space? If you have—well, I hope you liked it; for I cannot say that I did; but still, I wanted to judge of the sensation, and having made up my mind to get a deer, would have stopped a fortnight rather than be baulked. The shadows lengthened on the water. The sun went down. Mosquitos and bats succeeded the butterfly and blue jay, but still no sign of deer. Darkness set in. In the intentness of my watch prior to nightfall, I had neglected to select a comfortable spot to lie on. I now found myself apparently balanced on sharp stones, like the needle of a compass, in whichever direction I turned. It occurred to me that bears often came along the river to feed on dead salmon (indeed, we had seen many of their tracks), that at times they are clumsy and stupid, and that one might stumble over me by accident and cause a fight.

We killed a lot of rattle-snakes at the Soda Springs while I was there. It appeared to me now that this place was full of them. I heard their rattling distinctly. I longed for a pipe, but with stoical resolution I refrained from tainting the atmosphere. The trees assumed a thousand curious and fantastic shapes, quite incompatible with well-behaved vegetable life; in fact, I spent a particularly unpleasant night of it, and felt much relieved when the dawn of morning dispelled the gloomy visions and imaginations of darkness. Still, however, my long guard was unrewarded, and at nine o'clock Sam McNeil, who brought a pack-horse to carry back the expected buck, found me still watching, but unsuccessful. Would I ride back to camp for breakfast? No. I still had a morsel of bread. In the evening he might bring me provisions, but stir I would not till a buck lay slain. Sam went off possibly thinking me a lunatic, and for another hour I watched, now, however, varying the monotony with a book. At last my patience was rewarded, for on looking up to turn a page a deer stood before me.

So soft and noiselessly had it approached, I never detected the slightest sound. The rest was simple enough. A second after my bullet crashed through its heart, and thus ended my first experience of watching a lick. Another time I think I could (and did) improve on it; but having got through the first attempt, I felt that the next would be simple enough, and I learned from experience that I could soon accustom myself to solitary hunting if it became necessary. Except for the sake of food, I do not recommend anyone to undergo this ordeal, as deer are not worth it; but still, as bears are best got at by midnight watching, and an occasional vigil in darkness and solitude is at times a necessity during a sportsman's life, perhaps one trial by way of practice will do no harm, and I can guarantee that the second, if taken, will be far less irksome than the first.

A few Indians, "Diggers," occasionally camp for salmon-spearing near the river's banks, and it is not bad fun on a "lazy day" to see them picking them out. They seem quiet and well-disposed, though the distance from the "lava beds" is only seventy miles. These are famous as the scene of the last Modoc war, during which "Captain Jack," a noted Indian chief, baffled the vigilance and energy of the United States troops, killing several of them, though at length slain himself.

On several occasions, after fishing in the Sacramento, dead salmon were unavoidably left on the banks; as they were invariably taken off by bears, Mr. G. and myself determined one night to watch for them. Baiting a spot convenient to our ambuscade, which lay on the opposite side of the river, we took our blankets one afternoon to the selected place, and watched diligently all night, without, however, any success. No bear came near us, and a solitary wild duck, which I decapitated with a bullet after giving up all hopes of getting game more distinguished, was our sole reward.

Notwithstanding my own want of success, I can strongly recommend anyone staying here to "go in" for bears, as hardly a day passed that their fresh trails were not seen in the vicinity of our fishing, and immense numbers must be in the neighbouring mountains.

The mortality among salmon both in the McLeod and Sacramento rivers after spawning is very remarkable, and as the bears are in the habit of regaling themselves on the savoury morsels thus provided, to leave a few fish as a lure early in the season, before the novelty by repletion becomes worn out, is the best inducement I know of to get the generality of them to offer a shot. I nearly forgot to mention that the salmon of these rivers is as game a fish as ever swallowed hook. The mere fact of my having killed twenty-seven of them in one day, might induce people to fancy that strong tackle and muscle was all that was necessary, and an account of my successes, published in the *Field* newspaper, actually did produce a letter from some ignorant or jealous person, who, writing under the assumed name of "Phœnix," stigmatized the sport I had been enjoying "as a mere slaughter of useless and worn-out fish utterly unable to afford sport."

Owing to my having been on the Rocky Mountains on a shooting expedition, some time elapsed before this unwarrantable attack was brought to my notice; but as my letter in reply embraces pretty well the whole pith of Sacramento salmon-fishing, at any rate so far as the sporting qualifications of the fish are concerned, I give my letter on the subject at full length:—

"*Fishing in the Sacramento, California.*

"Having been for the last few months shooting in some of the most out-of-the-way places in the western portions of the United States, I have only just had brought to my notice a letter by 'Phœnix,' who, writing from California, criticises somewhat severely an account sent by my brother to your paper of the salmon-fishing in the head-waters of the Sacramento.

"Of all the bores a man can be inflicted by on this transitory sphere, a newspaper controversy is about the greatest; and were it not that 'Phœnix's' letter is calculated to mislead many fishermen, who next year may visit America for the centennial commemoration, I should not trouble you with this letter.

"Salmon, as 'Phœnix' observes, will look at nothing in these waters but roe. Day after day I have vainly endeavoured to tempt them with every description of lure. Every sort of fly—and I had some hundreds with me — failed to move them. 'Worms' was not their 'diet'; phantom and small trout they would not look at; they could not even be induced to 'spoon.' This being the case it merely became a question of fishing or not fishing.

"Now, salmon, with the assistance of a rod, are either killed by fly or bait, and I should imagine that only a lunatic would employ the latter where the former would answer his purpose. Still, during the seasons on particular waters, where a man might as well thrash a turnpike-road as cast a fly over the uncompromising fish, the latter method is constantly employed, and I have paid as much as £5 a week for permission to fish on Loch Tay at a time when no other could be used. At the commencement of the season at Castle Connell and other places I have been compelled to fish in like manner.

"I may be singular, but to me (as relative to fly-fishing) all bait work is alike, whether, roe, worm, trout, phantom, or minnow, and I only use them after experience has told me that flies are worthless.

"The use of roe in Europe is most properly condemned, as being unsportsmanlike and wrong; but in the Sacramento, not only will the fish look at no other kind of bait, but the river is so overstocked that hundreds of thousands of salmon perish annually during spawning time, and instead of the river suffering from so deadly a manner of killing fish, almost any method employed to thin their number would improve it.

"If 'Phœnix' thought proper to employ an Indian to spear him salmon, and then fished for them out of season, when they neither afforded sport nor were good for food, it is his own affair—'*Chacun à son goût.*' I neither did the one nor the other.

"Almost every day we ate salmon for luncheon, which we cooked ourselves by the river's bank, and most of us preferred them infinitely to trout.

"As to their affording no sport, I can only say that I have fished in Norway, Nova Scotia, Scotland, and Ireland, and have never handled gamer fish.

"One of my favourite casts (not with the two-hooked implement so well appreciated by 'Phœnix') was at the head of a large deep pool, into which flowed a heavy rapid. Close to where I stood a shelving bank afforded good landing-ground, but a steep rock and some overhanging trees prevented a fish being followed. The pool was so large and deep that a salmon seldom tried to leave it; still, occasionally they did, and when they did, used-up and powerless as 'Phœnix' describes them to be, I, at any rate, was unable to control their headlong rush. In case this inability might be attributed to either inexperience or personal decrepitude, I may as well state that I have killed salmon for over twenty years, commencing at the tender age of thirteen, when I landed my first fish. That the tackle I used was the strongest and best I ever had, that I walk over 14 stone, and was never a week sick or sorry in my life, and yet no less than five different fish compelled me to swim, with my rod in one hand, this long deep stretch of water, ice-like in temperature, from the small streams flowing from the perpetual snows of Shasta and other high points of the Sierra Nevada Mountains, and by no means the kind of water one would select for a bath in a shooting-coat. I could not get round the bank; I had to follow my fish or lose him, and I preferred to follow.

"On another occasion I saw a salmon, after running out eighty yards of line, take a great big backwoodsman a quarter of a mile down the river. A rapid here prevented his following, and as a last chance he threw his rod over after the fish. Fortunately no accident happened, and at the bottom the rod was secured. No sooner was the line tightened, than away rushed the fish; but Mr. Goodman getting before him, and beating the river with his gaff, he once more turned and again went up the rapid, the holder of the rod this time following, owing to having more line on the reel, and after twenty minutes' more severe play he was killed.

"These are the fish that 'Phœnix' characterises as 'having neither strength nor pluck,' the killing of which he designates as 'mere slaughter.'

"I do not know where 'Phœnix' fishes, or what kind of salmon he is in the habit of catching; but for my part, unless we can cross them with either a fox or a flying-fish, so that after an hour or so at the end of a line we can clap on a pack of hounds, or try them with a hawk, I do not know where to get a gamer fish than the salmon of the Sacramento. My friend, Mr. J. T. Goodman, one of the best fishermen in America, and a well-known man in San Francisco and all the West, saw these events occur, and will corroborate my statement, should corroboration be considered necessary.

"I shall not trouble you on this subject again. Should 'Phœnix' think proper to do so, I hope it may be with proper name and address. I shall be in California for salmon-fishing in July, and should much like to thank him for the courteous manner in which he criticised my brother's letter."

The Sacramento, Klamath, Shasta, and McLeod rivers, are not more than twenty miles apart, and come into order in succession. So that the very cream of each may be gathered by a man visiting them one after the other. In the Klamath and McLeod the salmon run very heavy, and in the Shasta they take a fly.

I felt quite sorry at leaving the Soda Springs. The fishing was so superb, everything was so clean, comfortable, and homely, and Campbell and Uncle Dick were such unaffected thorough sportsmen, and so very obliging and kind.

On the 16th of August we left by the Oregon stage, and after a somewhat dusty drive in an unpleasantly over-crowded coach, reached Redding at 12 P.M. We passed innumerable worked-out mining operations on the banks of the Sacramento, where some years ago the search after gold had been ardent and unceasing, and still a few straggling camps showed that there remained sufficient of the precious metal to render the river attractive to the industrious or sanguine. The ferries across the Sacramento, McLeod, and Pitt rivers, seemed excellent contrivances. We drove our six horses straight on board, and one man took the boat across by means of a windlass, without our having either to unharness or unload the coach. Notwithstanding the boasted superiority of American railway travelling over everything similar in the world, a European finds pretty well as many faults here as at home. The train leaves Redding at twelve o'clock at night with the mail and passengers from Oregon. These people are four days and nights on about as bad a road as can well be found, and will not reach San Francisco until late next afternoon—about double the time it takes in going between London and Edinburgh; yet there were no sleeping-cars, and American ordinary travelling ones are without exception the most unpleasant for purposes of slumber of any conceivable. Should the wearied traveller, notwithstanding the cramps and pains that attend the stowing away of legs and feet in the confined space obtainable on the two seats which form a single bench, succeed in getting to sleep, he is pretty certain to be awoke ere long by some garrulous native, and as each carriage holds thirty-six passengers, he has small chance of getting a nap.

Their regulations also with regard to baggage are to a sportsman inconvenient to a degree. Portmanteaus containing wearing apparel are checked, and much trouble doubtless saved; but gun-cases, fishing-rods, cartridge-box, and fishing-basket, are religiously tabooed; and as there are no porters, I had to stagger from place to place with my accumulated load of woes occasionally increased by a small portmanteau for immediate necessity, a bundle of wraps, and an odd book or paper.

My gun-cases were particular objects of suspicion, and each guard had a peculiar theory of his own in connection with them. Though within the margin of the recognised weight for luggage, none of them would allow them to be registered with my portmanteaus, and frequently would not permit them to be taken in the cars. Often I had to carry them to the luggage-van, where they were charged extra for. The rods, cartridge-box, and basket, were generally allowed in the Pulmans; but I always had to carry them about myself, which when changes were numerous, loose parcels many, and time limited, was excessively unpleasant. The railway officials were always civil and wished to be obliging, but they have their crotchets, and this crusade against the very ordinary baggage of an English gentleman, namely, his guns and rods, seems one of their hobbies.

I found that several English words in America had rather peculiar significations. Sportsman, for instance, means "blackleg;" shooting, they call hunting; and "democrat" is the term selected for their particular cognomen by the party who represent the Conservative interests of the country.

CHAPTER X.

Lathrop—Merced—American politicians—Tuolumne Grove—The Yo-Semite Valley—Garrote—Mammoth Grove of "Big Trees," Calaveras County—South Park Grove of "Big Trees"—Lake Tahoe—Fishing on Tahoe—Carson—Night ride on a "cow-catcher"—Visit to a silver mine—Gold—Earthquakes—Virginia City—Land of Mormon—Funeral of George A. Smith—The Tabernacle—A Mormon sermon—Sulphur Springs—The trowel-bayonet—The Great Salt Lake—Jackass rabbits.

At Lathrop we halted for dinner, and here I parted with my friends, Mr. and Mrs. G., who continued their journey to San Francisco. The next passenger-train for Merced did not go for five hours, and I was, after they left, somewhat disconsolately contemplating a large grizzly bear confined on the platform in a cage, and anatomically considering the best place for driving in a bullet if ever I got a shot at one,—a favourite habit of mine when examining captive wild beasts,—when I heard the whistle of a goods train, and finding that I could go by it at once if I liked, and save a long delay, I jumped on board and started.

Our track lay through a perfectly flat stubble-covered plain, and though it was interesting to know that much of the land we were passing over, though a common prairie and covered with shaparall and scrub not six years ago, was now yielding from fifty to a hundred bushels of grain an acre, the monotony became unbearable, and I was heartily glad when the journey ended. These great plains are horribly irksome. In England a man can amuse himself for hours—at any rate, I can—by selecting the places in a fence we are coming at, that, out hunting, I should ride for, and looking as the train passes to see whether my judgment was sound, or if I should have got a "cropper." Here the land was flat as a pancake, not a fence or tree to be seen, or even a bird, to break the never-ending stagnation of sameness.

Merced is a town of but little over two years' growth. It has a first-class hotel, "El Capitan," which is four stories high, and can accommodate two hundred visitors; and a handsome Court House, which would be an ornament to a town ten times its size and importance. From Merced the tourist starts by coach for Yo-Semite.

The rivalry that exists between the different companies renders a decision as to the route to be taken somewhat baffling, each tout swearing that the other's road is uninteresting or wrong, and that the unavailing regret of a lifetime will follow its selection. Being hard up for amusement to kill time, I made no choice until the different stages were actually about to start, and was considerably entertained by the skirmishes which continually took place at intervals during the day, between the rival agents to secure my dollars.

In the evening I was fortunate enough to hear a couple of republican members of Congress, who were what is usually termed "stumping the country," give vent to their pent-up patriotism by a violent attack on another body of political opponents termed "independents." The speeches took place opposite the hotel, and though the audience chiefly consisted of people belonging to the Democrat persuasion, they listened to the address of their antagonists with attention and forbearance, and gave them a far more liberal hearing, than a Radical audience at home would ever dream of giving Conservatives similarly situated.

A gentleman, called Bidwell, candidate for the post of Governor, was the chief object of their vituperation; and the fact of his owning a farm of some fifty thousand acres, which was all highly cultivated, and had been made so entirely by his own energy and capital, seemed their principal grievance and cause of complaint against him.

In the course of the speeches, one of the honourable gentlemen described how, from the summit of a neighbouring hill, he had beheld the vast plain covered with standing crops, amid which was situated this gentleman's country-house, and how his blood boiled at such an act of monopoly. "Am I," he cried, "in England or America? Is this the castle of some feudal baron—or the house of an American citizen? Am I under the Cross of St. George—or the glorious 'Stars and Stripes' of liberty and freedom? Citizens, this land should have belonged to you. Each hundred and sixty acres should have supported a happy family," &c., &c. As the property in question was by no means an unusually large one for California, and as there are any amount of millions of acres of equally valuable land in the States, still lying idle and uninhabited, I thought it a little rough on Mr. Bidwell, that, after taking so much trouble, an outsider should quietly distribute his property into one-hundred-and-sixty-acre lots; though goodness knows such political reasoning is not uncommon, as one of our own shining lights attempted a line of policy not very dissimilar with regard to other people's estates in Ireland.

All staging in America commences abominably early, and six o'clock one morning saw me start with a four-horse team for the Yo-Semite *viâ* Coulterville. I was fortunate in having pleasant companions for the trip, and during my stay in the valley we generally did our sight-seeing together. Coulterville is an almost deserted mining-town. In its immediate vicinity the surface of the land is burrowed and turned over in every direction, lasting monuments to all ages of the race for gold, which rendered California once so famous; but not till we reached Dudley's, a comfortable little crib where we spent the night, did the aspect of the country become a bit inviting, or show the slightest approach to pretty scenery. Next day the drive became more interesting. For miles we passed through the Foot Hills, covered with endless acres of forest; and gradually getting into the Sierra Nevadas, beheld the magnificent timber for which this part of the world is so justly celebrated.

All the trees were large, but occasionally we met some veritable giants among the sugar-pines, which ran frequently up to two hundred feet in height, often having a diameter of as much as nine feet at their base. Great, however, as these trees undoubtedly were, the Tuolumne grove of "big trees" (*Sequoia gigantea*), which we drove through in the afternoon, quite surpassed them. The stump of one, partly burned out, was over twenty feet in diameter, and many of the others were but little inferior to it in size. Most of them ran to a height of from two hundred to two hundred and fifty feet, and their huge stature and bulk certainly produced an effect on all of us of more astonishment and wonder than any trees had ever done before. One of our party, an American colonel, who had lost an arm during their late civil war, was justly indignant at the manner in which many of the trees were disfigured by idiots hacking their names on the bark. All through the Yo-Semite I afterwards found this to be the prevailing custom, and though I thought our own people were the greatest snobs in existence for cutting, hacking, and disfiguring trees, churches, and buildings of all sorts, I am glad to be able to add as a rider, to gratify my national conceit, that in this most unpleasant family failing our Yankee cousins lick us hollow.

We passed through some exquisite morsels of scenery, and at last reached the crowning point of all that is enchanting—the great valley of the Yo-Semite itself. Words are quite inadequate to do it justice, or convey to the reader anything of an idea of this marvellously beautiful spot. I not only never saw, but cannot even conceive anything more soul-inspiring or grand. What so many skilled writers have failed in attempting to describe, I shall not venture on; for I never read an account yet that brought the picture to my mind's eye that I now saw before me.

The road into the valley was just sufficiently wide to allow our leaders room to move along, but nothing could have passed us on the way. In some places the grade was exceedingly steep; the corners were invariably as sharp as they could possibly be made with the slightest regard to safety, and, the whole way down, the smallest move off the road would have entailed certain destruction for all of us. I occupied the box-seat, and was delighted with the manner our driver (the "Buffalo" he was called, and I do not know his real name) handled his team of five horses, the three leaders being harnessed abreast. With the brake hard on, we went at first a fair trot all the way. Over such ground a man should have a nerve of iron, a hand of steel, and the eye of a hawk, and my friend "the Buffalo" seemed to possess all of them. As I have observed before, there are no "whips" in the world that can touch the Californians—I do not mean to say that there are not a few "muffs" among them; but the general lot are marvels, and if you sit by the side of a good man on visiting the Yo-Semite for the first time, I do not think ages will ever efface your enjoyment of the drive.

There is little to choose in the matter of hotels. They are not bad, but, considering the length of time the valley has been declared a "national park," none of them are as good as they ought to be. Smith's Cosmopolitan Saloon and Bath-house is the only establishment among them that shows any of the enterprise and improvement that the Americans as a rule are famous for. If, immediately after your hot and dusty drive, Mr. Smith makes *himself* for the thirsty traveller one of his celebrated iced claret punches, a very happy termination to the day's journey will have been satisfactorily arrived at, as he is certainly one of the most clever manipulators of liquor in the States. *Apropos* of drinks, much as the Californians praise their wine to strangers, I observed they studiously refrained from drinking it themselves; and though San Franciscan bars are invariably crowded, I never heard any of the *habitués* ever call for the beverage they so frequently vaunt as equalling the wines of France or Spain.

Next morning we rode to the Nevada falls, 700 feet high and called by the Indians, Yo-wi-e; had luncheon at Snow's hotel, and after a swim in a deliciously cool little pond just above them, sent our ponies round, and walked to the Vernal, or Pi-wa-ack, which signifies a cataract of diamonds, and has about 350 feet of clear descent.

Our next expedition was to Mirror Lake, on whose surface during a clear still morning, the reflection of the "South Dome," 4737 feet above the Merced river, and the perpendicular face of smoothly cut granite on the side towards Tenaza Cañon, are as distinctly visible as one's own countenance when looking at a glass. The "Bridal Veil" fall, Po-ho-no, or Spirit of the Evil Wind, 940 feet, was also done. This was a very easy day's work, as, with the exception of a slight scramble of a few hundred yards over rocks to get to the immediate base of the Bridal Veil, both places were visited by carriage.

Glacier Point and South Dome formed the next trip. This, in my opinion, is the cream of the whole lot of points of observation to which trails have been cut, and strangers recommended to visit. By a winding zigzag path an altitude of over 4000 feet is gradually attained. As each grade in the road is ascended, fresh beauties in the valley are brought to view; cattle and horses become mere specks; until at last the grand old El Capitan—Tu-tock-a-mu-la—lies almost beneath us, and on looking over a rock at the summit, an apparently perpendicular wall shows a sheer descent to the bottom, and startles the gazer by its terrible abruptness and fearful depth. From this point one not only gets an entire view of the valley, absolutely looking down on the Yo-Semite falls, themselves 2634 feet, but gains also an extended range of the Sierra Nevada Mountains, which rise in serried peaks, pine-clad or snow-capped, far, far away in the distance. Nothing can be more beautiful or grander; and if time should be an object, and only one day be devoted by the hurried traveller to see the valley, he cannot do better than select Glacier Point as the one thing to be visited.

In the Yo-Semite are several very beautiful trees for cabinet purposes, and a German residing here has manufactured many pieces of inlaid work formed entirely from the woods found in the valley. The Manzaneta (*Arctostaphylos glauca*), the Buck-eye (*Æsculus Paira*), and the Laurel (*Tetranthera Californica*), all take a beautiful polish, and are much sought after for veneering.

I killed a few dozen small trout with fly in the

Merced river. The fish run small, and the water is very clear and much hacked in the immediate vicinity of the hotel; but by riding about eight miles down the river, tolerably fair sport can be obtained, and any one possessed of ordinary skill will easily capture from three to six dozen.

My friend Mr. G., who is, however, a first-class fisherman, constantly made much larger bags; but ordinary anglers will easily manage the numbers I have given them, though the hotel-keepers invariably talk of their extraordinary shyness, and pretend that the Indians alone are able to kill trout on the Merced.

Having exhausted the principal views of the Yo-Semite, though still wishing to linger, we tore ourselves away, and at the usual disagreeably early hour started one morning for the Mammoth and South Park Grove of Sequoias in Calaveras County, a three days' drive by stage from the valley. Our intention was to have halted for the night at Chinese Camp, which, with any regard to equalising the distance and comfort of next day's drive, would undoubtedly have been our wisest plan; but at Garrote we were seized upon by a predatory and plausible inn-keeper, who by the bribe of a butterfly to one man, and a swim to another, prevailed on the whole party to halt there, and I was perforce obliged to follow their example, though much against my will. The butterfly was described as being rare and beautiful; the bathing as refreshing as divine. The road, like all Californian ones, was dusty in the extreme, and cleanliness being next to godliness, only a good deal easier of attainment, I became somewhat reconciled to my fate, and cross-questioned our plausible friend as to the locality of the stream he had been describing. How far off was it? Oh, quite close—not a quarter of a mile,—and he would show us the way. Was it deep? Not very, but we could wade in nicely. Away started the Colonel and myself in the direction pointed out, and at last, after a hot and tiresome walk, of at least a mile and a half, came on the long-looked-for water. It was a dirty little mud ditch, not four feet wide, used for conveying water to some neighbouring hydraulic and placer mines. Not two inches of water ran over its slimy-looking bottom, and the wading *in* could only be accomplished by wading *through* two feet of soft mud. The butterfly, I am happy to say, was as great a sell as the bath; but I will do the fellow justice by saying that his feeding was good, his charges reasonable, and his house scrupulously clean.

Our next day's drive lay through a country burrowed and excavated in every possible direction by the seekers after gold. Round Senora parties were still busily engaged at this captivating species of toil, and several mines were pointed out by our driver which were yielding very heavy receipts above their working expenditure. Parts of the country were pretty, and particularly so near where we crossed the Tuolumne river by a ferry kept by an old Yorkshire man, who gave us several bunches of fine grapes. At Murpheystown, a small village entirely supported by a mining population, we halted for the night, and a good plunge in the clear blue water of an old worked-out and deserted mine over a hundred feet deep, reconciled us to our disappointment on the previous day.

The elections were still being busily pushed, and noisy politicians loudly proclaimed their individual opinions, until gradually in the small hours of the morning I went to sleep with the sounds of Republican, Independent, Democrat, and Dolly Varden, rapidly chasing one another through my bewildered brain, till Morpheus reigned triumphant, and temporary oblivion at last conquered all things. Next morning we again started, but this day only sixteen miles had to be accomplished, and a four hours' drive —the horses were bad and the roads hilly—landed us at the Mammoth Grove. In one of the narrowest and worst parts of the road we suddenly came on a waggon load of "campers." To pass abreast was impossible, and I soon had an opportunity of judging of one of the many resources of Californian travel. The driver of the waggon, unhitching his team, fastened them behind, and we, all getting out of our coach, clapped on to the pole and quietly dragged the obstructive conveyance over the almost precipitous bank, locked the wheels to prevent its sliding, and passed above in safety.

The hotel kept by Messrs. De Briges and Sperry at the "big trees" is comfortable and clean, and the *cuisine* far superior to anything we met with in the Yo-Semite. The approach to it passes between the Two Sentinels, each over three hundred feet high; the largest is twenty-three feet in diameter, and on the right-hand side lies the celebrated Mammoth Grove.

Description almost fails to give a person an adequate idea of the vastness and grandeur of these huge vegetable monsters, and even after viewing them, one is obliged to measure, to get inside, to walk round or crawl on the fallen ones, to gradually comprehend their enormous structure. One of these trees which has fallen is called the "Father of the Forest," and must have been four hundred and fifty feet high, and forty feet in diameter before it fell. Through a hundred feet of the trunk, which is hollow, I rode a moderate-sized horse without stooping my head. In 1853 one of the largest trees, ninety-two feet in circumference, and over three hundred feet high, was cut down. Five men worked twenty-five days in felling it, and as many as thirty-two dancers have figured together on its stump.

Near the stump lies a section of the trunk, twenty-five feet in diameter. And beyond lies the immense trunk as it fell, measuring three hundred and two feet from end to end. Upon this was constructed a bar-room and a bowling alley, which stretching along its upper surface for a distance of eighty-one feet, afforded ample space for two alley-beds side by side. I believe there are ninety-three of these sequoias in the grove, not including those under twenty years' growth, but out of the number there are ten, each thirty feet in diameter; and over seventy, between fifteen and thirty feet for the same measurement. All the largest have names nailed upon them, and "Starr King," three hundred and sixty-six feet high, is, I believe, the biggest standing in the group.

Having dawdled for a couple of days among these

monsters, and varied the amusement by catching a few trout in a small stream ("creek," they always call them here) running within a couple of miles of the house, we determined on visiting the South Park Grove, six miles distant from our hotel.

Horses, guides, and luncheon being forthcoming, we started off, and after an exceedingly pleasant ride arrived at a likely-looking stream about a mile from the grove, where, having my trout-rod with me and a cast of flies, I soon managed to kill sufficient fish to form an acceptable addition to our mid-day meal. The South Park Grove is far away the finest of all the groups of *Sequoia gigantea* yet discovered. It contains one thousand three hundred and eighty of these trees, many of them of immense size. Into a hollowed portion five of us rode our horses, which had plenty of room to turn without the slightest inconvenience, and the guide declared he had seen fifteen mounted people inside at the same time. A tall, wiry-looking man has located himself in this grove, and pre-empted the usual allowance of land about it. He took us to his house, which is formed in the hollow of a nobly-grown sequoia. It made a first-rate chamber, affording plenty of space for bed, table, and chair, and even allowed him room to offer, during very severe weather, stabling and protection to his trusty steed. In this singular abode, for eleven years, he had resided alone and happy. No rent to pay, taxes to afflict, or wife to torment him. He ate when hungry, and slept when tired; fished during the summer, and hunted bear and deer and did his trapping during winter, and was, according to his own account, perfectly contented with his lot. One of the chief charms of this grove at present, independent of its vast size, is that everything is in a perfect state of nature. The trees are undoubtedly much larger and better grown than any of those at the Mammoth Grove, and are not spoiled by having a lot of names, like so many signboards, stuck upon them. They are less visited, and are consequently less disfigured by Tom, Dick, and Harry hacking their uninteresting designations all over the bark; and, as no hotel or bar-room is in the immediate vicinity, silence and nature reign supreme. On the embers of an oak-bark fire I cooked our trout, and a delightful afternoon was passed in wandering quietly about this wonderful grove. The sugar-pines (*Pinus sabininai*) seem to attain more astonishing proportions in the immediate vicinity of these "big trees" than in any other locality. Some of them attain a height of two hundred and seventy feet, and not unfrequently a diameter of from nine to eleven and a half and twelve feet. Their proportions are, to my mind, far more symmetrical than the sequoia; and, notwithstanding the latter's enormous growth, I was often puzzled to tell, while looking at them together, which tree I admired most.

After leaving Calaveras our party broke up. Some went east, and others west; and, tumbling across another wandering baronet, we directed our steps towards Virginia City, the great centre of all silver mining; the modern Potosi in fact of North America. Mr. G. had given me a letter of introduction to Messrs. Mackay and Fair, the managers and part proprietors of the California and Virginia Consolidated Mines, at the present moment the most wealthy and best paying in the world, and H., thinking the opportunity of seeing them under their auspices too good to be lost, came with me, though he was in a red-hot hurry to get to Denver for the shooting.

The scenery from the train in the neighbourhood of Cape Horn was undoubtedly grand, and as the guide-books have it: "Timid ladies draw back with a shudder, one look into the awful chasm being sufficient to unsettle their nerves, and deprive them of the wish to linger near the grandest scene on the whole line of the trans-continental railroad." Had I not so very recently seen Yo-Semite, I might have admired it more, but under the circumstances I was rather glad when at 10 P.M. our train arrived at a station called Truckee, where, at a second or third rate kind of inn attached to the railway station, we were obliged to pass the night.

Our drive next morning from Truckee to Lake Tahoe, along the banks of the River Truckee, was one to be remembered. A well-kept road followed the river's bank through forest and meadow, forming a kind of cañon. On each side rose steep mountains, in some places showing extraordinary rock formations, whose fantastic outlines and queer conformation added considerably to the general effect of all around us. The river was clear as crystal and formed a very beautiful piece of water, spoiled, however, for trout fishing by the numberless saw-mills and mill-dams that are established along its banks; this part of Nevada being the great lumber region of the state, and Truckee City (almost every town of half-a-dozen streets, or even houses, in America is called a city) the principal depôt and chief market.

On our road we were pointed out the scene of a recent coach disaster, in which a couple of people were killed, and a few more badly injured. It seems that in going down a steep incline with a high bank on one side and a precipice on the other, the brake had carried away. The horses became unruly, and finally the stage was pitched about sixty or eighty feet down an almost precipitous declivity, killing and wounding the people mentioned. The horses were, I believe, all killed, and on examining the place, my only surprise was that the whole party had not suffered the same fate.

Our intention had been to cross Lake Tahoe at once and go on to Virginia City, but while waiting for the steam-boat which was to convey us across the lake, H. became so enamoured of a beautiful dish of trout, some of them running about five pounds, that he determined on staying to try his luck, a local fisherman promising to provide the necessary equipment, and I was only too glad of the delay. Lake Tahoe is really very beautiful. The water is singularly clear. Even on coral banks in the Indian Ocean, atolls rising from an almost unfathomable depth nearly perpendicularly, and celebrated for the extraordinary translucency of the blue water that surrounds them, have I never seen to greater depths. On a calm, clear, bright day, when the surface of the lake is unruffled, a white plate can easily be discerned a hundred feet beneath its tranquil waters. The counties of Eldorado and Placer in California, and Washoe, Ormsby, and Douglas in Nevada, share it between them. Its greatest depth is 1700 feet, its length twenty-two miles, and width about ten miles.

After a swim we repaired to the boat, where our fisherman awaited us, and judge of our surprise when the means of capture met our astonished gaze. A huge cod-line, armed with a hook large enough to kill a shark, was the rude and unsportsmanlike implement used for killing the speckled beauties, whose good looks we had both so much admired. No play and no sport could possibly be obtained, as neck and crop by main force the wretched fish is bundled into the boat. Of course fishing under such circumstances was a "dead sell," and not having our own gear with us, nothing could be done. The Tahoe hotel was exceedingly comfortable, and I can hardly recommend a pleasanter or more charming spot for any one willing to linger a week amid delightful scenery, with the certain knowledge of returning each day after his wanderings to a good dinner; but should he be an angler, let him remember to bring his own rod.

Our next day was somewhat eventful. It was polling day for California, and instead of being conveyed directly across the lake to meet the coach for Carson, we were trotted round to accommodate the different voters whose patriotism demanded their presence at the poll. The cruise was certainly pleasant enough, and one could hardly fail to admire the beauty of all around, but the delay nearly necessitated our spending the night in Carson, an event, under the peculiar circumstances of our being pressed for time, devoutly to be dreaded. On arriving at the pier, we were, as I expected, several hours late for the train; and not even the driving of Hank Monk, Mark Twain's "bête noir," served to do us any good.

Carson, the capital town of Nevada, seemed a bustling thriving spot. The shops appeared good and the streets crowded, but there was nothing of any particular interest to be seen or done, and we wanted to get on. All the passenger trains for that day had departed, and our only chance being that the manager of the line would give us permission to travel up on one of the freight trains during the night, we sent in our cards and requested an interview. This gentleman was no exception to the rest of his countrymen with whom I have had the pleasure of being brought into contact; and being as kind and obliging as all the educated Americans I have ever come across invariably are to Englishmen who require a favour and ask for it civilly, he readily gave the necessary order, which enabled us to reach Virginia City without stopping. At 10 P.M. our train started. The waggons were all quite full; the standing room on the engine (already pretty well crowded by the driver, stoker, and conductor) was hot and dirty; so a good-natured clerk belonging to the company, who came down to see us off, recommended our sitting just over the cow-catcher in front of the engine.

I remember once seeing in 'Punch' a cartoon which represented a director somewhat similarly placed, with the exception, that I think he had a glass of grog and an arm-chair. I did not envy his position even then, but little thought that circumstances over which I had no control would have ever led me to be situated infinitely worse off. Up we both scrambled, the whistle screamed, and holding on tightly by a stanchion, we dashed forward into darkness. Our billet had certainly the sensation of novelty to recommend it, and after confidence became restored by getting over the first half-dozen miles in safety, we lighted our pipes, and began somewhat to relish our queer ride. As well as we could make out, the line seemed occasionally to run over ground somewhat similar in places to Cape Horn on the Union Pacific. Lights and fires at times glimmered in the valleys many feet beneath us, and an occasional streak like silver told us that we passed a stream. Going through the tunnels produced an odd sensation. However, on the whole we both enjoyed the trip, and in a few hours our journey ended by the engine suddenly detaching itself from its burden, and halting at a "Round house" about a mile from the city.

The conductor I imagine went with his freight, as he did not take our fare and we never saw him again; the stoker disappeared likewise, and the driver was of an uncommunicative and slightly morose disposition, not given to answer questions. "Where are we to go?" asked H. "The engine stays here," was his laconic reply; and almost intimating by his silence that we might go to the d—l if it pleased us, he also vanished from our view.

Our position was so ludicrous and absurd that we both fairly screamed with laughter. Alone on an engine, in the dark, hampered with a lot of luggage, and not knowing where on earth we were, for a few minutes we could only look at each other and roar. There seemed every prospect of our spending the night by the wayside, when fortunately we discovered a couple of men smoking in the engine-house, who were of a more friendly and amiable disposition than the driver. They allowed us to leave our baggage in a place of safety, and telling us the town was about a mile off, pointed out the way, and H. shouldering a light portmanteau, we again started in the dark. Tripping over railway sleepers, barking our shins against unseen obstacles, at last we reached the town, a couple of as disreputable looking objects as well could be imagined. The road between Lake Tahoe and Carson is far and away the dirtiest in the West, which is saying a very great deal; and the blacks gathered on the engine, lying over the coating of dust picked up during our drive with Hank Monk, rendered us simply filthy. H. also carried his portmanteau himself, a thing very few free-born Americans ever dream of doing, and the remarks that greeted us on passing through a somewhat disreputable portion of the town were, if not complimentary, at least good-natured and amusing. "Where are you poor beggars going to?" "Pretty well played out I guess?" and "Have a drink?" were the various comments of the sympathising "innocents," who evidently took us for discharged miners or workmen on the tramp. At last we succeeded in getting comfortably settled in an hotel, and were glad enough to turn in after our adventurous but somewhat fatiguing journey.

Next day I presented my introduction to Messrs. Mackay and Fair, who were exceedingly kind, and sent one of their foremen to show and explain the workings of their mine.

Our first visit was to the robing-room, where, after divesting ourselves of every stitch of clothing, we were soon equipped in full miner's costume, of shirt, trowsers, thick stockings, boots, and an old hat. Thus apparelled we were conducted to the mouth of the shaft, and holding tightly to an iron bar running across the cage which held us, we rapidly descended into the bowels of the earth. Fifteen hundred feet were soon run down, and stepping out of the cage we were introduced to Mr. Lamb, the leading foreman of the gang of hands at present working, who giving us each a lantern, conducted us round the various workings, passages, and shafts ; pointing out what he deemed interesting, and explaining everything we saw. The heat in places was intense, but ventilation effected by engines worked by compressed air rendered it perfectly healthy. No noxious gases are ever developed, and naked lights are carried freely and without danger. In each shaft was placed a barrel of iced water, from which the tired miners drank copiously, as, stripped to their trowsers and pouring with sweat, they from time to time repaired to them for this grateful refreshment.

The quality of ore obtained in the various workings varied considerably, but some was of immense value, and so thoroughly impregnated with gold that even by the dull light of the miner's candle we could see the yellow flecks that betokened the presence of the precious metal. In these places we were literally surrounded by silver. The ground we trod on was silver, almost pure, and the sides of the shaft and the roof were formed of the same substance. A square, formed by cuttings some 200 feet long, was almost entirely composed of this extraordinarily valuable deposit, and according to the most reliable authority the estimated value of what we ourselves beheld was £74,000,000 sterling. The work on the men is severe, but as none receive less than sixteen shillings a day, and a foreman gets £750 a year, there is little difficulty in providing as many hands as are required. As the ore is excavated from the mine the vacant space is carefully shored up with timber, and eventually a solid mass of wood replaces the abstracted metal. It was singular to observe the commencement of the "find" in the shafts. As regular as possible were the marks which betokened the presence of the metal, which was preceded by dirt, clay, and porphyry. The end of a worked-out shaft always finished by showing silver, porphyry, clay, and dirt, in as regular a succession as the strata through which we entered. I was surprised at the extreme dryness of the workings; hardly a drop of water was to be found in any of them except what was used for drinking purposes, and occasionally water had absolutely to be pumped on the timbers to prevent dry rot.

Such enormous excavations as are here perpetually being carried on necessarily take proportionately enormous masses of timber to replace them. Hundreds of thousands of square feet of ore have to be replaced by an equally great quantity of wood, and whole forests are soon buried deep in the inmost recesses of the earth, peradventure after the lapse of many years to undergo a strange reconstitution, and bother some scientific discoverer as to how on earth such enormous masses of—whatever it may be—got together. The mere conveyance of these forests, doomed to such premature burial, was in itself a herculean labour, until the managers of the mine, at the cost of about a quarter of a million of dollars, built a water flume fifteen miles in length, which, from the heavily-wooded summits of the Sierras west and north-west from Huffaker, belonging to the company, conveys at little expense and with extraordinary rapidity all the timber they can possibly require. The flume is constructed of planks two inches thick, and built in the shape of the letter V. To gain a uniform grade it was found necessary to build it on trestle work and stringers from one end to the other, and this framework, which in some places is forty-eight feet high, is substantial enough to support a narrow-gauge railway, it being thoroughly braced longitudinally and across. All the main supports, which are five feet apart, are firmly set in mud sills; the boxes rest in brackets placed four feet apart, and these again rest upon substantial stringers. Mr. Fair described a trip he took by nailing a piece of board at the end of one of the V-shaped boxes, and being floated down by the workmen.

A strip of wood nailed across furnished a seat, and being once started, away he flew at the rate of twenty miles an hour for a commencement. The average grade is sixteen inches to sixteen feet, but the sharpest fall is three in six, which is, however, only for two hundred feet, and over this he flew at such a pace that he could hardly gain breath. H. and myself were both extremely anxious for a sail on such queer waters, and begged hard for a ride. Mr. Fair, however, declared the risk too great, that he had only gone down as a matter of duty, and that nothing would ever induce him to do so again. As the workmen go down it almost every day, this was all rubbish; however, he would not give us a mount, and we were both a good deal disappointed at his raising our curiosity without gratifying it.

At one of the richest deposits our guide begged we would take a sample of the ore, and seizing a pick, I set to work at the part being cleared out. It was astonishing with what surprising ease the pick detached large masses of metal, and selecting a small piece strongly marked with gold, I took it away in remembrance of our visit. I never saw anything more interesting than these extraordinary mines, and we both felt quite bewildered at the enormous amount of wealth we beheld all round us.

In connection with these mines, Mr. G. related a singular fact which I fancy is not generally known, but which must I imagine upset many a cherished theory on the subject of earthquakes.

While he was a resident in Virginia City, an earthquake of unusual severity one day terrified all its inhabitants. Houses shook, roofs fell in, and frightened women and children rushed into the streets thinking their last hour surely had arrived. After a few terrible shocks, the commotion subsided and tranquillity again reigned in the shaken town. Immediate apprehension for their own safety having ceased, the cry instantly became, "The miners!" Away rushed mothers and children to the mouths of the various shafts that honeycombed the mountain. Again terror, more intense than that caused by the fear of personal safety, seized the mother and the wife, and half dead with excitement, they reached the pit's mouth. The miners, astonished, looked at them, and could not make out what was the matter. The earthquake! "Guess they had felt no earthquake. What the thunder was up?" So indeed it was; and fifteen hundred feet under ground not the slightest movement of a shock, so severe on the surface as to cause the most intense alarm even among a population comparatively inured to such visitations, was even felt.

Having been through all the workings, a task that took nearly three hours in an atmosphere somewhat resembling the hot room in a Turkish bath, we bid adieu to our good-natured conductor, regretting that our unscientific education had not enabled us better to follow and comprehend the many descriptions he so kindly tried to make us understand; and once more getting on the cage we ascended to earth.

On our arrival we found a warm bath in readiness, and a glass of excellent whisky-and-water soon made us fit to examine the next process in the working of the metal.

Mr. John Mackay now kindly became our pilot, and showed the first process, where the large lumps of ore, having been brought up from the mine, are crushed by what, not knowing its correct name in machinery, I shall call a "mouth of iron." These iron jaws having broken in pieces the larger lumps, they are passed under stampers, ponderous iron rods shod with steel, which, rising and falling heavily with unceasing regularity, soon pulverise the already broken ore lying beneath their massive hammers. Water passing through this latter machinery turns the crushed metal into a kind of thick paste, which then passes into large circular pans; where water, quicksilver, and certain chemicals being added, the whole is kept constantly in motion by iron rakes radiating from the centre of the vat and revolving rapidly round it. The quicksilver seizes on the gold and silver, and finally settles in large flannel bags placed in boxes separate from but near the bottom of the vats, and this amalgam is fit for the furnace. Water carries off the superfluous dirt, but as this is often charged with precious metal, it is subjected to a still further examination by being caused to pass over coarse blankets laid on a small wavy kind of bed, which being charged with more quicksilver soon grasps the minute particles which have escaped seizure in the former process, and forming more amalgam likewise becomes fit for smelting. The amalgam being now all collected is placed in iron retorts and subjected to the action of fire. The gold and silver mass soon becomes liquid, the quicksilver passing away in a vapour, which being caused to pass through water, again consolidates itself and becomes available for further use. The molten metal is then cast into bricks which contain a certain amount of silver and a certain quantity of gold. To determine the accurate value of each is the next process. A corner of each brick is chipped off and sent to the assayer, who, determining the exact value of each metal in the brick it belongs to, registers the same and has the correct value stamped on the huge ingot, which is then fit for the market, and, I need hardly observe, finds a ready sale. The whole process, even to a tyro like myself, was exceedingly curious; but to a man versed in machinery, who could understand the beauty of the powerful engines, etc., he saw in play all around him, I can imagine it to be still more interesting and instructive.

Virginia City is well worth a visit on its own account, even without a trip to the mines. Few towns in the world are so lively, and a very few years back the lively nature of its inhabitants exhibited itself in constant shootings when they imagined things were getting slow. I was told by an old resident before I went there that it was a somewhat rapid place. "If you are in luck," he said, "you ought to get a man for breakfast;" which expression, I afterwards learned, meant that an account of a murder should be served up in the morning paper with my matutinal meal. Every other shop in the principal streets seemed to be a drinking saloon, and in most of them were established "hells" for the carrying on of the popular game of "faro." Drinking, gambling, and other unmentionable vices seem the chief occupation of the above-ground population. Underground I had seen them hard at work, and now I could witness their ideas of enjoyment. The two principal streets run parallel to each other and are about half a mile long. One consists of shops, stores, gambling-houses, and drinking-bars, the latter greatly predominating; and the other entirely of houses kept by Phrynes of various and manifold nationalities. Wages being high, everything was proportionately extravagant, and the ordinary charge of the common street shoe-black was a quarter-dollar (a shilling) for cleaning one's boots.

I had expected to have seen people wearing the proverbial red flannel that is supposed to designate the son of toil in this particular industry, but it was quite the reverse; "biled shirts," the western American name of white ones, were the rage, and H. and myself suffered severely by our contrast to these wonderfully got-up gentry. Mr. F. had put our names down as hon. members of the Washoe Club, but never dreaming that there was more than one club in such a place, we omitted to inquire its name, thinking "the club" would be sufficient. On going there we missed our way, and H., addressing a gentleman with flashy diamond studs in a very much "biled shirt," asked him to be kind enough to tell us the way to the club. "The club!" he replied. "What club?" H. was nonplussed, but managed, Englishman-like, to stammer, "Oh—ah—why—don't you know? *the* club." Our friend looked at us both from top to toe with a perplexed expression of countenance, evidently taking stock of our probable social position. Neither of us had diamond studs or a black coat. I wore a rather seedy hat. I think the hat decided him, for with a spit of relief he answered, "Guess you want the Miner's Club: straight down two blocks and turn to your right." H. looked bewildered, but it was somewhat more than delicious to see a member of "White's," the "Marlborough," and goodness knows how many of the best clubs in London, quietly pooh-poohed for not wearing a "biled shirt," and when the possessor of the diamond studs was out of hearing, we both laughed till our sides ached. Eventually we did arrive at the club, and found it an exceedingly nice and comfortable one, and every member in it quite willing to be kind and obliging.

Before 1861 the State of Nevada, now the richest mining country in the world, formed part of Utah; and prior to that, in 1848, being a part of Alta California, it belonged to Mexico. The whole country is more or less covered with mines, good, bad, or indifferent, and their names on the "Share List" are legion. The Comstock lode is pretty well known throughout the world; for the others, those who care about such things know well enough where to get detailed accounts, and those who do not would not care to see them enumerated here. With regard to its wealth, I may state without exaggeration that the streets of Virginia City are paved with silver. A curious statement, but nevertheless a true one, as the metal used in laying down the roads has been found on analysis to be composed of dirt which if worked would return a very fair profit per ton.

At about two o'clock one morning I was awakened by bugles, horns, whistles, and all kinds of music.

Wondering what new and peculiar phase of life in America I was about to witness, I jumped out of bed, and on throwing open my window needed no interpreter to explain the cause. The whole town seemed in a blaze. Fire-engines shrieked, men shouted, and women in scanty apparel rushed wildly about the passages of the hotel. I proceeded to rouse out my companion, and after a couple of bad shots at his door, of which I forgot the number, discovered him sleeping tranquilly through all the turmoil. On getting into the street we found that a livery stable about a block off had been entirely destroyed, and that the Odd-fellows' Hall, a handsome brick edifice, was now battling with the flames. At one time there was every prospect of Virginia City emulating Chicago in its holocaust. The houses are nearly all built of wood, and on their shingle roofs a perfect hailstorm of fire was being rained down. Many people packed up all their effects, and piling them in the streets, quietly sat on them, waiting to see how things would turn out; while others repaired to the saloons, considerately opened for so festive an occasion, and nerved themselves by a morning cocktail for the coming struggle. The fire brigade, a volunteer one, did its duty well, and after a hard fight the flames were got under and the excitement subsided.

Having exhausted the chief wonders, and visited the commencement of a shaft Messrs. Mackay and Fair intend running 4000 feet deep, we took our departure, and after a tiresome delay at Reno, an unimportant little town, twenty-one miles from Virginia

City, we once more found ourselves in a Palace sleeping-car, and *en route* to the East.

We had breakfast at Humbolt, a small station with a scanty garden, in which was a pond and a couple of Mandarin ducks. The country all around is barren and arid. Alkali incrustations render white the surface of the ground, and sage-brush seems the only vegetable produce. On the platform lay a huge mass of sulphur in a solid lump; it was a desolate place, and we were glad to get on.

The Humbolt cañon is curious; the river running through it rather slimy and green. We dined at Battle Mountain; elevation 4508 feet. Slight improvement in the aspect of the country. More grazing land, and a few cattle were to be seen from the train. A lot of children were in the car who raced about from end to end, knocking over books and incessantly disturbing one's papers. Occasionally they varied the amusement by howling loudly, while their mothers looked complacently on without endeavouring to stop them, evidently well pleased with the healthy condition of the disagreeable little animals' lungs. I certainly did pine for the ease and quiet of an English first-class carriage, in which, thank Heaven, such bores can be avoided. We fed again at Elko; elevation 5065 feet. Badly divided time, only a few hours having elapsed since the previous meal. We passed the one thousand mile tree west from Omaha, and at last arrived at the Mormon town of Ogden, in the territory of Utah. Here we had breakfast and parted company—H. going to Denver, to shoot in the North and South Parks; while I continued my journey towards Salt Lake City, to study Mormonism in its own headquarters.

I arrived there on Sunday September 5th, in time to witness the funeral solemnities of one of Brigham Young's shining lights—Mr. George A. Smith; his First Councillor, Church historian, and President of the Twelve Apostles. This Apostle became identified with the Mormon Church in its very infancy, and participated in its travels and trials from New York to Ohio, to Missouri, to Illinois, and finally to Utah. Most people in Utah suspected him of having been the willing instrument that Brigham used in compassing the massacre of the emigrants at Mountain Meadows; and had Mr. Smith lived another year, he would in all probability have been indicted and tried for that fearful crime. The Tabernacle—a huge building, looking at a distance more like an enormous inverted boat on a pedestal than anything else I can think of—was crowded to suffocation. Over ten thousand people were congregated within its walls, and it would have been impossible to have had a better opportunity for inspecting these strange beings.

I was chiefly struck by the extreme ugliness of the greater portion of their women, and by the shocking manner in which they were dressed. I never saw such a lot of frights, and can quite understand their jumping at polygamy, as a last chance of becoming entitled to even the fractional part of a husband, after failing to secure an entire one in the various parts of the world they may have come from. The plainest women find no difficulty in getting married. Becoming servants immediately after the ceremony, in a country where domestic labour is almost impossible to be procured, unprepossessing as they generally are, they represent a certain amount of value to their owners; and as they are systematically worked, they soon a good deal more than pay for their keep. The men looked thick and brutish, and in no part of the world have I seen so unprepossessing a set of whites, or such a vast quantity of ugly men and women congregated together, as were assembled here to assist in burying their departed Apostle—Mr. Smith.

While Brigham Young and some of the Apostles were eulogising the departed saint, whom they endowed with every earthly virtue, I had time to examine the interior of the building. It was tastefully decorated with flowers, and round the gallery were various inscriptions, such as, "Brigham, our leader and friend"; "We thank Thee, O God, for a Prophet"; "Utah's best crop—children." In the afternoon I again attended service in the Tabernacle, and this time heard a sermon on secular matters. The service was tedious and dragged out and lengthened to a considerable extent by the administration to the entire congregation of the sacrament. Several loaves of bread having been broken in small fragments were handed round to the people, who never left their pews; and shortly after large mugs of water followed. The organ was a fine one, and the music and singing fairly good. One of the "Twelve Apostles" addressed the saints (they all call themselves saints in Utah) and took them to task roundly on their various short-comings. He complained that they were paying too much attention to the laying up of wealth, while at the same time they begrudged the Church her accustomed share; that they were adopting the vices and bad habits of the Gentiles who had thrust themselves in among them, and that while walking in the streets he had absolutely seen saints smoking pipes and cigars, without even having the grace to seem ashamed of such a thing. He believed some of them drank; but at any rate they would never prosper if they smoked or took snuff. The women caught it next. They were going to the bad also. Many of them used tea and coffee, and perhaps sugar. They were departing from the simplicity of that mode of life laid down as best by their teachers, and he could hardly tell to what depravities such behaviour might not lead. He gave tongue for about half an hour, and talked more bosh during that space of time than any man I ever heard before or since.

I put up at a Mormon hotel, "The Townsend House," and can strongly recommend it. The proprietor, a Mormon, was extremely obliging, and does all in his power to make his guests comfortable. He took me to call on Brigham Young, and drove me about the city, showing and explaining the various objects of interest. Just about this time the excitement caused by the trial of Lee for his participation in the Mountain Meadow massacre was still going on; and many of the atrocities perpetrated by the Mormons were constantly being published in the daily papers. There is not the slightest doubt but that the leaders of the Mormon Church encouraged assassination in the most methodical and wholesale manner; the confessions of some of their own disciples who were actually engaged in these outrages showed that such atrocities actually did occur; and to me it seems strange that the Government of the country did not, and do not, take some active steps in avenging the victims.

Putting aside the wickedness and absurdity of the religion, and the unscrupulous villainy of the sacerdotal power, which in Mormonism is omnipotent, there is much to be admired in the industrious, frugal, and simple customs of the people. Finding a desert, they converted it into a garden, and Salt Lake City is laid out with the strictest regard to both health and convenience. Every street is about eighty yards wide, and has broad side walks well sheltered by locust or other ornamental trees; streams of clear running water border each side, and every house is surrounded by a garden laden with fruit-trees. The town is built on a gentle slope, behind it are the lofty ranges of the Wahsatch Mountains, and I doubt if it be possible to find any town in the States better planned for either comfort or scenic effect.

Gradually handsome buildings are beginning to be constructed. The Temple, when finished, will certainly be an attractive and ornamental structure, its very unusual style of architecture perhaps constituting its principal charm. The Prophet's favourite wife, Amelia, has had a handsome house just finished for her particular benefit; and wealthy Mormons in various parts of the town are building residences that would be considered fine anywhere.

Fresh discoveries of mineral wealth are almost daily taking place; and when confidence, so entirely destroyed by that gigantic swindle the "Emma Mine," again returns, and once more Gentile capital becomes invested in the country, I expect to see not only Salt Lake become a wealthy and prosperous town, but the Mormon faith rapidly become shaken, and the power of their Prophet and his apostles sensibly decline.

Not far from the town are two sulphur springs, over one of which has been built a bath-house. The water is kept at a temperature of 90°, and besides hip-baths they have constructed a very fair plunge one. A mile farther another stream of strongly-impregnated sulphur water, with about 130° of heat, rushes from beneath a solid rock. The odour, which is extremely unpleasant, can be detected at least half a mile off, and the stones and herbage growing near its banks are both tinted with a brilliant emerald green.

A small garrison of United States troops are quartered at Camp Douglas, which is built commanding the town and about two miles from it. Mr. A., the brother of an old schoolfellow, living at the hotel I was staying at, drove me over, and I met with every kindness and attention from the officers. I saw here, for the first time, the new American bayonet, "Rice's trowel bayonet with the Chillingworth attachment,"* and cannot speak too highly of its admirable qualities. It is simply a sharp-pointed strongly-built trowel, of eleven inches in length,

* See Appendix B.

exclusive of handle, and three and a half inches broad—quite sufficiently formidable as a weapon of offence; while for throwing up cover rapidly for infantry troops exposed to an enemy's fire it is simply, as a tool, unparalleled. With it a man can chop wood, build a wall, bake a cake, and stab or cut down his enemy. I see no reason why, without impairing its efficiency, one side should not be partially filed into a saw. An officer, who had seen troops drilled to its use, informed me that in less than ten minutes he saw a company completely shelter themselves (on rather hard ground into the bargain) from musketry. Our "shelter-trench drill," with its necessary accompaniment of picks and shovels, is as childish and grotesque in comparison to the handy implement used by the Americans, as the Indian bow in modern warfare would be to the Henry-Martini breechloader. Another exceedingly useful invention employed by them is the stacking "swivel," *i.e.* a small hook-swivel placed on the upper band of the rifle, which weighs almost nothing, and enables the men to stack their arms regardless of any inequality of ground. Were it the slightest use to urge our War Department to adopt any improvement not emanating from themselves, I could not advocate too strongly the adoption of both these plans in our own service.

Clintons station and hotel on the Great Salt Lake is about a three hours' ride from the town. The country on each side of the line leading to it is flat, and in some parts marshy. A few wet splashes, which we passed through just before first coasting the lake, were covered with wild duck; I also saw a few snipe, and should fancy the shooting there in winter would be pretty good. The mosquitos on this part of the line were fierce and bloodthirsty as tigers, and quite took possession of the cars, driving most of us who were not extra thick-skinned to take refuge on the platform, where the current of air prevented them effecting a lodgment. After passing Black Rock we stopped at Clintons, nicely situated on the Lake, and looking directly on Church and Antelope islands. On the former Brigham is accused of having stowed away the plunder so fearfully obtained by the massacre at Mountain Meadows. A small steamboat for the use of excursionists lay at a pier near the hotel, and a few bathing boxes were erected for the use of visitors.

I was somewhat curious to test the buoyancy of these waters, and shortly after arriving was floating about on their surface. The sensation of such extreme buoyancy is certainly curious, and for an indifferent swimmer I daresay pleasant. I could stand upright without motion. Lying on my back I could keep both feet entirely out of the water, with my arms also at the same time extended upwards to their full stretch. In breast swimming I could keep both legs above water from the knee joints, merely paddling with my hands; in fact, in any position it was difficult to sink. Swimming a distance was, however, difficult and tedious, as when on my breast the extraordinary buoyancy of the water had a tendency to throw the feet and legs right up in the air, which naturally forced the head forward and kept an unpleasant strain on the neck to secure its elevation. Diving was next to impossible, and the slightest drop of water getting into one's eyes caused extreme pain. The day was fine and the lake as smooth as glass, and I pottered about very pleasantly for over an hour, floating and paddling on its surface experimentalising with its peculiarly buoyant properties, when in one of my efforts I got and swallowed a mouthful of water. Great goodness! what a mouthful it was. The most nauseous medicine I ever tasted was nectar to it, added to which, it possessed a burning acrid power that almost took the skin off my mouth. I tried no more tricks, and feel convinced that the strongest swimmer in the world, even the famed Captain Webb, would be unable to live beyond thirty minutes in rough weather on Salt Lake. Three such mouthfuls as I swallowed would kill a water-buffalo "let alone" a man.

Round the lake, and extending for many miles on each side of the long flat valley in which it is situated, runs a curious but distinctly marked water line on the hills, a hundred feet or so above the water's present level; and at some distant and long past period, Salt Lake must have covered an extent of ground at least double its present area.

Among the sage-brush growing on the large alkali plains in the vicinity of Salt Lake, there are at certain seasons innumerable hares, or as people persist in calling them here, "jackass rabbits." They really are the true prairie hare (*Lepus Campestris, Bachman*), and not the jackass rabbit (*Lepus callotis, Wagler*), who is not to be found in either Utah or

California; but as every description of hare or rabbit, with the exception of the "cotton tail," is called "jackass," I suppose we must let it pass and adopt the national cognomen. A couple of Mormon gentlemen, hearing I was anxious to get a day at them, very kindly drove me out some ten miles across the plains, and passing the River Jordan, a muddy sluggish stream that runs into Salt Lake, we shortly afterwards commenced operations. Although not the best season of the year, immense numbers of them were scattered through the sage-brush, the only plant growing on these alkali bottoms. We found them rather wild, still they afforded good sport, and as the cover was in places somewhat thick, it required tolerably quick shooting to knock them over.

Judge H., to whom I had an introduction, and who had been residing for some years among the Mormons, explained many of their eccentricities, and told me many stories about these extraordinary people; and though tempted to give some of the benefits of his experience along with my own impressions, and "let out" on them, I will be merciful to my readers and spare them a dissertation on such a well-worn subject as Mormonism, contenting myself with an adoption of Bret Harte's remarks concerning the "long-tailed gentry," to whom in some things they are very similar, viz. "ways that are dark and tricks that are vain."

Salt Lake City could hardly be visited at a more favourable time of the year for witnessing it under its brightest garb than during the month of September. The fruit-trees were laden with peaches, apples, plums, and pears. The gardens were brilliant with flowers of many colours. Trees with their spreading branches threw a cool and grateful shade on all the side walks. Sparkling water rippled by their sides. A delicious fragrance perfumed the air, and whatever one may think of the Mormons, it is impossible to go away otherwise than charmed with their capital town. Utah, like Nevada, California, and many of the Western States, abounds in silver. For some inexplicable reason the wise people of Salt Lake City got it into their heads that I was a capitalist, and I was constantly beset with offers of mines for a mere song, that only required some of my superfluous wealth to develop into second editions of the Comstock Lode.

It is quite impossible for any man with an ordinary amount of brains to shut his eyes to the indisputable fact, that from the immense quantities of silver being poured into the market, a very serious and important change must shortly take place in this great circulating medium, and one which, coming with such extraordinary celerity as it really is doing, is certain most seriously to affect the whole world.

Financiers and legislators cannot look to this matter too soon; and accepting for a solution of the difficulty the argument of short-sighted or wilfully blind people, who assume that the adoption by America and other countries of specie payments will be sufficient to absorb the surplus, will only lead them more and more astray.

Up to a very recent period, Mexico was the only silver producing country of any importance in the world, and the greater portion of the bullion even sent from there came from but one mine—that of Potosi. Since those days, silver has been discovered in all directions, and were the country in a fit state to warrant the introduction of foreign capital, most of these mines could be made to pay.

The mines of Utah are many of them returning a high dividend on the very small capital expended in their primary working, and fresh deposits of ore are being discovered daily by people without any capital at all, and are consequently untouched. The Emma Mine is strongly suspected by the knowing ones at Salt Lake of having a rich "Bonanza" but a very few hundred feet below the distance worked by its present shareholders.

On the mines in Nevada it is impossible to touch without going into a matter of statistics and figures too wearisome for a short gossiping book of travels, but let it be borne in mind that, in only one mine out of the several hundred that exist in a small portion of Nevada, I saw myself ore which, still unraised, represented seventy-four millions of pounds sterling.

It has only been very recently that people have systematically looked for silver at all. Up to this the rage has merely been for gold. Experienced and resolute men are now prospecting in all kinds of wild and out of the way places for metals that a few years ago were rarely searched for by men educated to their task. Silver, more or less, exists in all the Western States; even Alaska contains it; but were not another mine to be discovered, those that exist at present are more than sufficient to halve the present market value of silver, if they were only properly worked.

In San Francisco the vulgar but successful speculator in mines has his dinner menu engraved on a silver plate, which each guest puts in his pocket and takes away; but if it even became the fashion to pocket the spoons, the flow of silver is too incessant and steady to feel the drain.

I have studied this subject at far greater length than it is necessary to enter upon here, and feel convinced that the depreciation of the metal, owing to the immense quantities produced, will soon become so decided that statesmen will be compelled to take the matter very seriously up, and the sooner they take their task in hand the better.

CHAPTER XI.

Cache Valley—Chicken shooting—A bear hunt—A few words concerning bears—Ogden—Laramie City—Fort Sanders—A scout on the Rocky Mountains—American tents—Rarefaction of the air—A long shot—Sage-hens—Beaver-dams—My first elk—Lost on the mountains—Our game bag—Murders by the "Noble savage"—A few words about Indians—The Pi-Utes superstition—Chiefs—Squaws—Religion—Cards—Sioux or Dakotas—Preparation for war—The Black Hills—The beginning of the end—President Grant—North Platte—Buffalo—The Loup Valley—Anecdotes of the frontier—Fort Hartsuff—Prairie fires—Prairie dogs—Tame elk—A close shave—Another elk hunt—Buckshot—A large band of elk—Not dead yet—Wolves—A complete spill.

From Salt Lake City, I travelled about one hundred miles north through the land of the Mormon, to the small town of Franklin in the territory of Idaho, where I heard good prairie chicken shooting was to be obtained. Mr. A. came with me, and we got comfortable quarters at Keeney's hotel. En route, we joined forces with another gentleman who was bound on the same errand, and during our stay in Idaho we had a very pleasant time.

The greater portion of the road to Franklin lay through Cache Valley, one of the most fertile and best-cultivated pieces of land in the territory. Mormon towns, designed on plans similar to that of Salt Lake City, lay like so many gardens nestled at the foot of the hills; Corinne, situated near the west bank of Bear River, being the most important. A large salt slough of several miles in width was passed just before getting there, and a large river crossed by a substantial looking bridge, under which floated a solitary pelican quite undismayed at the strange racket above him and a pistol shot with which he was saluted from one of the cars.

This town does a considerable freighting trade with Montana and other Northern sections, but for any one visiting the Yellow-stone I should recommend their going straight through to the end of the Utah Northern line, then taking coach for Virginia City—Montana, and to fit out and make all other necessary arrangements from there. Logan is another Mormon town of some importance on this line. It has a brass and iron foundry, saw and planing mills, a fine new temple, and is, to use a common expression out here, "quite a place."

In coming over the divide from Bear River to Logan River a fine view is to be obtained. To the southward, Corinne, Brigham City, Call's Fort, Honeyville, Deweyville, and Hampton lay before us; while to the northward some half-dozen tree-embowered towns could be taken in at the same glance.

The prairie chicken shooting turned out quite as good as it had been represented, and my companions knowing the habits of the bird, we had little difficulty in making large bags each day we went out. During the mornings and evenings they were scattered about the prairie and in the neighbouring grain fields, but during the heat of the day they all crowded for shelter to the small willow-shaded streams, where there was no difficulty in finding them, and where we got shots at times quite as fast as one could in any "hot corner" of a well-preserved covert in England. Their flight is like our own grouse, to which bird they bear a strong family resemblance, and indeed to which class they belong. As every species of hare in the West is called a "jackass rabbit," so is every kind of grouse called a prairie chicken. Blue grouse, sage hens, pin-tailed grouse, and willow grouse are all chickens; and these birds about Franklin, though called chickens on all sides, are in reality willow grouse (*Lagopus albus, Audubon*). The shooting was as good as it could be; we soon fired away all our cartridges, and were meditating a flight, when one evening news was brought to the hotel that a bear had been tracked some distance up the hills by a noted Mormon hunter, who, singularly enough, was christened Orson Broadbent.

Mr. Broadbent was quite a local celebrity from his successes as a bear hunter, and, offering next morning to pioneer us to the spot, we made the necessary arrangements for starting. The following account of the hunt I afterwards found published in the editorial correspondence of the 'Ogden Freeman,' and give it *in extenso*, as a sample of American journalism. The story chiefly existed in the editor's imagination, who happened to be staying at Franklin at the time, the only correct part of his statement being that we really did kill the bear. Orson Broadbent, getting the carcass, sold it, and it was eaten quite as rapidly as described. My friend Mr. A. has been given "brevet rank," and the skin fell to me.

TWO ENGLISH LORDS ON A BEAR HUNT—HOW THEY BAY THE GRIZZLIES —BEASTS MORE FEROCIOUS THAN THE BENGAL TIGER—A FAMILY DRIVEN OUT OF THE COUNTRY BY THEM.

Soda Springs, Idaho, Sept. 18, '75.

THE CHASE.

Sir Rose Price, an English Baronet, and Sir B. Argall, another English nobleman, who has invested largely in Utah mines, came to Franklin, and enjoyed the sport of a grizzly bear hunt while we were there, a few days ago. A noted bear hunter, Mr. Orson Broadbent, had discovered that one of these mountain terrors was feeding in Birch Creek Canyon, about four miles from town, and notified the two British Lords that he would pilot them to the spot if they thought they had lost any bears. The gentlemen accepted the proposition, were furnished by their landlord, J. W. Keeney, with a most suitable covered carriage, drawn by a handsome span of blood bays, driven by John C. Barrow, familiarly known as "Rambling Jack;" and after a cautious journey of three hours' duration, the great uncouth hunter—Broadbent—accompanied by Jas. H. Handy, announced that they were in the vicinity of the game, when every weapon was made ready, the dogs brought to presence, and action prepared for. It was soon known that his majesty, Bruin, watching the party from his closely ensconced point of observation in a thicket of birch willows, wild rose bushes, service and hawthorn brush, and when Broadbent entered the lair, a rush, accompanied by a hoarse growl, made chills creep over the nerves of some of the party, but only gave confidence to Sir Rose Price, who had tried and proven his famous breechloader among the jungles of Patagonia and Central Africa; nor was Sir Argall at all disconcerted, although he was a neophyte in the chase of such monsters. And now that both the Lords had an open field and a fair fight, at the crack of their trusty weapons the grizzly dropped, rolled, reared, and pitched with headlong ferocity, and unearthly yell after Sir Rose, but when within ten feet of the African hunter, a well-directed shot from Argall gave him another tumble; and then the two powerful dogs took part in the sport. One giant canine, best described as a cross between a bull and a mastiff, was reduced to jelly by a single blow of the left paw, while his mate was torn half in two by a grab with the right. Then did bruin renew the charge against Sir Rose Price, and before he could recover his wits he too lay sprawling under the bear. All the spectators were horror-stricken and stood aghast, as they supposed the brave man was so completely within the jaws of death, that rescue would be an impossibility, though all were in a moment agreeably surprised when they saw the long knife, dripping with hot blood, withdrawn from the heart of the brute, and all gave a prolonged cheer as the bear rolled over, dead, and Sir Rose leaped to his feet unharmed. The fine specimen of game was taken to Franklin, and after being dressed for the butcher's stall, weighed eight hundred and seventy-five pounds, and yet he was only three years of age. The robe was placed in the hands of Broadbent to be tanned for the Lords. The game was put on sale at the market of H. T. Smith, who sent one quarter to the Beardsley House, Ogden, and a choice piece to THE OGDEN FREEMAN, the remainder going off like hot cakes to residents of Franklin. We must not omit to mention that Mr. Black, route agent of the Utah Northern R. R., was a participant in the hunt, and that he and H. W. O. Margery also received each a present of the rarity. The fat on the tenderloin was three inches thick.

The public are notified that such game is so plentiful about Franklin that in many places they have made serious inroads upon the stock; and the family of Wm. Bradshaw, comprising himself, wife, and four children, were so annoyed by their inroad upon their hogs that, after nine swine had been taken out of the pen and devoured, Mr. Bradshaw considered it unsafe to remain with his family, and therefore left his homestead—driven away by bears. This was on a travelled road along Deep Creek, six miles from Malad City, Idaho.

Mr. Keeney will furnish the most superb outfits for hunting parties, and Broadbent will admirably guide any persons desiring a grand bear hunt in the neighborhood of Franklin.

Sir Rose Price expresses himself as fully impressed that the Bengal tiger is not near so spirited a battler as the Rocky Mountain grizzly. He is delighted with the sport. Sir Rose presents the appearance of a much travelled man and an intrepid hunter.

A great number of bears have this year been seen in many parts of the country. Within thirty miles of Salt Lake City I heard of several being noticed, but almost invariably they are given a wide berth. A man will tell you of having seen "grizzlies," but if asked "Did he kill any?" generally replies, "Guess I never lost no bar, and don't want to find none."

Notwithstanding all this, the bear is not half so formidable a beast as he is represented, and killing a tiger on foot (not from a tree or an elephant remember—any "muff" can do that—but fairly face to face in the jungle) is far and away a more dangerous game in every respect, and requires much more nerve to do it. A ball properly placed will kill a bear as easily as a snipe; and this bear who was so near eating the two "English Lords" fell stone dead at the very first fire, which was delivered at about five yards' distance and took effect in the brain, the ball entering one inch over the left eye.

A man hunting grizzly bears alone should always have a dog. Not "a giant canine best described as a cross between a bull and a mastiff," but a well-plucked ordinary cur, such as all really valuable bear dogs generally are. I have passed within a few feet of a bear in cover without being aware of it, until a dog brought to the place immediately afterwards found out and started him from the very spot I had almost walked over. A couple of good active curs who will bark and snap at the bear is all one wants. At this time of the year Master Bruin is found in thick copses of fruit-trees or berries, where it would be almost impossible, as well as extremely dangerous, for a man to get out a bear without their assistance. The instinct of nine bears out of ten is to retire when they first discover the presence of men; but if wounded, or with cubs, they will quite as generally show fight. It is worth remembering that, when taking a body shot at bear, *their heart lies low.* I had been told this by old hunters, and took the first opportunity of convincing myself, by anatomical examination, of the correctness of their statement. A knife blade four inches long can reach it comfortably. In tolerably open ground, a cool man armed with a breechloading rifle has nothing to fear, as a bear nearly always stops when wounded, no matter how slightly, to bite and growl, and could be filled with bullets, even before coming unpleasantly near. This latter plan, however, spoils the skin, and one express bullet, properly placed at close quarters, will generally be found quite sufficient.

Franklin is at present the terminus of the Utah Northern in Idaho and point of departure for mails and passengers going north; the line is, however, gradually being pushed on towards Montana, and I fancy the importance enjoyed by the town at present will soon decline. It is built on the usual plan of all Mormon settlements, *i.e.* in large blocks, every house with a garden and plenty of fruit-trees, streams of water on each side of the broad streets, and trees planted on the side-walks for shade. Having slaughtered chickens until I was tired of firing at them, I retraced my steps to Ogden, where, as on a previous occasion, I had to pass a night, waiting for my train. Ogden is built at the entrance of a cañon which runs from the Wahsatch Mountains, and is a nice-looking town on the usual Mormon plan. Fair trout-fishing can be had on the river, but at some distance from the town. Two rival hotels are at the station, and only a few yards apart. One is on the Union Pacific line, the other on the

Utah Northern. On the arrival of every train they both bang gongs, and as they seem to fancy that the fellow who hits hardest and longest will attract the greatest amount of custom, the noise they kick up by both night and day is simply fiendish. There are plenty of better hotels in the town, which is about half a mile off, and one escapes this horrid row by going there.

I nearly omitted mentioning that any one desirous of seeing the "noble savage" can get plenty of him all over Utah. At Corinne, just before I went there, about three thousand camped near the town. Ogden has generally a tribe or so loafing about; and as the Mormons encourage and feed them for purposes of their own, there are usually plenty idling the time away, with dirty blankets, painted faces, and half drunk.

A ride of twenty-four hours in a Pullman, with rather over the average number of children and babies, brought me to Laramie, in the territory of Wyoming, which I had been recommended to make my headquarters for shooting in the Rocky Mountains, and where I accordingly made a halt.

Laramie City is situated on the east bank of the Big Laramie River, one mile below the crossing of the old California emigrant road of 1849, and seven miles below the crossing of the overland mail and stage road near the centre of Laramie plains. This magnificent plain or park, comprising two million acres of land at an elevation of 7170 feet above the sea, is entirely surrounded by two spurs of the Rocky Mountains—on the eastern side by the range of the Black Hills, and on the western by the Medicine Bow range.

The Territory of Wyoming boasts of enjoying real universal suffrage, the franchise being actually extended to females; and Laramie is celebrated as being the first (and I trust it may be the last) place in the territory, and probably in the world, where a female jury was ever empannelled. The enactment passing this singular ordination by the Council and House of Representatives of the Territory of Wyoming is dated the 10th of December, 1869, and runs, "That every woman of the age of twenty-one years, residing in this territory, may, at every election to be holden under the laws thereof, cast her vote. And her rights to the elective franchise and to hold office shall be the same under the election laws of the territory as those of electors." On the 7th of March, 1870, at the District Court, several ladies sat on the jury, hearing and deciding on various cases. From this date, women's rights in Wyoming seem to have been firmly established, and a licence legally given them by their territory to neglect their domestic duties as wife and mother as much as seemeth to them fit.

Fort Sanders, a military post established in 1866 for the protection of workmen engaged on the Union Pacific line and the then infant town of Laramie, is about two miles from Laramie Station. I had with me a letter of introduction to Colonel B., who was commanding the post, and shortly after my arrival I delivered it in person. My reception was both courteous and hospitable. The Colonel would not hear of my remaining in the hotel at Laramie, where I had engaged rooms. He sent off immediately for my traps, and once more I was comfortably living my old barrack life, and enjoying the novelty of witnessing and criticising a new service, while waiting for the shooting party which the good-natured Colonel had almost immediately offered to get up. The headquarters and band of the 2nd Cavalry and one company of the 4th Regiment of Infantry formed the little garrison, the remaining portion of both regiments being engaged in looking after Indians in different places about the post, varying in distance from one hundred to a thousand miles. Three troops of the former were on escort duty to the commissioners, at the great council being held for negotiating the purchase of the Black Hills from the Indians, so that but few officers were at the post.

Some fair duck and hare shooting is to be had in the immediate vicinity of the post, and antelope are within a couple of miles. At this season of the year the climate was all that one could wish for, and the clear blue of an Italian sky seemed added to an atmosphere indescribable for its extreme clearness and invigorating purity. The Rocky Mountains are indeed during the early autumn months the very quintessence of perfection of climate. For these few months I know of nothing in Europe or anywhere that can touch them, but preserve me from being here in winter. Sanders is on a bleak flat plain, without the slightest protection of tree or hill to shelter it from the fearful storms so common on the mountains; "blizzards" they call them. During these blizzards man and beast alike suffer, and on one occasion during the winter of '74 the spirit thermometer showed a register of 49° below zero.

A couple of days after my arrival the following appeared in garrison orders:

HEADQUARTERS, FORT SANDERS, W. T.

September 19*th*, 1875.

SPECIAL ORDERS, No. 91. } (*Extract.*)

* * * * * *

III. Captain *Wm. H. Powell*, 4th Infantry, *W. P. Clark*, Adjutant, 2nd Cavalry, and 1st Lieutenant, *J. L. Fowler*, R. Qr.-Mr., 2nd Cavalry, with an escort of eight (8) men, will proceed to-morrow on a scout to the vicinity of Sabille Pass and Laramie Peak, making a careful examination of all roads and passes leading from the country known as the Black Hills to the Laramie Valley.

An itinerary of the march and accurate account of the distance travelled, as determined by an odometer, will be kept, and on return of the party a map of the country scouted over, with a full report of the trip, will be submitted.

The topography of the country as compared with the maps now made will receive especial attention, and changes needed carefully noted.

The Quartermaster's Department will furnish the necessary transportation.

* * * * * *

By order of

LIEUTENANT-COLONEL A. G. BRACKETT,

W. P. CLARK, LT. & ADJT., 2ND CAV.

This order entailed the most perfect combination of duty with pleasure that it has ever been my lot to witness, and on the day specified off we started in the highest possible spirits. A four-mule waggon carrying tents, bedding, and food, and a light ambulance formed our transport. The escort were mounted, and we each had a led horse for the chase. Springfield and Express rifles, with a thousand rounds of ammunition, and several varieties of shotguns formed our "battery," and thus equipped we were fully prepared for grizzly bear or Indians, the only two dangerous animals we were likely to come across.

The Indians anywhere within a hundred miles of their reservation are never to be trusted. They rob and scalp indiscriminately any small or unwary parties they fall in with, to use a common western expression, "all the time;" and as the Government rarely permits their being followed into their reservations, even when troops are in hot pursuit of stolen cattle, they are in my opinion rather encouraged to run the risk than otherwise. Officers have told me that they have constantly seen the stolen cattle they were in pursuit of over the border, having just crossed before they could seize it, and that the "noble savages," knowing well the existing order which protected them, testified their confidence in its efficiency by derisive motions of exultation and contempt.

On a wet snowy morning, unusual to find at this time of the year, we left Fort Sanders, our route lying over the plains that stretch away for many miles to the north and south. Our first day's march was uneventful, and chiefly exemplified the comfort of travelling in a well-covered and easy-going ambulance, in contradistinction to riding in the blinding sleet; my only experience hitherto, during bad weather, while on hunting parties. A few hours brought us away from all signs of civilisation. As far as the eye could reach towards north and south lay a huge rolling prairie well sprinkled with antelope, both single and in herds; we had not time, however, to waste in stalking these wary creatures, and after a march of twenty-seven miles we camped for the night not very far from Wyoming. The government tent of the American service is a far more comfortable habitation than the regulation "bell" of our own. The men are provided with what are termed "A," and the officers with "wall," tents; and as the canvas they are constructed of is lighter and easier to pack than ours, they combine the advantages of having more room with less weight to carry. Our beds were formed of buffalo robes, and the amount of luxuries forthcoming at dinner-time fairly surprised me. A comfortable table to sit at, and arm-chairs to smoke in afterwards, were good things I little dreamed of ever enjoying on a hunting expedition in the wildest part of the Rocky Mountains. Next morning we had a sharp frost, severe enough to throw a coating of ice over the water in my bath. The snow and rain had disappeared, and for the rest of our trip we had the most charming weather conceivable. The extreme purity and lightness of the atmosphere at this great elevation above the sea gives to out-of-door life in these mountains a charm that I have never felt elsewhere. Everything under its seductive influence becomes *couleur de rose*, and one seems to inhale exhilarating draughts of pure ozone more vivifying than all the brandy-cocktails in a San Franciscan bar.

Our line of march ran for some miles close by and parallel to the Union Pacific Railway. Large sheets of zinc or tin, torn from the roofs of the carriages by the prodigious force of the wind during winter storms, strewed the way, and at intervals snow-sheds and snow-fences protecting the line showed the kind of weather one might look forward to in January or December.

On striking off from the railway the country became wilder and game more abundant. We passed over a succession of bluffs, and from the top of each invariably saw herds of prong-horned antelope (*Antilocapra Americana, Ord*), the only representative of its species inhabiting the continent. They were extremely shy, seldom offering a shot closer than four hundred yards, and a good number of rounds were fruitlessly expended. We only got one during the day, which I killed by a chance shot at rather over a thousand yards with an American Springfield rifled musket, calibre forty-five. The ball went in at the eye, passing through the neck, and it being such a singular shot we measured the distance, which was exactly a thousand and ninety yards.

Though tolerably familiar with the appearance of many of the vast tribes of the antelope species inhabiting Eastern Africa, I had never before met the "prong-horned," and was glad of an opportunity that added a new head to my collection.

This animal is nearly the size of our ordinary fallow deer. The hair is everywhere very coarse, thick, spongy, and easily torn apart, somewhat resembling the South African "klip-springer," whose hide is so eagerly sought after by the Dutch boers for saddle cloths, and I think these antelope skins would answer very well for the same purpose. The head is broad, much hollowed on the forehead; the ridge of the muzzle narrow, high, and convex; the outline of the head narrow and tapering. The horns are situated very far back, are much compressed antero-posteriorly, with a broad, compressed, pointed snag directed upwards and forwards; beyond this anterior snag the horn becomes rounded and tapers to an acute and compressed tip; when near the tip the direction of the horn, instead of being upwards with a slight outward divergence, changes abruptly and bends inwards and a little backwards. The terminal portion of the horn is smooth and polished; the basal, on the contrary, is generally warty and roughened by angular tubercles of greater or less size.

The geographical distribution of the American antelope is pretty well indicated. According to Dr. Richardson, it is found as far north as the north branch of the Saskatchewan in lat. 53°. It is spread all over the plains between the Missouri River to the Rocky Mountains, and as far west as the coast range of California and Oregon. To the south it reaches the Rio Grande at its mouth, and probably extends some distance into Mexico.

In some places we passed large tracts covered with sage-bush, and frequently put up and shot a very handsome bird called the "sage-cock" (*Centrocercus urophasianus, Swainson*). They are one of the numerous birds that come, as I have described, erroneously under the head of "chickens," being often confounded with the "prairie-hen" of the plains. This bird varies much in size, the male being considerably larger and heavier than the female. They are like huge grouse, feathered to the toes, about the size of turkeys; and one of unusual growth, which I shot during our trip, measured forty-eight inches from tip to tip of its extended wings. The weather still continued magnificent, and moving quietly onward by easy marches averaging twenty-eight miles, we reached on the third day our camping-ground on the North Fork of the Laramie River, about nine miles from Laramie Peak.

Our tents were pitched on a level sward at the mouth of a cañon, through which for about eighteen miles coursed the North Fork of the Laramie, a small stream apparently full of beavers, whose beautifully-built dams shored up and kept from drying during the heat of summer many a mile of river. When first I saw these wonderfully-constructed works of art, I felt certain that I was looking at some new description of fish-trap made by the Indians; and wondered if they were in the habit of visiting them often to get what I supposed they contained, and if many came together. The sticks were planted with an evenness and regularity that quite surprised me; and unless I had been told by one of our party who the builders really were, should have been quite satisfied in my own mind that it was a particularly clever fish-catch.

Shortly after camping, Lieutenants C., F., and

myself mounted and started up the cañon. Mr. F. knew the country well, and had only a month previously killed two bears, besides elk and mountain sheep, while hunting over the same ground, and was consequently sanguine enough about our getting sport. We had some terribly rough ground to ride over along the river bank, and for the first eight miles saw nothing. C. was on one side, and F. and self on the other. I began to fancy we should have a blank day, when suddenly F., who was leading, sprang off his Indian pony, and crouching down motioned with his hand to look ahead. I did so; and there, not a hundred yards from us, standing in the river and almost concealed by its high banks, stood a band of four magnificent elk. I did not get the "elk-fever," but I was certainly for a few seconds quite lost in admiration as I gazed on these superb creatures.

Some confusion exists in the name of this animal, the term "elk" having been applied by several European writers to the moose (*Cervus alces*, or *Alces malchis*), an animal entirely different and not half so handsome, though of about same size. These were, however, the true American elk (*Cervus Canadensis, Erxleben*), sometimes called wapiti by Barton and Leach. They evidently were quite unaware of our presence as we were well to leeward; and the ground being favourable, I really believe we might have got within forty yards undetected, had not the mule Lieutenant C. was riding suddenly given a most hideous bray. The elk immediately sprang in alarm upon the bank, and simultaneously C. and myself opened fire. The band now gained an open space, and I can hardly conceive a more beautiful sight than that of these four lordly beasts, with their immense antlers thrown well back on their shoulders, trotting in bewilderment about the plain as the bullets from they knew not where came whizzing by them.

The whole picture was replete with beauty. The winding river, the heavily-meadowed plain, the lofty and precipitous sides of the cañon on one bank of the stream slightly wooded, and the beautiful clear volatile atmosphere of the Rocky Mountains, all combined to render the sight one never to be forgotten. The two elk we had first fired at were hard hit, and leaving the band, who soon trotted out of sight, came back towards the river, evidently with the intention of standing at bay. One of them took to the water close by where I was standing, and was soon put out of pain by a bullet behind the shoulder delivered at about twelve yards, and the other received its *coup de grace* from C. about a hundred yards farther up the river.

They were both in splendid condition, and had magnificent well-antlered heads. Had it not been for C.'s musical mule I believe we should have killed the entire band; but, as it was, getting two out of four was pretty good luck; after having performed the obsequies for the dead, and hung the heads on a tree out of reach of wolves, we returned to camp highly elated with our fortune.

Next day was devoted to getting in the elk, and looking for bear. We saw plenty of signs of bruin,

ACT THE FIRST.—"I GUESS HE'S DEAD ENOUGH."

See page 329.

UNIV. OF MICH.

some not twenty minutes old, but had no bear-dog and were unable to get him out of cover. Once Mr. C.'s dog, a setter, came bolting out of a thicket, and rushed, with tail depressed and hackles standing, between his master's legs. C.'s back was turned at the time, and I never saw a fellow hop round quicker, as he certainly thought the bear was right upon him. We beat the ground with almost reckless closeness, but were unable to unearth Master Bruin, who seemed somehow to be aware of the hot reception awaiting him, and was quite determined not to show.

The whole of the country is so intersected with cañons travelling on horseback becomes extremely difficult, and a novice can lose himself with most uncomfortable ease. Once while hunting "mountain sheep" (*Ovis Montana*), an animal similar to the mouflon (*Caprovis Musimon*) of Sardinia, with Lieutenant C. and a sergeant, we lost our bearings, and after some hours' wandering became quite bewildered, those horrible-looking ravines being on every side. After riding many miles, we determined on venturing to cross a cañon along whose sides we had crawled a long time vainly endeavouring to find a practicable place for descent, and which we felt certain lay between us and the one containing our camp. The more we looked, the less we liked it; but the sun was getting terribly low, and in a short time we knew darkness would close upon us and our fate for the night be sealed.

C. had gone on an exploring expedition by himself, and had we imagined most probably either broken his own or his pony's neck long before this. One thing was quite evident, the cañon must be crossed; so the sergeant and myself began a closer inspection of the yawning abyss preparatory to attempting the descent. Had it not been for an accident it is quite certain we should have never got down. Seeing a couple of openings, I led my mule towards one, telling my companion to try the other, and arranging that whoever found a practicable road should shout for the other to come to him.

Half an hour spent in a state of extreme nervousness in endeavouring to lead down places where only monkeys could climb, convinced me of the impossibility of descending by my route, and retracing my steps I went to the place reconnoitred by the sergeant. It looked quite as bad as my own, but I saw his trail for some distance until it became lost on the rocks, and arguing that, bad as it looked, where one mule could go another could follow, I pushed on, considering at the same time the odds were at least fifty to one in favour of my animal furnishing a meal in a very few hours for coyotes and wolves, and wondering how on earth the sergeant managed to get down. Several times I tried to go back, but that really *was* impossible, and, to make a long story short, I at last succeeded in reaching the bottom. What was my surprise on getting there to hear a shout, and to see my friend the sergeant hard at work half-way up the side, looking uncommonly like a fly on a wall, on the old route I had deserted, as being impracticable.

It appears that he had given up his first attempt, as I had mine; we had both crossed to the places first tried by the other, and both went down them, fancying the other had already accomplished the feat. On looking from the bottom at the place we had descended, it seems as if we must have dreamed we came down there, and had any one told me that he had taken any four-footed animal over such a place, it would have required considerable experience of his veracity ere I could have believed it possible. Our good luck stuck to us, for more by that than by good management we had stumbled into the very cañon which contained our camp, and got back by nightfall; but it was the merest chance in the world, and we narrowly escaped being three or four days lost on the hills. We had neither blankets nor food, and considering the amount of Indians in the vicinity always on the *qui vive* for scalps, had we not blundered on the right trail, our position would have been dangerous as well as disagreeable.

On our return journey we passed some beautiful natural meadow land, well watered and admirably adapted for agricultural purposes, but unsettled owing to its dangerous vicinity to Indian reservations. All along the North Fork of the Laramie this land seemed equally valuable, and it appears hard that a country so fertile should still remain in its native and primitive condition, owing to the dangerous proximity of these savages, who would most certainly run off with both scalps and cattle, were settlers to venture, situated as things are at present, to establish themselves in the locality.

Lieutenant F., who was guide and had arranged the expedition, intended on starting to have hunted on the Horse Shoe, a two days' farther march from the

North Fork; but the journey up quite tired our animals, who were rather a poor lot owing to the best teams being away in the Black Hills with the troops at the "great council," and we had to return without getting the cream of the sport we expected. We hunted instead on and about Laramie Peak, the highest point of the Rocky Mountains, and, though we should probably have killed more game on the Horse Shoe, our trip was enjoyable and pleasant as it well could be, and the bag, which consisted of 2 elk, 17 antelope, 35 blue grouse, 54 sage-hens, 28 duck, 25 hares, 2 rattlesnakes, and a badger, was sufficiently mixed to show that the sport obtained was both excellent and varied.

One of the first things we heard on our arrival at Fort Sanders was that three white men had been killed and scalped on the very ground we had been shooting over, while we were up there. The following is from a local paper; but the account of the other poor fellows, who were both scalped, I lost.

Special to the 'Sentinel.'

FORT LARAMIE, Sept. 23.

The body of a man by the name of John Little was just brought into this post. He was killed by Indians near the mouth of the North Fork of the Laramie, about twenty miles from this post and not far from F. M. Phillip's ranch. Some of his stock had been run off, and he went in pursuit of it last Sunday, which was the last time he was seen alive. His body was found yesterday. The ears are cut off, and his nose and chin look as if they were shot off. He is also shot through the body. There were supposed to have been only three Indians in the party that killed him.

As hunting on the Indian frontier is invariably attended with considerable danger to small or badly-armed parties, and as the most unceasing vigilance even in large ones is required to prevent the loss of cattle, an unprotected train of horses and mules being a temptation no Indian can withstand, a few words concerning these people may not come in amiss, particularly now that the Black Hill question is directing general attention to Indian affairs. My host had been many years on the frontier, and much of my Indian information I got from him.*

The principal Indian tribes between the Pacific and about here are the Pi-Utes (or Water Utes) and the Utes, many of whom reside in Utah, and are some of them converts to the Mormon religion; the Shoshones or Snakes; the Dakotas or Sioux, and their cousins the Arapahoes and Cheyennes. The Pi-Utes are the same, or nearly the same, as the Digger Indians of California, though perhaps not as degraded. There are two reservations in the State of Nevada possessed almost entirely by these Indians. The first is on the Truckee River, and near the southern extremity of Pyramid Lake, where the Indians are headed by Win-ne-muck-a, who is the war chief of the nation; the second is on Walker Lake and along Walker River, where the Indians have for their leader a gigantic and at the same time amiable savage, named Big George, who is their peace chief. These Indians are still nearly in a wild state, and seem to have very little respect for any authority save that of the military. They wander about at will, and seem to have direct connection with the tribes of the north, by means of trails which reach out to the N.W.

* See Appendix C.

across the Mud Lake Plain, on to the Madeline Plains, and thence to the head waters of the Sacramento and McLeod rivers, where I was salmon fishing some pages back. There is a considerable quantity of game on the reservations, but the principal reliance of the Indians is on fish. For winter supplies great numbers of rabbits are killed, their meat smoked and dried, and their skins made into robes. Besides the Indians on the reservations, there are other small bands which roam through the northern portions of the State of Nevada, and commit many depredations on the white settlers. With these frequent skirmishes occur, and their numbers are rapidly diminishing. These fights, however, sometimes assume the proportions of respectable actions, and the stand made by the Pi-Utes on the Truckee reservation in 1860 is even now spoken of with terror by the people of that region. In this action young Win-ne-muck-a moved about like the genius of destruction and incited his braves to deeds of daring and cruelty. Ormsby, the leader of the whites, was killed, and the volunteers driven in confusion off the field.

The Indians are very superstitious, and some of their proceedings are of the most puerile description. Their doctors or medicine-men depend in great part on their knowledge of sorcery to effect a cure, and it requires considerable fortitude to become an Indian doctor, inasmuch as he who loses a patient forfeits his life. When one of their number falls sick, the Indians gather about and dance near the patient during the whole night, singing in the meantime a weird monotonous song until daybreak, when, becoming almost frantic in their gestures and movements, they chase the witch far off on the plain. They claim that the patient is bewitched, and that they can hear the voices of the witches in the night breeze. One Pi-Ute doctor said that when he died, if the Indians would cut him to pieces, the pieces would all unite again immediately, and that he would ascend into the heavens in a cloud of smoke. This was too much for Indian curiosity, and a bystander despatched the doctor with a blow of his knife. The body was then cut to pieces, but much to the disgust of all present the remains of the poor wretch refused to move, and were left on the ground as food for wolves.

It is a mistake to believe that their chiefs, as such, have much power over the members of the tribe. If their war expeditions are of considerable importance, their chief leads; but in making war or preparing for any enterprise of moment, the darling wish of the Indian heart is to meet, and smoke, and speak in council. It is here that the leaders are most at home, and it is here that they make their greatest effort to impress their superiority upon the other members of their tribe. In these councils everything is carried on with the greatest decorum, and no speaker of any nation is more careful of his oratory. They have a war and a peace chief, whose power is very limited; and several sub-chiefs, who occupy about the relative position of a county justice of the peace in civilised communities. The laws of property are well understood among them, and he who owns several ponies is considered a person of no mean importance, and is respected accordingly.

Labour devolves upon the squaws, and in summer-time they are engaged in getting grass seeds, pine nuts, &c., which are preserved for winter use. In fact they do all the drudgery of the camp, and while travelling carry the loads. An Indian who has any pretension to being a leading man has as a general thing two or three wives, who roam about in the most abject and miserable condition. As to cleanliness among the Pi-Utes, it does not exist even in name. Filth, morning noon and night, is always to be found. Their lodges are poorly constructed, and when a locality becomes so dirty as to be no longer endurable, the lodge poles are pulled up and the band moves off to some new and clean place. So it is from year to year, always moving, always careworn, and always, when outside of the reservations, in constant dread of the American soldiers.

In the summer of 1865 the Pi-Utes were very troublesome, and killed Lieutenant-Colonel McDermot, who was at that time in command of the district of Nevada, while he was out on a scout. Active operations were at once instituted against them, and two most successful actions were fought against them by Major Smith and Captain Conrad. These, in addition to several minor skirmishes, taught the savages that it would be well for them to be more careful of their behaviour in future. The north-western portion of the state has been kept quiet for a long time, and the bands about Quins or Queen River were nearly all brought in as prisoners through the exertions of my friend Colonel Brackett in the autumn of 1867.

As to religion, it is doubtful whether these Indians

have any belief whatever of this kind. An Indian religion at best is but a miserable affair, and the Pi-Utes seem destitute of any. They are a revengeful and cruel race, but are not devoid of industry, as their labour upon the farms in Long Valley and upon the Truckee attest. They do a little work in Virginia City at sawing wood and other light jobs, but it is impossible to get them to work underground in the silver mines.

Young Win-ne-muck-a is a man of a good deal of mind, and is moreover one who is really anxious to improve the condition of his people. He wishes them to have farms, and to raise large herds of cattle and horses. Old Win-ne-muck-a is among the wild Indians of the north, where he has gathered about him a large band of renegades from the Pi-Ute, Shoshonee, and Snake tribes. He became incensed against the whites on account of the cruel and unnecessary murder of his wives and children near the banks of the Pyramid Lake by a party in 1864, and then and there swore he would have a terrible and unrelenting revenge against civilised people. He has more than made his threat good, and several massacres which have taken place in Northern Nevada can be traced directly to him. In early times the Pi-Utes had a terrible war with the Washoes, and after desolating them carried off all their horses and many of their best-looking women. For years the Washoes were kept in subjection, and it was only after the whites settled the country that they again got the right to own horses and arms, and keep their women for themselves.

As a tribe the Pi-Utes are singularly free from the vice of intemperance. Most tribes take to intoxicating liquors with a love which is only given up at death, but these Indians do not like liquor, and as a rule it is difficult to get them to take it. Their women are virtuous, and unchastity is punished with death. This may appear strange among a people who seem to be so utterly degraded, but still it is true. The poor women lead a sad and unhappy life, and one which to a civilised being seems utterly hopeless, but among all the sins committed by them that of unchastity is not numbered.

Gambling is a besetting sin of the Indian men, and they risk all they have, ponies, horses, bows, arrows, and whatever else they own, on a game called by the whites "Pi-Ute Poker." In this game five cards are dealt out to each man, and one pile is left in the centre. The one nearest the dealer picks up a card, and if necessary discards one, and he who can first get three pairs takes the stakes. I remember watching one of these games for some time at Virginia City, and a queer-looking card party they made, as "bucks" and "squaws" sat in a circle under the shade of a deserted house, perfectly indifferent to the din of engines and machinery at work all round them. The men were all painted with red and yellow colours, and wore white low-crowned felt hats, evidently recently purchased. The women sat together, some of them with children in the curious wicker-work cages slung on their backs, and appeared, as far as I could judge, to play against the men. Plenty of silver was in circulation, and one good-looking squaw, who was gambling freely, had quite a pile of dollars by her. As to the number of these Indians it is a difficult matter to judge, but there cannot be over four thousand of them in Nevada, with perhaps two thousand more in Oregon, Idaho, and Utah. There is also a small band in Northern Arizona. Outside of the reservations they are rapidly diminishing, and a few years hence all of them will be numbered with the things that were. They are departing for ever; the smoke of their council fires is becoming less frequent; the plains and mountain sides of Nevada will soon cease to echo back their footsteps, and all will be gathered to "the land of the hereafter."

The Shoshonee or Snake Indians number about eight thousand, and wander through Idaho, Northern Utah, Wyoming, Montana, Southern Oregon, and California. The small tribe who under Captain Jack gave so much trouble at the lava beds, about sixty miles from where I was fishing in Northern California, was composed of about equal numbers of Modocs and Snakes. The tribal relationship between the Shoshonees, Bannacks, and Comanches is very close, and any one speaking the Shoshonee language could travel without difficulty from Mexico to Oregon. Of course each band has its peculiarities, but in the main they are much alike, and if they could be combined, would form one of the most powerful Indian confederations in America.

A Shoshonee brave in full dress is a very great dandy, and thinks no "small beer" of himself. He has a hunting shirt of tanned buckskin, with heavy fringes of the same, ornamented with rows of white and pink beads on the shoulders and outside of the sleeves. His hair is carefully combed out and adorned with brass bosses. Large hoops of brass form his earrings. His moccasins are highly embroidered. His trowsers are gay-coloured and fit loosely. An embroidered belt hangs over his left shoulder, and a tomahawk completes his equipment.

The Sioux are a nation numbering nearly forty thousand, and are by far the most numerous and powerful tribe of the North American Continent. In their own dialect these Indians call themselves Dakotas. For centuries past they have held sway over the whole of the north-western portion of the United States lying near the head waters of the Mississippi River, and along a great portion of the Missouri. They have been and are "the lords of the plains;" and every man and animal that has passed through their country for ages past has done so only with their permission. They are brave, hardy, and warlike, and able to bring into the field such numbers of men as to override their weaker neighbours and keep them in the proper degree of subjection. In general terms, all Sioux Indians living north and east of the Missouri River are Santee Sioux, while those living south and west of that stream are Teton Sioux. Of late years, however, these names have got greatly mixed up. This tribe is divided into several bands; named respectively, Sisseton, Warpeton, Cuthead, Brulé, Ogallala or Red Clouds, Minneconjou, Yanctonai, Yankton, Uncapa, Two Kettle, Sans-Arc, Blackfeet, and Santees Proper. It must not be understood from this that all these bands are clearly and fully defined. The Indians have a way of mixing themselves up from time to time, so that it is utterly out of the question for a white man to make out much in regard to them. When any depredation of a peculiarly aggravated character is committed, the Indians help one another, and endeavour to make it appear that they themselves are unable to find the criminals, on account of the number of different bands. These bands occupy an immense extent of country, and are able on occasions to bring into the field more than five thousand warriors well armed and mounted.

For years past they have dictated their own terms to both white and red men, and have declared their intention to continue such a course in the future. The members of this tribe are personally brave, and all the men are trained soldiers and hunters. They make no concealment of their supposed ability to defeat the people of the United States whenever and wherever they are so minded, and point to the various battles in which they have beaten the whites in proof of this assertion. Nothing but an overwhelming defeat and humiliation will convince them of the absurdity of this belief.

They have plenty of horses, the very best kind of arms, a full supply of ammunition, and it will be no joke to conquer them; but whatever may be the cost, it will have to be done sooner or later, and the recent discovery of gold in the Black Hills must shortly bring things to a climax.*

* This was written prior to the recent war and the slaughter of General Custer and his entire command.

The Sisseton and Warpeton bands have two reservations. One at Lake Travense, Dakota, containing 1,241,000 acres, where there are 1500 Indians. The other is near Devil's Lake, Dakota, where there are over 700 Indians, including the Cutheads. These Indians lived in Minnesota at the time of the frightful massacres in that state, and murdered many people, including both women and children, in cold blood.

The Yanktons, numbering about 2000, are located in the extreme southern part of Dakota Territory, on the east side of the Missouri River, about fifty miles from the town of Yankton, upon a reservation of 400,000 acres. This reservation is nearly all rolling prairie set apart for them by the treaty of 1858, of the tract then ceded by them to the United States. They have not been much inclined to work, and, although there is good land within their reservation, are poor, having still to be supported in a great measure by the Government.

The Uncapapa, Blackfeet, Yanctonai, Sans-Arc, Brulé, Two Kettle, Minneconjou, and Ogallala bands are located at five different agencies—viz. the Upper Missouri or Crow Creek Agency, on the east side of the Missouri; Grand River Agency, at the mouth of the Cheyenne River; the Whetstone Agency (so called from its former location at the junction of the Whetstone with the Missouri River), on the White River, about 225 miles west of the Missouri; and the Red Cloud and Spotted Tail Agency in Nebraska.

The Indians at the agencies number in the

aggregate over 22,000. They have a reservation set apart for them by the treaty of 1868, containing about 25,000,000 acres lying west of the Missouri River and north of Nebraska. For years these Indians have been hostile. They are doing everything in their power to prevent the completion of the Northern Pacific Railroad, and show their deep-rooted hatred to the whites on every possible opportunity.

For several years past the Sioux have been laying in an ample supply of arms and ammunition, for the purpose of commencing a war upon the people of the United States; and late atrocities committed by them would seem to indicate that they are now, not only ready, but anxious, to have the war commence.

The Northern Pacific Railroad has always been a thorn in the side of the Sioux, and many of them have sworn by the ashes of their fathers that it shall not be built. They say the road will destroy their land, and the engines will sing the death-knell of their people. The Great Spirit is angry with them for allowing the road to be started west of the Mississippi River, and the shades of the dead of their deserted graveyards watch at night in the hollow caves of the mountains, while they wail over the degeneracy of their children, who are about to be overcome by the white men. The sun goes down in blood; the storm clouds gather in the Spirit Land; and the children of the nation—if any are left—will become pigmies, who will have no dwellings except in the branches of thorn bushes.

It is impossible to tell how long the Sioux have

had possession of the country which is now occupied by them. They were found on the grounds they now occupy when the French discovered them, and were known as Naudowisses. As they required new lands, they made war upon the neighbouring tribes, and carried their conquests far to the north and west. They always had able leaders, and this no doubt is the secret of their successes. They are a stolid race of men, and only seem to get thoroughly waked up when murdering or robbing. Their cruelty to prisoners taken by them knows no bounds. When found they were a powerful nation of Indians, and have held that power until the present day. At times they have pretended to be friendly with the whites, but this was only to get some great advantage over their Indian enemies. In diplomacy they are fully equal to the whites, and in almost every instance where they have made treaties they have retained a decided advantage to themselves. In peace and war they are cunning, revengeful, and sneaking, and little or no dependence can be placed on what they say. As winter approaches these Indians become very friendly to the whites, as they wish to get as much out of them as they possibly can in the way of food and ammunition; but when spring-time returns they commence depredations which last until the grass begins to die on the prairies, and there is no longer anything left for their horses to eat. In the summer it is easy for them to hide their women and children in the mountains, where there is no difficulty about getting enough for them to subsist on; but during the cold winter months they live in the thick bushes near the margins of the streams, and behave comparatively well. Soldiers might almost as well attack a whisp of snipe as attack those Indians during the summer months, as they disappear with almost equal facility; but in winter, when they have all their camp equipage with them, they can easily be overcome and severely punished.

Red Cloud and Spotted Tail, two leading men of the Sioux, have been at Washington to visit the Great Father, and both have an abiding sense of the power of the United States. This seems, however, to have very little effect upon the majority of their tribe, who are panting to be on the war-path with all its dangers and excitements. The older Indians are content to stay in comfortable lodges and behave themselves; but the young men scorn such effeminacy, and long for the day when they may meet their foemen (no matter who) in the shock of battle. One of them, talking in his broken way, made this statement, as related by Colonel Brackett: "Me got heap of horses; heap of squaw; plenty good grub; but me no got scalp. All the time squaws say, 'Why you no get scalp, same like oder Injen?'" Here is the secret of the desire to go on the war-path—it is to get scalps, in order that they may make a great figure in the eyes of their nation, and be honoured as becomes a great warrior.

This desire to get scalps may soon be gratified.

At the time I write news has just been published of the utter failure of the Commissioners sent by the United States to treat with the Sioux for the purchase of the Black Hills. Spotted Tail, Chief of the

Brulés; Red Cloud, Chief of the Ogallalahs; Red Dog, Orator of the Sioux nation; Little Bad Man, Chief of a northern band; Swift Bear, a Chief of the Two Kettle band from the Cheyenne Agency; Lone Horn, Chief of the Arrapahoes; and nearly three hundred chiefs of lesser note were present. After a council which lasted about four weeks, the Indian demands were so preposterous the Commissioners had to break up the conference, and both parties retired disgusted. A short explanation concerning the cause of this unusual Commission is perhaps necessary to some of my readers, and a very few words will suffice to put them in possession of the leading facts.

In the Black Hills, a part of the Sioux reservation, large and valuable deposits of gold have recently been discovered. This news becoming widely spread, numbers of men rushed to the spot regardless of the fact that the land belonged exclusively to the Indians. The United States troops were then despatched to preserve the integrity of the Indian reservation, and soon, by a judicious mingling of the *suaviter in modo* and *fortiter in re*, persuaded the miners to retire; informing them that a Commission would shortly be appointed from Washington to treat with the Sioux for the purchase of this part of their territory, and that they might then legally resume their labours. The miners retired, and the Commission sat. The Indians demanded $70,000,000 as the price of the land. Red Cloud, in his speech, said six generations of Indians had passed away. The only condition on which the Sioux nation would sell the hills would be a guarantee that the Indians should be provided for during the next six generations. An Indian generation is one hundred years. He said he considered the hills more valuable in the precious metals than the entire wealth of the United States. He proposed to ask a large sum for them; the principal to be put at interest, and from the latter to derive sufficient to keep the Sioux nation. In addition he wanted for each head of an Indian family six yoke of oxen, a waggon, a span of horses, harness, a bull, a cow, a sow, a boar, a sheep, a ram, chickens, coffee, tea, sugar, rice, cracked corn, beans, dried apples, and a host of other articles. He enumerated also house and furniture, the same as white men. He said the Government were trying to make a white man out of him, and he wanted to indulge the white men. The other chiefs' demands were equally preposterous, and seeing that there was not the most remote probability of a settlement ever being arrived at, the parties engaged separated, each mutually disgusted with the other.

The miners all this time were quietly watching the conference, and those who left the Hills upon the understanding that the Government were about to purchase them are now preparing to return. All negotiations having failed, neither fear of the Indians nor dread of the troops will scare these hardy and desperate men from their race for gold. There is not a town of the smallest importance anywhere near the Hills where these men are not quietly fitting out. The Government being unable to manage affairs, they will do so themselves; and a very short time will see the ambition of the young Sioux braves realised, and every opportunity be given them for gathering scalps. A few stray murders have already been committed. During the time I was hunting in the vicinity of Laramie Peak, three white men were killed and scalped in the very section of country we were wandering over. It is, however, the beginning of the end—Gold, the great civilising agent of the world, is hard at work—and nothing can now stop the tide of adventurous and desperate men flocking in on the coveted possessions. These forerunners of civilisation, though in themselves unscrupulous, vindictive, and cruel as the savages they are destined to replace, will soon become possessed of a firm footing. The legitimate trader will rapidly follow in their footsteps; the settler will gradually appear; and in time railroads and a distinct form of municipal government will render the at present dangerous and formidable Sioux as innocuous and peaceable as the few remaining Indian tribes so rapidly becoming extinct.

During my stay at Fort Sanders, President Grant passed through Laramie, and, all the officers going to pay their respects, Colonel B. was good enough to invite me to join them. On arriving at the railway station I found a small crowd of people waiting for the President's arrival, and not long afterwards his train drew up and halted by the platform. I never saw less enthusiasm at the reception of any distinguished individual than was displayed here. For some moments the crowd seemed undecided as to who was the President, and a man near me shouted out, "Which is Grant?" "I guess he's that red-faced coon in a plug hat," replied another, in a by no means *sotto voce* tone; and this information seeming to be sufficient, the mob shortly afterwards raised a faint cheer. The Governor of the territory now announced to the assembly that he had the pleasure of introducing to them the President of the United States; and General Grant, coming forward and leaning over the platform of the car on which he was standing, extended his hand mechanically to be shaken by the crowd assembled to do him honour. Every one so disposed gave it a wring, but during the entire operation, which lasted for several minutes, I never once saw his Excellency open his mouth. The hand-shaking business having at length terminated outside, Colonel B. and the rest of us went into the car, and shortly afterwards I had the honour of being presented to the President of the United States and Mrs. Grant, who was travelling with him. His Excellency evidently thought it hard enough work to do all the hand-shaking required, as he rarely said a word to any of us. With Mrs. Grant I had a few minutes' conversation, and on making my *congé* she was kind enough to express a hope that I would call on them at Washington. Accustomed to witness the enthusiasm which invariably welcomes not only Her Gracious Majesty, but all people of any eminence visiting England, I was certainly astonished at the quiet undemonstrative manner with which the Chief Magistrate of their nation was welcomed in America; and considering the President's great successes as a soldier, as well as his abilities as a ruler, I certainly expected that some kind of ovation would have welcomed his arrival.

Shortly after the little episode of the presidential visit one of the officers was ordered to Nebraska on court-martial duty. Prairie chicken shooting in this state is celebrated; there was also a chance of getting elk, and I willingly accepted an invitation to join him for the trip. Our first halt was at North Platte, a mushroom town named after the river, which winds along the fine alluvial bottoms of the prairie, affording plenty of opportunities for irrigation, when an increased population provides the necessary labour. At present agricultural enterprise appears limited to the raising of stock, but very few years can elapse ere thriving farms line, at any rate, the immediate vicinity of the railway that passes through such favourable ground. A one-company post is situated about a quarter of a mile from the town, and sixteen miles farther off is Fort Macpherson, which generally contains a more considerable garrison.

From North Platte one gets into the buffalo country. Close to Macpherson they are often found in large quantities, and even near the town of North Platte they are frequently killed. But a very few years back these prairies were covered with them, though the accounts of slaughter which everywhere greeted me renders it more than probable that by the time my prophecy concerning the farms is fulfilled a buffalo will be as rare as a dodo. At present the best place to find them is on the Republican, where they still abound in herds occasionally so large that as far as the eye can reach the plains seem alive with them.

Our next halt was at Grand Island, a small town named after an island on the Platte about two miles distant. A good deal of the country here seems cultivated, but it has the same level unpicturesque appearance that characterises for many miles each bank of the river, and I was glad to break the spell of monotony inseparably attached to travelling through flat land in a railway carriage. Our party consisted of six officers besides myself, and our destination was Fort Hartsuff, a post on the Loup River, two days' drive from our starting-point. In pleasant company one can dispense with, or at any rate cease to crave after, lovely scenery; and though our route lay along the side of the Loup River, through, for many miles, a rolling prairie without a tree or hill to enliven it, we all managed to enjoy the drive immensely. The non-shooters went in a trap by themselves, and the shooters in a light spring waggon with a four-mule team. We had plenty of time to take things leisurely, and as each field of Indian corn was invariaby full of prairie chickens we had some very pleasant sport along the road, until we arrived at Beebys, a small wayside farmhouse, where we halted for the night. The houses in the Loup Valley are built in a style of architecture quite peculiar to the locality, and only on the island of Feenish, a small barren sandbank on the coast of Connemara, have I ever seen anything like them. Partly owing to the extreme severity of the winter, and partly owing to a great paucity of timber for building purposes, the ground selected for the site of a house, in nine cases out of ten, is so close to a steep hill, that by a little judicious engineering the occupant is enabled to burrow a room out of the mountain. These houses, though small, are comfortable enough, being cool in summer and hot in winter, but their appearance has a look of originality and desolation not to be found elsewhere. Beebys was no exception, and a queerer-looking crib I have seldom put up at. Accommodation was necessarily somewhat scanty, but we found a capital hostess, got excellent food, and our party of seven were glad enough to settle down for the night in a room of some twelve by fourteen feet, with but three beds between us, where we chatted and smoked well into midnight.

What fun it was listening to the stories my companions told of frontier life. They had all been for years away from civilisation, and had all passed through the extraordinary scenes consequent on first settling strange lands, many hundreds of miles from the arm of law or the reign of order. Some of the early episodes of life in Arizona, where a rush upon mining had collected hordes of the greatest ruffians on the continent into a comparatively small space, would have afforded groundwork to a sensational novelist for at least a dozen volumes. One gentleman, a Mr. James Duffield, figured prominently among those most celebrated for a contempt of life in the small community that had the honour of his society. "A man for breakfast," was to him quite an ordinary affair, and among the desperadoes in Arizona he was looked up to and reverenced as became so prominent a citizen. Envy, inseparable from greatness, however, took possession of a neighbouring ruffian, whose fame as a quick shot was completely eclipsed by the greater villainies of Duffield, and actuated by acute jealousy he stated publicly his intention of whipping the immortal James on the very first convenient opportunity. News of this sudden usurpation of authority was soon brought to Duffield, and shortly after the rival claimants met in Arizona. The new man, well primed with whisky, swaggered loudly into a saloon frequented by Duffield, and, with much bluster and many strange oaths, demanded to be shown his enemy, whom he did not even know by sight. Duffield with extreme courtesy, for he prided himself on manners, came forward, and offered to point out the man he was looking for, if the gentleman in question would come into the street, and on his accepting the proposition, immediately shot him down when clear of the doors; then raising his hat to his prostrate foe, said, "My name is Jim Duffield, and them ere," pointing to the bleeding orifices in the bewildered sinner, "are my visiting cards." After this no one disputed his authority until his death, which occurred somewhat suddenly about six months afterwards.

Another story was told of a stranger, who, while on a visit to a resident in the town, was invited by his host to take a drink. Having decided on the tipple, the barman, with the peculiar grace which belongs to professors in this particular branch of industry, commenced manipulating the liquors, *i.e.* pouring them from glass to glass, sometimes over a shoulder, and at others from above the head, varying the operation, however, by occasionally seizing a shot-gun, and presenting it at the door right across the stranger's nose, which unfortunately appeared always to be getting in the way. On looking round to find out what had caused this unusual pantomime, he just saw a figure bob back, and again the manufacture of the drink went on, only, however, to be interrupted by the again sudden production of the fowling-piece, which was always as conveniently handy as lemon squeezers or nutmeg grater to the presiding genius of the bar. This comedy was gone through some four times before the drinks were handed over; no remarks on the subject were made, and his friend quietly smoked his cigar as if it were an affair of no kind of importance. Would he have another drink? Thank you, no. He had particular business at home. A letter to answer—a telegram to send—anything, he mentally added, to get away from this confounded place. They reached the house, and were shortly afterwards at dinner, when suddenly the host's child, a boy of ten years old, rushed into the room in the highest state of glee. "Bill got him Pa—Bill got him," he loudly exclaimed. "Got him; got who?" "Why, Pa, Bill got that fellow he was trying to shoot when you and Mr. —— were having your cocktail." It seems that Mr. Bill, the barman, had turned the gentleman who was shot out of the saloon; and that individual, very drunk, had retaliated by trying to shoot Mr. Bill, who with a shot-gun was equally anxious to pot him. Neither party could for some time get a favourable chance of doing execution until at last virtue was triumphant, and Bill the barman reigned supreme.

These stories owe everything to the manner in which they are told, and lose much by being written, but still they serve to illustrate, both being perfectly true, the extraordinary state of existence of the first inhabitants of mining towns in the settled territories.

Our next day's drive was more interesting. Settlements were more scattered, hills began to crop up, we constantly passed for miles close to the banks of the river, and prairie chickens were sufficiently numerous to keep us in active employment until we reached Fort Hartsuff, just in time for dinner.

Fort Hartsuff, a small one-company post, was, when I visited it, held by a detachment from the 23rd Regiment of Infantry. It is situated a few hundred yards from the North Fork of the Loup, and under its protecting wing has lately sprung into existence the few log-houses that constitute the city of Calamus. The Commanding-Officer, a Brevet Colonel, highly distinguished in the late war, during which he had been severely wounded, happened to know many of my old friends in the "old country," and on the duties of the court-martial being satisfactorily concluded, I accepted his very kind offer to remain behind and have a hunt from his command after black-tailed deer and elk.

Six miles distant from Fort Hartsuff, along the banks of the river (and there are no farms over a mile from them) civilisation and the latest settlement end. Both forks of the Loup, as well as the Loup River itself, are somewhat singular, their breadth being greatly in excess of their depth. In no other country have I seen the bottom so uniformly treacherous, and in few places on either are there any really good fords. For many miles the average depth seldom exceeds six inches, yet, owing to quicksands and shifting bottom, no crossing is possible. In this respect the Platte and all other rivers in the State of Nebraska are very similar, and the few fords that exist are generally only known to the herds of buffalo and wild Indians who wander through the country. Forty miles to the south-east, on the South Fork of the Loup, lies the Pawnee preservation; the Yanktons are sixty miles farther; and eighty to the north-east are planted the Santees. The Missouri lies eighty-five miles due north through a country possessing but little water and very imperfectly known; indeed, up to the present I fancy it has never been surveyed, and possessing few attractions for white settlers, is generally tenanted by small wandering bands of Indians, who unhesitatingly scalp any small parties of whites they may come across during their peregrinations on this debatable land.

Once I went on a four days' hunt among the sand hills. We camped each night by a small water-hole and carried fuel with us. Like waves of the sea the hills extended far beyond our sight. Sparse vegetation covered them, but occasionally some of the valleys were fairly meadowed; and as farther to the northward the head waters of the Elkhorn and Beaver rivers are known to flow, I should fancy that a party sufficiently strong to be able to afford to defy Indians might get good hunting, as certainly the ground must be perfectly undisturbed. We killed black-tailed deer, antelope, and white-tailed deer, besides a few pin-tailed grouse, but met with no elk, though occasionally we saw some old trails.

It is hard at this season of the year to count with any degree of certainty on finding game even in their favourite and most-resorted-to feeding grounds. The reason was obvious enough. Each night the distant horizon was illuminated to the sky by gigantic prairie fires, which at times completely surrounded us. The long grass is now like tinder, and when once fired, no one can possibly tell where the conflagration will end. For days, weeks, or months the fire may still sweep unrelentingly onward, destroying winter pasture, and scaring the timid denizens of the plains to places unfrequented and pasturages unknown. Hunting parties cannot be too careful at this season both in lighting and extinguishing their fires. If I heard of one case I heard of at least twenty, where incautious men had burned up their camps, waggons, and even mules, through carelessly firing the grass; and on one occasion I narrowly escaped being burned out myself. In lighting our camp fire the grass about it became ignited, and had it not been for the prompt manner with which Buckshot, our guide, seized his coat and beat out the flame, we most undoubtedly would have lost our tents. The safest plan is to dig a small trench round the intended fireplace; the party should then arm themselves with horsecloths to beat out the flames in case of their extending, and carefully burn all grass within a radius of five yards from the fire to be, which will then be comparatively safe.

Apropos of fires, when travelling in an Indian country much precaution should be taken, particularly by small parties at all desirous of retaining their scalps. Because a man is not afraid of Indians, it does not at all follow that he should be such an egregious ass as ever to give them a chance of getting what frontier men term "dead wood on him;" an expression, I take it, indicative of the seasoned stock of a rifle being brought into close proximity with a sleeping white man's head. The hunters on such occasions should halt at least an hour before sunset. The fire should be made of the driest wood obtainable, so as not to make any perceivable smoke, it being remembered that an Indian can see smoke where a white man sees nothing; and after having cooked and eaten their dinners, watered their horses, and smoked their pipes, by which time it will be nearly or quite dark, they should quietly march on for a couple of miles farther, and sleep without fires till dawn. In very dangerous places, of course one of the party should remain awake, but unless they are all very thick-headed, the mules will make quite enough noise on the approach of Indians to let any average hunter know that something unusual is up. No man with the slightest pretension to be called a hunter will neglect these precautions, and, as a general rule, in hunting parties, it is only fools who get scalped. If any one thing more than another "riles" a good man, it is for some lazy idiot to say, "I ain't afraid of Indians," as an excuse for his not troubling himself with ordinary means of safety. No man worth his salt *is* afraid of Indians, or afraid of anything on earth (barring the tip of a bailiff or a protested bill, and I've known a few plucky fellows funk them most confoundedly); but a good hunter and brave man will never be above circumventing, by his own caution and knowledge of woodcraft, the savage on whose native prairie love of sport and adventure may send him wandering.

One more hint may be useful. If, notwithstanding these precautions, the cheerful war-whoop of the noble savage should in the small hours of morning echo round the camp, don't seize your rifle and rush out like a stampeded mule, but seize it and *crawl* out. You will pretty soon know whether their little game is cattle or scalps, but in either case you will be better able to form an opinion and decide on further action lying on the ground than standing exposed to the bullets of the Red-skins probably concealed in the neighbouring bushes, who may after all have raised the shout to stampede your cattle, and who will only give a few volleys from their place of vantage without risking a closer engagement.

During the prairie fires two or three farms near Hartsuff were entirely destroyed, through their owners neglecting to make a "fire-guard," *i.e.* burning with care a belt twenty yards wide round their most valuable land and houses, as a preventive to the spread of any fires so common on the prairie. Round the fort a good-sized guard was cleared out, and farmers who neglect such precautions deserve to suffer for their carelessness.

In this part of Nebraska there are a fair sprinkling of prairie dog towns. Why the odd little beast should be called a dog (*Spermophilus ludovicianus*) I don't know, as he certainly is not a bit like one. They are small rodent animals of a brown colour with white bellies, and somewhat resemble a guinea-pig both in size and shape. The Indians eat them, and as they live principally on grass and roots I don't see why they should not be pretty good. Their burrows are the mischief; and many a cropper and many a curse have they caused the reckless or excited sportsman when galloping after wounded elk or buffalo.

I was charmed with the number of tame elk about Hartsuff. Some of them were a couple of years old, and fed quietly with the cattle, whom they never cared to leave, and were quite as tame and domesticated. When pleased they make a little plaintive cry, more melodious than the squeak of an infant, and not so loud as the cry of a hare; but I know no sound so touching in its sweet tone of entreaty, or so perfect a combination of an appeal and salutation coaxingly blended, as the beautiful cry of a young elk. Occasionally they have been trained to harness, and "Buckshot" drove a pair about Omaha. They are, however, liable to sudden frights, and sometimes startle horses in other men's traps not accustomed to seeing them; but for sleighing in such a wild outlandish place as this, where there are few horses to frighten and no trees to run against, I cannot imagine a more delightful team.

I had a rather close shave one day while out shooting with Colonel C. I had just killed a prairie chicken, and was firing at another with the same barrel, when my gun burst badly. One barrel flew about twenty yards to my right, and fell within a few feet of the Colonel, the other went fifteen yards to my left; the stock was shattered, and the small wooden portion which acts as a lever to the gun opening and closing went, I know not where, as we never saw it again. The cartridges, which I had loaded myself, only contained three and one quarter drams of powder. No foreign substance could possibly have been in the barrel, as I had discharged it not a minute previously, and of what could have caused such a terrible blow-up I have not the faintest idea.* Nothing but the oldfashioned way I have of holding my gun saved my left hand. When an exceedingly small boy, my father (who was about the very best all-round sportsman I ever met) taught me to carry my left hand just touching and partly inclosing the trigger-guard; explaining at the same time that by doing so I should save my fingers in the event of a blow-up. This habit, contracted in extreme youth, stuck to me through life; and though once tempted by a very crack pigeon shot to alter my style, the old leaven was too strong, and instinctively I returned to the first taught lesson, and by doing so unquestionably saved my hand, the wooden piece before mentioned, which nine out of ten among the dove-slayers at Hurlingham hold on to, having been blown, I naturally presume, to "smithereens." As it was, I only had my head slightly cut and the forefinger of my left hand bruised.

* I discovered afterwards that the fault lay through the extractor being improperly bored by a drunken foreman. The maker, after inspecting the barrels, acknowledged the error as one for which he was responsible and supplied me with a new gun.

On the strength of my remarkable escape, for I never before even read of such an unusually bad burst in a fowling-piece where the holder of it was not seriously injured, I do most strongly recommend every one to adopt my system of holding a shot-gun, which is quite as handy as any other, and infinitely safer. In adopting this plan, allow the left hand to slide close home to the trigger-guard during the up swing to the shoulder. Quick shooting is as easy this way as any other, and, though no pigeon shot, I have killed from twenty to thirty-five brace of snipe a day in China with the old muzzleloader, and walked all my birds up into the bargain, having no dog. This is quite quick enough for any sportsman, and though nowadays the bursting of a gun is, I am happy to say, more unusual than when muzzle-loaders were in vogue, and excitable spirits in a hot corner were apt to ram two charges into one barrel, still accidents may occur; and I must again urge, at any rate, young men who have not contracted the Hurlingham system to endeavour to adopt mine.

Having failed in finding elk to either the north or east of the post during the three and four days' trips we had taken, the Colonel determined on trying a more extended journey to the north-west, on the land lying between the North Fork of the Loup and the River Calamus. Our outfit comprised a strong springless waggon with four mules, which was to be game bag; and another light hunting-waggon with a faster team, in which we ourselves were to ride, and which was so full of springs that at sharp turns there was no small difficulty in sitting so lively a conveyance. The Colonel having built this trap himself was exceedingly proud of the performance; and on smooth roads with no sharp corners it really did him credit.

Since a certain distinguished statesman, who shall be nameless, ruined promotion (as well as some other things in the British army he interfered with) by his non-purchase system, I think this waggon might be adopted with a certain degree of benefit to the service, and am certain it would soon become popular with at any rate the younger officers, if their seniors would only ride in it.

We carried tents, had led horses, and were guided by the scout and hunter of the post—Conrad Wentworth, better known as Little Buckshot. Buckshot was quite a type of his class, and an uncommonly good type into the bargain. Rather under the average height, but perfectly formed and wiry as steel, about five-and-thirty, and weighing little over ten stone, he was just the very cut of man suited to hunt elk, Indians, or buffalo, and he knew the tricks of the one quite as well as he did the habits of the other. His duties as scout were varied and numerous. At one time he hunted Indians, and at another game, and was pretty successful with both. Of course such men have many narrow escapes during a life spent on the Indian frontier, and at least one of Buckshot's will bear reciting, as illustrative of the caution and presence of mind requisite in such a calling.

He had been on a hunt with a couple of other men, in a country known to be pretty hot with

Indians, and on camping for the night was much annoyed to find that, during his temporary absence to water the mules, his two companions had lighted a large fire. Kicking off some of the blazing logs, he pointed out the folly of such a proceeding, and urged them to shift camp after eating, and sleep without any fire. The night unfortunately was cold, and the men would not hear of moving. They knew as much of Indians as he did, they said, and had frequently hunted over the ground before; one would remain awake, and nothing was to be feared. A strange feeling, Buckshot told me, made him uneasy; an indescribable sense of something, he knew not what, being about to happen prevented his getting any rest; but permitting himself to be overruled—indeed, his arguments were quite unheeded — he lay down, telling the man who watched first to call him when the moon rose, at which time vigilance became more necessary. A few hours afterwards the mules commenced snorting, to which Buckshot directed the attention of the man on watch. He went towards them, but returned almost immediately saying it was only a coyote; and on his way back threw a lump of bark on the fire, which immediately blazed up; and said, in reply to the remonstrance of his more sensible companions, "Oh, Indians be d——d! I ain't going to freeze to death." He had hardly crept under the blanket when there was a sudden yell. The war-whoop of the Indians resounded in the night air, and a volley was fired into their bed-place from the bushes. One man never spoke again; the other merely said,

"O Jesus;" and Buckshot, who lay between them, rolled unhurt over his dead comrade away from the fire. One Indian, who was close to him, he shot with a revolver, and then tearing off a white handkerchief he wore round his neck, he dashed towards the mules, bending to the ground and under cover of some bushes. On reaching them he found an Indian untying the lariat, who, in the dark mistaking him for a brother savage, addressed him in the native tongue. He was on the point of sending a bullet through him when he recollected that the shot would at once attract the others, and struck him over the head instead with the pistol as hard as he could let drive. The mule, half untied, broke loose and galloped down the cañon; and this saved his life. The Indians, hearing the mule make off at such a pace, imagined she must have been ridden, and immediately commenced firing at her. It was too dark to distinguish a rider even had there been one, and as the mule was not shot down for nearly two minutes, Buckshot had time to get well away from the immediate vicinity of the fatal scene. For some time he was undecided how to act; however, he at last determined to make for his post, some twenty miles off. He had no shoes, and the ground was covered with cactus plants, which penetrated and cut to pieces his feet, as well as the coat which he wrapped round them. The twenty miles, however, *had* to be done, and daybreak saw him reach the fort, unharmed by Indians, but so lacerated about the feet that three months elapsed before he could again put on a boot.

On our first day's march we forded the Calamus, and camped on the banks of the North Loup; and on the second and following ones we hunted a few miles off among the hills nearly parallel to the line of march taken by the waggons. The weather was delightful: clear sunny days with a sharp keen air, and hard frost at night, sufficiently cold to freeze water in our tents, though a small stove for wood was burned in each of them. White-tailed deer, antelope, grouse, and chicken fell before us, but still no signs of elk. We had a capital cook, a German, who dressed venison wonderfully; so we shot, and ate, and prayed for better luck in future. At this season of the year elk are always in bands, and are consequently not easy to find, owing to their not being scattered; and in such a country as we were hunting in, consisting as it did of innumerable hills and cañons, a large band might easily be passed without detection, unless, of course, one hit upon their trail.

At last the happy day arrived. Early one morning Buckshot came on the trail of a large band of elk, and soon after we were in hot pursuit. The wind was in the right direction, and about three hours' riding, following carefully the trail, brought us in sight of the band, who were entirely unsuspicious of the slightest danger. Picketing our horses, we now commenced the stalk on foot, and the ground being favourable got within forty yards of where they were making their mid-day halt. It would be difficult to imagine a more perfectly beautiful sight. I should fancy about eighty of these magnificent animals, of different ages, sexes, and sizes, were in the band. Some were lying down, and others quietly feeding. Our position was on the brow of a small steep sand-ridge, thickly covered with long grass at the top, through which we could watch quietly the movements of the band without a chance of being discovered. A good stiff breeze blowing directly from them to us prevented the possibility of their getting our wind, and there being no danger of anything alarming them, we lay for at least five minutes perfectly still, to admire so grand a sight, and get quite cool and collected after our long stalk.

How poor Landseer or Rosa Bonheur would have enjoyed such a sight! Of all animal creation, I consider the elk is beyond question the handsomest. The bulls were full maned, and almost black about the neck and muzzle. Some of the old ones had grand heads, but the greatest number were about one and two years old, and with antlers not fully grown. The cows were very handsome, and in splendid condition; and there were many this year's calves, as graceful and pretty as they well could be. Picking out our favourites, we now got ready. I selected a fine bull, who was certainly not over fifty yards from where I lay, and taking a deliberate aim, sent a bullet directly through his heart. Buckshot's rifle missed fire, and the Colonel knocked over a grand old bull, who was sent kicking to the ground. We then blazed away at the nearest elk, and knocked over three others. In the excitement of firing at the retreating elk, we paid no attention to those already fallen, and were disgusted and surprised to see the Colonel's first love, who was the finest of the lot, trotting steadily away and well out of range. Cutting the throats of the fallen ones as quickly as possible, we mounted and galloped after the band, who, having neither seen nor smelt us, were by no means greatly alarmed; and after a sharp spin of some four miles, keeping well to leeward and out of sight, again struck the band. This time we got within about a hundred yards from where they were quietly feeding at a walk, and once more did considerable execution. It was now getting late; we had as much meat as the waggon could carry, and though we might certainly have struck the band a third time, as they had never either seen or smelt us, we tempered mercy with prudence and rode back to camp.

It is surprising what a number of elk get off, after having been apparently mortally wounded, and considered even beyond the assistance of another shot.

Lieutenant H. once shot a fine bull who rolled over, like the Colonel's had done, seemingly *in articulo mortis*. He had on the occasion a new knife, which he was most anxious to christen, and laying down his discharged rifle he advanced to flesh his weapon. The elk, however, appeared to object to be operated on, and kicked lustily whenever he approached to put his charitable project into execution. Now an elk's kick is worse than one from an unshod horse, and the Lieutenant, being well aware of his danger, dodged about from side to side in a decidedly cautious and wary manner, trying vainly to get a safe chance. This game lasted over two minutes, at

ACT THE SECOND.—NOT DEAD YET.

See page 329.

UNIV. OF MICH.

the end of which time the animal, disgusted with the clumsy efforts being made to send him to a better world, concluded to remain a little longer in this one, and, quietly jumping up, galloped off and was never seen again.

A still more amusing incident happened to Buckshot. He also one day knocked over a fine bull who fell apparently quite dead, as he pitched right over on getting the shot, with one of his fore-legs entangled mid his branching antlers. Buckshot came up to cut his throat, and to save the trouble of picketing his pony, tied the end of the lariat to the elk's hind-leg, while he dragged the body round to a more convenient position for performing the obsequies. The movement cleared the entangled limb, and the elk, who was only "creased," *i.e.* shot through the thick part of the neck and momentarily paralysed, jumped up, and, with the pony fastened to him, galloped off as strong and well as if he had never been even touched. The sight must have been as ludicrous a one as well could be imagined. Buckshot raced after the pair, shouting, "Whoa, whoa, Billy!" not daring to fire lest he should hurt his pony. How it would have ended one can hardly tell, had the elk, instead of keeping up the gallop, not foolishly turned round to fight the pony, whom he could not stand any longer dragging at his heels, while still within easy range of the scout's rifle. The movement was favourable. This time a bullet sped more true, and the poor elk really tumbled over dead.

On going with the waggon next day to bring our

game to camp we found a most unusual thing had happened. A large pack of wolves had been before us and eaten all up but five, and some of these were also partially torn. None of our party had ever known an instance of these brutes touching game the first night before, and though there were any quantity of them in the Rocky Mountains, and we often left game out when killed far from camp late in the evening, I never knew it occur.

We got some very pretty deer-shooting occasionally. Once I remember having a long and very interesting stalk after three white-tailed fellows with Buckshot. It lasted over an hour on not particularly easy ground; however, we came within range at last and killed them all.

By this time we had loaded our large four-mule waggon with elk, deer, and antelope, until it would not hold another beast. We had eaten parts of others, and had varied the entertainment with duck, pin-tailed grouse, and prairie chickens, so nothing was left us but to return to Hartsuff, lest our meat from being so long packed should go bad. On our way we saw any quantity of geese, and the river at times appeared alive with wild-fowl.

On starting for our hunt, I think I mentioned the lively nature of the Colonel's pet waggon, and on the return journey it gave us a sample of what, under unfavourable circumstances, it really could do.

We had successfully forded the river, and were trotting quietly down a rather awkward ravine with a stream running at the bottom of it, when something startled our team, and to our horror away they stretched at a gallop down the hill; a corner was turned rather sharply, and in a moment all save the Colonel were sent flying. The driver and a sergeant on the box-seat first shot into the air; I flew about three yards over where they lay sprawling, pitching on my shoulder; and Buckshot, who was on the back seat, being the lightest of the party, took a spin over all of us, a shower of rifles and guns coming with him. The waggon, which had never fallen over, then righted itself, and the mules, with the reins hanging at their heels, took their now greatly diminished load over the little stream in their stride, the waggon jumping like one quite accustomed to such cross-country usage. Up the opposite hill they then tore madly, the Colonel sticking to his post like a man, and trying, though unsuccessfully, to fish up the reins. This pace was, however, too good to last, and on reaching the top the solitary inmate jumped out, and, running across a small place where the road made a turn, stopped the team without further damage.

I have seen a good many fellows upset, but never witnessed such a complete clearance before without the trap coming to grief also. I had been riding all the morning; my spurs were still on when the spill took place, and to give an idea of the force with which we must have been shot out, one of my strong hunting spurs was torn off my boot and left in the waggon, yet, notwithstanding this very considerable drag, I was sent spinning through the air well clear of the wheels. The inventor—a true Hibernian—was delighted with the agility displayed by his favourite trap, and fervently expressed his opinion that not another vehicle in the two Americas was capable of such a performance. I really believe he was right; but it would be a sweet thing for a "Seniority Corps," and the service might adopt it with advantage.

This little episode wound up our hunt, and we shortly after arrived safely at Fort Hartsuff. We had enjoyed a very jolly trip, had some really fine shooting, and notwithstanding the eccentricity of the lively waggon, and the several attempts it made to break our necks, I cannot thank my friend the Colonel too much for all the kindness and hospitality I received at his hands, and the "good time" I had at Hartsuff.

After our hunt the weather got decidedly cold. Once or twice the thermometer went several degrees below zero, and occasionally a keen icy wind struck across the prairie which cut into one's bones like a knife. Life under canvas, with one's cattle picketed out, is not under such circumstances generally very pleasant, and once more I got ready for a start east.

CHAPTER XII.

Leave Fort Hartsuff — Rapid growth of Western towns — Omaha — Chicago — Hotel life in America — Canada — Toronto — Sleighing — Niagara — Montreal — Summing-up — A chivalrous American — Hospitality of the U.S.A. Officers — Tale of a snuff-box — The end.

On the 28th of November, 1875, we left Fort Hartsuff. A considerable amount of snow covered the prairie, and large masses of ice floated down the Loup, chasing each other over the shallow rapids finally to be checked and piled up in a large heap at the first still and frozen pool of water below them.

On this occasion, I am happy to say, the lively waggon was not brought into requisition, and comfortably ensconced in a well-hung and cosily-covered carriage, we gazed over the desolate-looking plain, and watched the flocks of wild geese and ducks, who appeared intent on migrating to warmer climates. Even the wolves seemed tamed by the cold, as at times they waited on the road until almost within pistol-shot, and Buckshot more than once handled his revolver, and got ready to fire.

At Beebys we halted for the night, getting, however, a little more room than on the occasion of my former visit; and after another cold drive the following day, the piercing wind being far more responsible for our discomfort than any particular lowness of temperature, the thermometer being only 4° below zero, we arrived in the evening at Grand Island, where we put up for the night at the railway station hotel.

The rapidity of growth peculiar to these Western towns is very striking to an Englishman accustomed to the slow progression of our rural districts. How very few villages or small towns that we remember in our early youth that are not still either villages or small towns, now that old age has bent our frames, and remorseless Time stands watching the few remaining grains of sand still to run before he mows us over. Here they never cease to grow. Grand Island had increased considerably even during my short hunt on the Loup. A new hotel of very considerable dimensions was about to be opened, several fresh edifices had commenced making their appearance, and the bustle and activity displayed everywhere showed that this little town was no exception to the general rule of rapid progression so noticeable all over the West.

An uninteresting railway journey brought us to Omaha, where we arrived on Thanksgiving Day, and of course found everything shut up and stupid; the inhabitants being too busily engaged in either eating or getting ready to eat turkeys to think of opening their shops or anything else. It is a disagreeable time for a traveller to arrive in a strange town, and I advise others to avoid doing so.

There is nothing of any particular interest in or about Omaha. It is at present the headquarters of the army for service on the nearest Indian frontier, or the military department of the Platte, and is built on the western bank of the Missouri, which was almost frozen over when we got there. During my stay a rifle match formed one of the holiday attractions. Major Henry Fulton, the champion shot of the late American team, was one of the competitors, and put fifteen shots in succession into either centre or bull's-eye, at a range of eight hundred yards, and during a by no means favourable day either. It was magnificent shooting, but I should very much like to see his practice at antelope, judging his own distance. In 1854 a few squatters settled on the site of the present town. In 1870 the construction of the Omaha and South Western Railway gave a fresh impetus to what was even then a fast-increasing city, and now a population of over 20,000 inhabit the state capital of Nebraska, with every likelihood of attaining far higher numbers. Some of the public buildings are creditable, still the town is not a particularly attractive one to visitors unconnected with it by business, and I was not sorry when a run of little over twenty-four hours farther east brought us to Chicago.

Of all the extraordinary towns in the United States, Chicago may certainly be looked upon as being the most so. Twice almost entirely destroyed by fire within an unprecedentedly short space of time, it has on each occasion risen like a Phœnix from its ashes, invariably improved by the fiery ordeal. If it continues burning and improving at the same rate, there is no telling to what pitch of magnificence it may not ultimately arrive. It is built on the shore of Lake Michigan, one of the huge inland seas of fresh water for which this continent is famous, and owes much of its prosperity to its favourable situation. The last great fire was during the Fall of 1871, when the town was almost entirely destroyed. It is now quite restored. The streets are well paved and broad (very different in this respect from New York, which without any exception I consider the most disgracefully paved town I have ever visited), the business houses are large stone buildings and very handsome, and the town is of immense extent and still growing. A charming drive in course of construction along the border of the lake and a small park outside the town are worth looking at. The municipality have every reason to be proud of the city waterworks, the entire supply being obtained from Lake Michigan, about a mile and a half out from its banks, whence by means of two immensely powerful engines, the largest I believe in America, a constant and liberal flow of deliciously pure water is conducted over the town. We put up at the Palmer House Hotel, without any exception the finest, best conducted, and most comfortable one I ever saw in America. The reception-rooms were almost regal; the bedrooms were simply the perfection of comfort, each having a handsome marble bath in a small chamber attached to them; the cuisine was excellent and liberal; attendance the best I have ever seen; and the charges not a bit higher than the tariff at any ordinary first-class house.

Hotel life in America is an institution peculiar to

the country. Owing to the difficulty in the first place of obtaining good servants, and the uncertainty of keeping them afterwards for any length of time, when the great fundamental principles of all republics (liberty and equality) firmly take root, many families reside entirely in hotels. These people therefore become a fixed income to the proprietors, and all possible means are adopted to attract them to their establishments, and to retain them afterwards. Year after year families inhabit the same suite of apartments, only too glad to escape the expense and annoyance of housekeeping in a country where, notwithstanding the theoretical advantages of equality, very few care about introducing it to social life, or tolerating it among their domestics.

Chicago is well supplied with newspapers; indeed, the amount of this class of literature all through the United States is very remarkable. The smallest towns have a "Daily," and even Calamus City, which only consisted of a few miserable log huts, sported a printing-press and a weekly paper. The Chicago style is somewhat unique, if not absolutely bewildering. For instance, in one of the leading journals, dated November 27th, I noticed an article containing an account of a recent execution, which, headed in large black letters, announced the following startling intelligence: "Jerked to Jesus"; "Four Senegambian butchers were wafted to heaven yesterday from scaffolds"; "Four of them died with the sweet confidence of pious people," &c. &c. &c. Some of the other articles were well written, and I was astonished at seeing such indecent vulgarity in what was in other respects a clever and well-conducted newspaper.

From Chicago we went to Toronto in Canada, our luggage undergoing a slight inspection at Sarnia, a small town on the frontier. I was surprised at the marked difference in the aspect of the country and appearance of the people, and could hardly have believed it possible that the distinction between two races of similar origin and language should have been so decided. The farms were smaller, the fields and inclosures smaller, and the people more intensely English in appearance, speech, and costume. The refreshments at the railway stations were cheaper, but savoured more of the "stale bun" and "scalding soup" system we are cursed with at home, than the liberal tariff that generally characterises American tables similarly situated; and though delighted with the unmistakable evidences of English nationality in other respects, we did not find the feeding a change for the better, and occasionally pined for the well-supplied tables of Lathrop and Merced in the "Far West."

Toronto is a handsome well-built town, situated on the shore of Lake Ontario. Some of the public buildings are fine, and the university is exceedingly beautiful and well worth a visit. We put up at the Queen's Hotel, and though it did not rival the Palmer House in magnificence, it certainly deserves a word of praise as being one of the most comfortable houses I ever stayed at, and far superior to anything at Montreal or other parts of Canada we passed through.

I find myself now getting on such a well-worn and beaten track that I am disinclined to bore my reader with an account of places he in all probability knows more of than I do, and shall therefore touch but very lightly on the few remaining towns we visit before I cease my wanderings. King Street is the fashionable promenade. A heavy fall of snow and an unusually "cold snap," as it was termed, had arranged everything for sleighing, and every vehicle was at once called into requisition and every waggon put on sliders. Nothing could be gayer than the scene in the principal streets during the fashionable hours of from three to five, when all the well-appointed equipages turned out with handsome fur robes trailing far behind them, almost touching the snow.

Sleighing is certainly a delightful amusement, and if a man be fortunate in having a crack team and a pleasant companion of the opposite sex, I am unaware of any sort of driving that can touch it. The calm, cold, clear atmosphere, the tinkling of the bells, the pure snow, the warm robes, and the pretty girl—all form a combination which, added to the smooth gliding action of the sleigh, renders the experience one often to be longed for when snow and sleighs can only be thought of among the long-departed and never to be recalled pleasures of the past.

The theatre was pretty good. I went one night and saw a wretched play badly acted, but the interior of the building was well got up and of larger size than those of most provincial towns in England of more than double the population.

From Toronto I went to Niagara, and find some

difficulty in analysing my feelings in connection with its extraordinary and wonderful Falls. My first sense was one of disappointment. From earliest childhood I had heard and read such gushing accounts that reality naturally fell short of expectation; but after a time their magnificence seems to grow on one, and eventually their marvellous grandeur unrolls and steadily impresses itself most thoroughly. What I had expected to see, I am sure I don't know; but with such food for fancy as one gets in Niagara, I imagine the first impression of many must be that of disappointment at the first sight.

The pleasures of Niagara are, to me at any rate, dreadfully marred by its surroundings. Guides, touts, photographers, vendors of curiosities, Jewesses, and harpies of every description abound. All kinds of Cockney ridiculous names are given to every point, rock, or extra spray of water. You are besieged at every step with solicitations to purchase rubbish.

A perpetual demand for fifty cents seems to be the "current" topic of conversation. If you look over a rock, it is fifty cents; if you look up one, it is fifty cents; for everything you do, it is the same price; and I was rather surprised when a stranger to me said, "Good morning," that he did not charge fifty cents for his civility. Photographers chase you with a prepared plate for a Niagara in the background. Pertinacious and brazen-faced Jewesses insist on your shelling out dollars, and show unmitigated disgust if your expenditure falls short of their expectations; and when, to escape from these nuisances and enjoy a solitary weed, I found what I imagined to be a secluded spot on Goat Island, before I had been allowed a quarter of an hour's quiet enjoyment of the truly magnificent rapids, I heard a voice from behind request me to remain perfectly still, and that he would shoot me in twenty seconds, and on turning round found a ruffian quietly "covering me" from under a cloth-covered camera.

Of course lots of people like all this. They enjoy their guide's twaddle. They purchase Indian curiosities (manufactured on the spot) with sweet confidence as to the genuine nature of the commodity. They get photographed at every possible opportunity, the picture being very much of themselves and very little of Niagara. If it were not so, the nuisance would cease to exist; but with it all, they certainly spoil at least three-fourths of the pleasures an ordinary mortal can derive from one of the most marvellous sights in nature. One sees and becomes impressed, but enjoyment is out of the question. As well talk of enjoying Nilsson or Patti, in their favourite and most exquisitely rendered passages of Opera, with a monkey chattering in the stall behind you; playing a salmon with an enthusiastic crowd criticising your actions (I went through that experience once on Galway bridge, and did not like it); or enjoying a *chef's* most sublime effort, ten minutes being allowed for the trial.

I hardly know what to recommend, as escaping these bores altogether is impossible. I can only suggest that the best plan is to see the Falls during the day, and enjoy them at sunrise, before the tormentors are out of bed. Such early rising is a little rough perhaps on some people, but nevertheless it is one's only chance, and it will repay them amply. The majesty of Niagara is stupendous, but cannot make itself properly felt with a running accompaniment of photographers and touts.

From Niagara I went to Montreal, a curious old town with a large population of French extraction, who still retain the language. The St. Lawrence was frozen across, and I came in for an exhibition of some of the wonderful skating Canadians of both sexes are celebrated for. Not being provided with letters, and not knowing a soul in the town, there was not much to be done in the way of amusement. I heard a good many people regret the loss of the English regiments, and from the enthusiasm displayed at the parade of a volunteer corps I can quite imagine what a "good time" the regiments fortunate enough to have been quartered here in the old days must have had.

There is a wild natural park overhanging the town; rocks, trees, and their surroundings being quite in a state of primeval simplicity. From some points of it a most exquisite view is to be obtained of the surrounding country. For many miles the River St. Lawrence winds away in the distance, a lofty range of mountains in the States being also occasionally visible. There are not many views better worth seeing, and on a fine day it is quite enchanting. Some of the public buildings and a few private residences are handsome well-built stone edifices. The streets were well laid out, and as the weather was cold, bright, and clear, gaily-painted sleighs, with their musical accompaniment of bells outside and "belles" in, enlivened the scene, and gave an air of festivity to all about them.

After a few days devoted to sight-seeing, an account of which I will mercifully spare my reader, I started for New York, and after an uninteresting railway journey, and a rigid examination of luggage by the custom-house authorities, arrived safely at the great commercial capital of the United States.

Here as an author my wanderings end. Washington, Philadelphia, Baltimore, Richmond, Boston, and all the great eastern cities are far too well known to require description, and are only interesting to the European as being the means of giving him an insight to American society, their manners, their customs, and the working of their municipalities and legislature.

On these few topics I shall lightly touch ere concluding, and having had ample opportunities and facilities for judging of each, will be at any rate impartial in my "summing up" of the people among whom I have been living for over a year, and from whom I have experienced great and unvarying kindness and hospitality.

Unmitigated flattery would be a sorry recompense for such treatment, and I even confess, but without departing from my "platform" as an impartial witness, that holding political views diametrically opposite to anything republican, it has almost been a source of satisfaction to find, on inspection, inquiry, and diligent investigation, that the institutions of the country are very far indeed from being perfect; that bribery and corruption is reported common in both

Senate and Congress; and that the suppositious virtues which, according to the reiterated statements of our leading Radicals in England, appertain to all republics in general, and the United States in particular, only really exist in their own over-imaginative and highly-wrought conceptions of a modern Utopia based on republican principles.

While at Washington I witnessed the impeachment of a Cabinet Minister (General Belknap) for selling Government appointments. Another member of the same council was roundly accused by some of the leading newspapers of having in various ways benefited himself to a very large amount at the expense of his country, and though we are informed by Scripture "that a little leaven leaveneth the whole," the undoubted high personal character of Mr. Fish, the Secretary of State, one of the few men of social rank and fortune who have entered the political arena, seemed utterly unable to leaven the immediate associates he was brought directly into contact with.

That corruption to a very lamentable extent exists in the country, I have not only the personal statements of very many prominent and distinguished citizens, who deplore an evil they are unable to remedy, but also the accounts given almost daily in the public press, whole columns of which are filled with histories of the swindling operations of what they felicitously term "rings," on the principle, I suppose, of there being "no end" to them. There are Indian rings, whisky rings, municipal rings "*a la* Boss Tweed," and every conceivable ring that can be thought of, but none with the ring of true metal.

Universal suffrage, unaccompanied by either an educational or property qualification, is the fundamental root of all these evils; and to universal suffrage all the existing ills, in all existing republics, distinctly can be traced.

No one but a mule in stupid obstinate perversity, or a mole in blindness, can fail to see these glaring evils in the Constitution, or can help noticing that, in consequence of them, men of the highest social and hereditary rank are conspicuous by their absence from the legislative councils of their country; and yet, after a few weeks' sojourn in the States, our Radical members of Parliament come back bursting with false information, and give vent, in lectures and addresses to confiding and credulous constituencies, to their ill-conceived ideas of republican purity.

Some people are possibly misled by results, and unintentionally draw false conclusions from apparent facts. This is a mistake a superficial observer is very liable to fall into, and merely looking at the growing prosperity and wealth of the "Far West" as an accomplished and *bonâ fide* realization, he is apt, having republican proclivities, to ascribe the cause to an adoption of his political views, of which mistake a very slight study of the true reason would soon disabuse him.

The future greatness of the American nation will undoubtedly come from the West; and, without having been West, an individual, no matter how far-sighted and deep-thinking he may imagine himself, will fail, not only in grasping whence the real wealth and prosperity of the nation must eventually be derived, but where also already much of the primary causes of success and contentment exist in a degree not to be met with in Europe.

A boundless extent of territory teeming with agricultural and mineral wealth is still entirely unoccupied. Crop after crop can be raised for many years to come of the very finest grain, simply by scratching the earth and dropping in seed. None of the artificial resources known to older and impoverished lands are here ever thought of, and superphosphates and guano, bone-dust and top-dressing, are subjects entirely unknown and seldom even read about. The mineral wealth of the Pacific States is simply incalculable, and will assuredly cause a revolution in the value of precious metals which will make itself felt with startling severity ere very many years go by. For years to come the Western emigrant will be entitled to claim his one hundred and sixty acres of land; and, undoubtedly, none but the idle, the vicious, or the infirm need suffer poverty in America. There is no country in the world whose prospects of future greatness are so apparent to the meanest comprehension, but to ascribe such prosperity to the peculiar republican form of its government, or to the effect of universal suffrage, is as ridiculous as to suppose the worn and impoverished land of Europe, decrepit from the hundreds of years of close and exhaustive agriculture to be simply the effect of monarchical institutions or hereditary legislation.

Had the Americans that strong sentiment of loyalty to a reigning family which happily pervades most European countries, it would serve as a cement to bind them together; but lacking this adhesive quality, and being governed entirely by individual interests, each unit in the community feeling an inward consciousness that ill luck alone prevents his being Chief Magistrate, a position that he feels eminently fitted to adorn, the conflicting interests of east and west must eventually rise to the surface, and though nothing seems likely to disturb the Union for at least another seventy years, my ghost will be much surprised if it ever witnesses another Centennial.

The reply to my remarks, from a native, I know well enough, would be that I misjudged entirely; and that their sentiment to the Union was as strong in every degree as ours to a monarch. He would refer with pride to the late civil war, and point to the lives laid down, and treasure expended, in a cause for which he also would possibly be willing to die, forgetting, or at any rate losing sight of, the fact, that lives and money were being spent quite as recklessly by the Confederates to abolish the Union he so fondly loves, and that the wealth and intellect of the country were at one time pretty equally divided in the matter of that sentiment which most Americans now imagine pervaded the entire nation. To prove that my ideas are not singular or even original, I may as well quote the words of the celebrated "Fisher Ames," an American of much eminence, who, living as far back as the revolutionary period, saw even then the growing tendency of the rapidly thriving young Republic. While speaking of the future state of the country, his prophecy ran as follows: "We will eventually become too expansive for Union, too sordid for patriotism, and too democratic for liberty." How far these warnings have proved correct, or are likely to prove so, the reader can judge for himself; but I certainly have found nothing myself in the republican institutions of the Two Americas to make me wish to see such a form of government introduced among us in England.

It is a positive relief, after having found so many faults in the constitution, to be able to allude to other American traits of which one can speak nothing but the highest praise.

In no part of the world, England or anywhere else, will a traveller meet with more uniform kindness and hospitality. With all classes it is precisely the same. During my wanderings I was brought into close contact with every description of person; the rich, the poor, the cultivated, and the rough; but never once in any part of the United States, in the meanest ranche or most primitive mining camp, did I ever experience the slightest discourtesy or lack of kindness. Often and often perfect strangers put themselves out of their way to do me a good turn, and nothing can ever obliterate from my memory the remembrance of the unmitigated good-nature, hospitality, and friendliness of feeling I have invariably experienced.

That such a feeling should exist, many people who have merely read the occasional bitter outpourings of the American press, when the "Bird of Freedom" is on one of his lofty flights, will hardly conceive possible; but, notwithstanding their occasional caustic speeches, there is a deep undercurrent of goodwill towards all Englishmen, which only requires "circumstance" to bring out in its brightest and most genuine character.

It may not be out of place while on this topic to allude to my first experience of this good feeling, which I assert that all true Americans (not Fenian Irish counterfeits) entertain in their hearts for us; and I use the words "in their hearts" advisedly, as occasionally the surface outpourings of the nation very much belie their innermost sentiments, and a momentary bitterness of speech is only like the hasty quarrel of really dear friends, who each may be ashamed afterwards of a sharpness of temper which betrayed them both into expressions which neither seriously meant.

In June 1859 I was present at an attack on the Ta-ku Forts at the mouth of the Pei-ho River in the north of China, an affair which I regret to say terminated in our receiving a very severe repulse. In a most disagreeably short space of time three gun-boats and two despatch vessels were sunk by the severity of the enemy's fire. Admiral Sir James Hope, who commanded, was seriously wounded, and after about three hours' further sharp practice all the gun-boats were so knocked about and hard pressed in engaging the enemy's batteries, that hardly any were available for towing the "storming party" (who were waiting in junks anchored off the forts out of range) into action.

At this juncture the captain of an American frigate —Commodore Tattenal—volunteered his services. During the very severest part of the action he pulled in his galley to visit Admiral Hope, who had hoisted his flag on one of the gun-boats, to express sympathy and volunteer assistance; and not to be behindhand in good feeling, his boat's crew, during their chief's visit to the cabin (where the Admiral lay wounded), improved the occasion by "falling in" at one of the guns and fighting it until he returned on deck. Commodore Tattenal then permitted a small steamer under his command to assist in towing the boats containing the storming party into action, an affair which I came out of with a bullet through my leg, my clothes cut to ribbons by others, and considering myself exceedingly lucky in getting off so cheaply, as nineteen men out of my small company of fifty-three were either killed or wounded. In proportion to the numbers engaged, our "butcher's bill" was one of the severest on record, and on leaving our Admiral's ship the American Commodore had his coxwain, who was sitting beside him, cut in two by a round shot.

I make particular mention of the severity of the fire, as I wish to show that Commodore Tattenal's courtesy was no mere holiday form, but the deep-seated, true, chivalrous feeling which men of the same blood should always entertain. He had no earthly necessity to do what he did. His nation was at peace with China. He risked his commission and whole prospects in the service by his undiplomatic behaviour, and all —to use his own memorable words—because "blood was thicker than water." So may it ever prove, and may the English-speaking races always entertain, irrespective of differences in government, the same undercurrent of good feeling so nobly exhibited by Tattenal and his men at the Taku Forts.

The more one sees of America, both of people and country, the better one likes both; and I trust that the present Centennial Exhibition now going on at Philadelphia may be the means of inducing many Englishmen to travel through the States, and return with that feeling of friendship and goodwill for their American cousins which propinquity with them is certain to engender.

Should any visit America after reading these lines, let me advise them to pay particular attention to three subjects—i.e. Canvas-back ducks, Terrapin, and Madeira. This to the uninitiated is a hint worth remembering.

In the streets of New York I have seen more pretty girls, in a shorter space of time, than in any other town I have been in. Nearly all have beautiful hands and feet, and dress both expensively and well, though there is rather too much of a display of diamond earrings and jewelry in the daytime to constitute what we should consider exactly consistent with "good form" in England. It must surprise a stranger, the first fine Sunday he walks down the Fifth Avenue, to see not only so many pretty women, but the extraordinary number of undoubtedly expensive costumes all of them appear in. This extravagance of apparel is by no means confined to a particular "set," and where on earth so many people find the money to dress in the way they do is to me a perfect wonder. I don't think the men are so extravagant as we are, and as the greater portion of them occupy all their time in making money, they seem to derive their chief pleasure and satisfaction from seeing their wives and daughters spending it, having neither time nor inclination for such frivolities themselves. A few among them buy pictures, but as they have neither expensive country-houses with estates to keep up, grouse moors and deer forests to pay for, nor even amuse themselves by maintaining large studs of horses to chase the "wily fox," their personal expenditure is necessarily comparatively small, while their generosity to their wives naturally becomes proportionately greater than that of poor beggars living under "effete monarchies," who have to pay like fun for amusements that can be had for nothing in America. No wonder American ladies proudly and emphatically declare that their men are the best husbands in the world.

The *jeunesse dorée* of New York endeavour to assume English manners, and do so with only indifferent success. This is, however, a defect in their education that time will gradually correct; and I daresay, with constant study, in a few more generations, they may become nearly as affected as the class at home they so vainly attempt to imitate.

American society is sociable, charming, and delightful; and experience soon tells one that the shoddy representatives so frequently met while travelling in Europe are but very poor specimens of the nicest people in New York, Washington, or the "Hub."

I do not mean to say that the power of money is not occasionally felt. A yacht and four-in-hand are as powerful passports to society in New York as the same appendages most unquestionably are in London, and a wealthy snob is as attractive to fortune-hunting mothers in one town as in the other. Shoddy, however, to be tolerated, must be polished, and the specimens one occasionally meets with in New York are less objectionable than members of the same fraternity abroad.

In the Western States money reigns supreme, nor is society particular as to how it was come by, so long as the possessor has a decent cook and is liberal in dinners. Two of the élite of San Francisco kept a fifth-rate drinking saloon before a lucky mining speculation raised them in the scale of social importance, and their partners, who are equally distinguished for enormous wealth, commenced life in an even less ostentatious manner. The Boston people consider intellectual qualifications a necessity, and the Washingtonians some kind of rank, either political or diplomatic; but any English gentleman is certain to get on well with all of them, and will like the people.

Of all the good fellows in the world I really believe the U.S.A. officers are about the best. It is simply impossible to do them justice in describing their kindness and hospitality to any one bringing letters of introduction who may visit their posts. No trouble is too great if they can only give you a "good time," and no inconvenience you can possibly put them to is considered of the slightest moment if they can add to your comfort or enjoyment. They are all highly educated, the course at West Point being one of the most thorough a man can receive, and among the many pleasant recollections I carry with me, there will be none more highly valued than the remembrance of days and nights, in camp and prairie, passed in their society.

During the early part of the winter, in New York, I constantly met General George A. Custer of the United States Army. He was a fine, dashing, gallant officer, with a splendid record, earned in many a well-contested field during the war against the South. A mutual love of all field sports brought us a good deal together whenever we met casually in society, and eventually led to his asking me to serve on his staff as a volunteer aide-de-camp during the coming spring, when he had been promised the command of an expedition being fitted out for a march into the Yellowstone country, promising, in the event of my accepting his offer, that he would guarantee I should kill bear, elk, mountain sheep, and buffalo.

Knowing the General to be as charming a companion as he was a thorough sportsman, it did not take long to make up my mind to join him; and for the rest of the season we had long conversations, whenever we met, as to the "good time" we should have together when we had once started on our hunt.

The spring approached and everything was in readiness for the field. We expected an occasional brush with the Sioux Indians, into whose country we were about to penetrate, but as to anything really serious in the way of fighting, it never for an instant entered either of our heads.

I got my hunting-gear together, and Custer, passing through New York on his way to Washington, breakfasted with Lord M. and myself the morning before he went there, and arranged that I should have everything packed and ready to start within an hour after receiving his telegram; his command at Fort Abraham Lincoln only waiting his return to take the field. I little thought tne day I heard General Belknap, the Secretary of State for War, impeached before Congress for selling Post Traderships, that that very impeachment should have been the indirect means of saving my life.

General Custer proceeded to Washington and gav his evidence, which unfortunately for himself was so indirectly damnatory to the President's brother, as well as to the Minister of War, that General Grant, taking advantage of his position as Commander-in-Chief (through being President), vindictively superseded him in the command, after having in a most insulting manner kept him waiting a whole day in a chamber at the White House, when seeking an audience. Poor Custer wrote me word he was not to go; but the press took the matter up so warmly, and public opinion ran so high on the subject of the injustice of his treatment, that eventually the President, as a kind of compromise, permitted him to join the expedition he was to have commanded, though only in a subordinate capacity.

His last letter to me from Fort Lincoln said he was about to take the field in command of his regiment, under General Terry, who had superseded him; that of course he could not put me on his staff, not being in his altered position entitled to one; and that as he had only received twenty-four hours' notice of his being permitted to go at all, was unable to ask me to join him ; and that also it was dangerous, from the quantity of hostile Indians being on the war-path, to travel through the country without an escort, which, as all the available men were away on duty, of course I could not get.

The rest is a matter of history. General Custer, while on a scout in the vicinity of the Little Big Horn River, with a force chiefly composed of men belonging to his own regiment, and numbering some three hundred sabres, struck the Sioux Indians under their celebrated chief, "Sitting Bull." What exactly transpired will never be known with any degree of accuracy, as not one single soul out of the entire party lived to tell the tale.

General Custer, his brother and nephew, with fourteen officers were among the slain, and had I received his last letter a few days sooner, or had a Cabinet Minister not been impeached, there can be no doubt but that I should have shared their fate, and that probably at the present moment my scalp would be adorning an Indian lodge-pole. I was greatly disappointed when I first heard I was not to go. My traps were packed, and all was ready, but it only shows the truth of the old provèrb, "A man never knows when he is well off," and I can truly say I have much to be thankful for, but I little thought while writing my impressions of the Sioux or Dakotas in the Rocky Mountains, that my prognostications concerning them should to a certain extent be fulfilled actually before the words I had written could be put in print.

A singular incident happened shortly after my arrival in New York, which speaks so highly for the people connected with it, and really is in every way so remarkable and almost romantic, that I cannot help relating the story.

Having taken up my quarters at the Everitt House, my name, among many others, was announced in the list of arrivals. A few days afterwards I received a letter from a firm of lawyers, stating that they had received instructions from one of their clients, who had seen my arrival in the papers, to find out if I was any relation to a baronet of my name, who many years ago had been travelling through the country, and who had left some property in the possession of their family for more than fifty years, which they were extremely anxious to return. On replying in the affirmative, an interview was appointed, and, very much to my satisfaction and surprise, an exceedingly handsome and valuable gold snuff-box, with my coat of arms engraved on the lid, and an enamelled mortuary tablet in the interior, containing a list of names, dates, and deaths of various members of my family for many generations, was handed over to me.

As I was perfectly unaware of the existence of the box, and had never even heard a soul speak of such a thing, obtaining possession thus unexpectedly of so valuable a family relic was extremely gratifying, and in the warmest manner I expressed to the lawyers my gratitude to the lady for the great obligation she had placed me under. The gentleman who conducted the matter, smiling blandly at my warmth, said, "My dear Sir Rose, it is almost impossible for you to be more delighted at obtaining so interesting a family relic, than my client is in getting rid of it. Mrs. P. is a very old lady, and was left it many years ago by her husband, who begged her if possible to return it to your family. This on various occasions she attempted to do, writing frequently to England, and once to yourself, her letters never apparently reaching their destination. On seeing your name, quite accidentally, she immediately communicated with me, and her delight, in at last being able to fulfil her dead husband's wishes, and return your snuff-box, quite equals yours in receiving it."

Having spent an entire season in New York society, as well as six weeks at Washington during the very gayest part of the year, I feel tempted to give my impressions; but remembering the manner in which I was received, and the very great hospitality I enjoyed, I will not venture on so delicate a subject, notwithstanding my advantages, lest unwittingly I should wound some one.

I know well enough by not doing so I shall disappoint many of my American friends who occasionally like their literature "highly seasoned." This cannot be helped. It will be sufficient merely to say, that I thank them much for their very great kindness, having really had in the very fullest acceptation of the term, "Such a good time."

My yarn is now spun. I have endeavoured to curtail it as much as possible, and avoid prosiness. It being only a gossipping narrative of what came under my own immediate observation, the first personal pronoun unavoidably comes somewhat prominently into play; however, that is an infliction that all readers of travels become accustomed to, and if I have bored them very much, I can only apologize, express sorrow, and regret for their sakes that a more experienced writer had not undertaken a description of an uncommonly pleasant rambling journey through "The Two Americas." *Vale.*

APPENDIX A.

THE 'BOXER.' (See page 94.)

HAVING seen by the *Times* of a recent date, under the head of "Naval and Military Intelligence," the official trial of the *Boxer*, I find it necessary to call attention to the subject.

It states—"A trial of the engines of the *Boxer*, composite screw gun-vessel, at the measured mile off the Maplin Sands, has been very satisfactory, an average speed of about nine and a quarter knots per hour having been attained—a higher rate than had been expected. The vessel has returned to Chatham Dockyard, and has been moored in the Medway. Her fitments are almost completed, and she will soon be ready to be commissioned."

This is evidently the old gun-boat rejuvenated. Now a ship on trial doing its measured mile is a very different thing from the ordinary steaming of the same vessel, and should by no means be accepted by the uninitiated public as a sample of the ship's ordinary performances.

During a trial of this sort, the boilers are kept at full pressure by picked stokers who do not usually belong to the ship's company; the coal is the best the dockyard can supply, and naturally very far superior to coal unselected and picked up anyhow at out-of-the-way coaling-stations in foreign parts; and the whole trial is superintended by a class of men attached to the dockyards who are employed especially for these purposes.

I was on board the *Rocket* during her trial trip at Sheerness, during which trial nothing could have been more satisfactory, and yet she proved afterwards to be a veritable dummy.

It is impossible to attach too great importance to the necessity of having efficient and serviceable gun-boats, and one cannot overrate their immense utility in time of war.

That there are considerable difficulties in the construction of what I must term "efficient gun-boats," I will readily allow; but while millions have been squandered in expensive failures like the *Captain*, and many others it is needless to enumerate, comparatively nothing has been attempted in perfecting a class of vessel that has invariably proved itself of vast consequence on many important occasions, and whose very economy in construction should alone render it at any rate an object of consideration for those who have the designing of our Navy.

Speed under steam; strength to carry two guns (one of heavy calibre) and fight them continuously if needed, as in case of bombardment, without racking herself to pieces; capacity for turning rapidly in a confined space; sufficient sailing property to enable her to take long voyages by these means alone, within a reasonable space of time, and thus save fuel for important occasions—all these combined in a vessel with not over eight feet draught of water are the chief qualifications for success, but which up to the present time have certainly never been arrived at.

There are many difficulties in arriving at these combinations, though I feel certain they can be overcome. Being compelled to have so small a draught of water as eight feet necessitates a gun-boat's bottom to be almost flat, and consequently having no hold in the water, while sailing as "close hauled" as she sometimes is obliged to be, her amount of lee way is incredible. This being allowed, why should not a lee-board be adopted? It will certainly make a man-of-war look like a Thames barge, but I take it appearance is of small importance where utility can be arrived at; and many a time during our tedious passage from Mazatlan to San Diego, I felt certain, from observation, that had the *Rocket* been so provided, our days of discomfort would have been considerably shortened.

I quite expect to have my idea either ridiculed or pooh-poohed, still it is worth a trial; and as fitting up a lee-board would cost comparatively nothing, it certainly ought to be attempted, unless some other better plan can be suggested for enabling a round-bottomed shallow-draughted vessel of considerable length and no hold whatever on the water to beat to windward in a roughish sea. One thing is at any rate quite evident. Our present class of gun-vessels are defective, and it is some one's duty to see that a more useful and better sort be forthcoming, and that shortly, *as the time when they will be needed cannot be far off.*

I see by a recent paper the following intelligence. "Loss of a gun-vessel.—H.M.S. *Lapwing* has been reported lost in a great gale near Chefoo. The *Lapwing* was a double-screw gun-boat, with three guns, and was of 774 tons and 882 (nominal 160) horse-power." I am only surprised we do not see this sort of thing oftener, and it is only owing to the very great care and caution of the officers that it does not occur.

APPENDIX B.

(See page 263.)

THE trowel-bayonet. While in the vein for making suggestions, I wish again to draw attention to the trowel-bayonet, a description of which is given at page 263. In these days of military progress, when arms of precision are so equally distributed among European nations, a very little weight on either side of the scale may turn the balance, and most unquestionably whichever side holds the smallest advantage has immense odds in its favour.

Most people who pay any kind of attention to military matters will, I fancy, allow that the days when battles were won by charges of the bayonet are practically ended; and a Government like that of the United States, who have lately had all the experience of a long and severe war in their own country, ought to be considered no mean judges of a weapon which, without hesitation, they have adopted for their army.

The system of tactics most likely to find favour (at any

rate for the commencement of all great battles) will cause the frequent use of long lines of skirmishers on each side, and where the ground is open a decided advantage must necessarily accrue to the men who, armed with the trowel-bayonet, have the ready means always at hand of throwing up or otherwise improving any natural cover they may take shelter in.

With an army so numerically weak as ours, it behoves the authorities to render the small force they have the control of as efficient as possible; and though the adoption into the service of this novel weapon would possibly meet with opposition from the pipe-clay school of soldiers who study appearances more than utility, I cannot help believing that the practical man would immediately see its advantages over the present comparatively useless bayonet, and gladly approve of the change. Shelter-trench drill, as taught when I had the honour of serving, was a harmless amusement, utterly inapplicable to active service or the requirements of advancing or retiring lines of skirmishers; it, however, pleased the authorities of the day, and the details for its performance may even now be given in our drill-books.

APPENDIX C.

(See page 293.)

My chapter about Indians was written shortly after a hunting expedition in the Rocky Mountains, where we had been over ground frequently visited by Sioux, and during which hunt three white men had been murdered by them within a very short distance of our beat. Colonel Brackett, commanding Fort Sanders, kindly gave me his copious notes on the various tribes he had lived among, and his evident knowledge of the subject, particularly as relating to the Sioux or Dakotas, has been amply exemplified by recent events connected with their rising.

My prophecy, written after the Great Council at the

Black Hills, has already been literally fulfilled (page 205), as to the eagerness of the young "Brave" to get scalps, though I hardly thought it possible that those of a general officer and three hundred soldiers would have formed the contribution of a single day.

A general press despatch from the mouth of the Big Horn on the 1st July, 1876, gives the following particulars of General Custer's disastrous expedition against the Sioux Indians.

At noon on the 23d June, 1876, General Custer, at the head of his fine regiment of the twelve veteran companies, left camp at the mouth of the Rosebud to follow the trail of a very large band of hostile Sioux leading up to the river and westward in the direction of the Big Horn. The signs indicated that the Indians were making for the eastern branch of the last-named river, marked on the map as the Little Big Horn. At the same time General Terry, with Colonel Gibbons in command of five companies of infantry, four of cavalry, and the Gatlin Battery, started to ascend the Big Horn, aiming to assail the enemy in the rear. The march of the two columns was so planned as to bring Colonel Gibbons's forces within co-operating distance of the anticipated scene of action by the evening of the 26th. In this way only could the infantry be made available, as it would not do to encumber General Custer's march with foot-soldiers. On the evening of the 24th Colonel Gibbons's command was landed on the south bank of the Yellowstone, near the mouth of the Big Horn, and on the 25th was pushed twenty-three miles over a country so rugged that the endurance of the men was tested to the uttermost. The infantry then halted for the night, but the department commander, with the cavalry, advanced twelve miles farther to the mouth of the Little Big Horn, marching till midnight, in the hope of opening communication with General Custer. The morning of the 26th brought the intelligence, communicated by three badly-frightened Crow scouts, of the battle of the previous day, and its results. The story was not credited, because it was not expected that an attack would be made earlier than the 27th, and chiefly because no one could believe that a force such as General Custer commanded could have met with disaster. Still the report was in no way disregarded. All day long the toilsome march was plied, and every eye bent upon a cloud of smoke resting over the southern horizon, which was hailed as a sign that General Custer was successful and had fired the village. It was only when night was falling that the weary troops lay down upon their arms. The infantry had marched twenty-nine miles. The march of the next morning revealed at every step some evidence of the conflict which had taken place two days before. At an early hour the head of the column entered a plain, half a mile wide, bordering the left bank of the Little Big Horn, where had recently been an immense Indian village extending three miles along the stream, and there were still standing funeral lodges with horses slaughtered around them, and containing the bodies of nine chiefs. The ground was strewn everywhere with bodies of horses, cavalry equipments and buffalo robes, packages of dried meat, and weapons and utensils belonging to Indians. On this part of the field was found the clothing of Lieutenants Sturges and Porters pierced with bullets, and a blood-stained gauntlet belonging to Colonel Yates. Farther on were found bodies of men, among whom were recognised Lieutenant M'Intosh, the interpreter from Fort Rice, and Reynolds, the guide. Just then a breathless scout arrived with the intelligence that Colonel Reno, with a remnant of the 7th Cavalry, was entrenched on a bluff near by, waiting for relief. The commander pushed rapidly on, and soon came in sight of a group surrounding a cavalry guard on a lofty eminence on the right bank of a river. General Terry forded the stream, accompanied by a small party, and rode to the spot. All the way the slopes were dotted with the bodies of men and horses. The General approached, and the men swarmed out of the works and greeted him with hearty and repeated cheers. Within was found Major Reno, with the remains of seven companies of the regiment, with the following named officers, all of whom are unhurt: Colonels Benteen and Wier; Captains Felix Mayland and Macdougal; Lieutenants Godfrey, Mathey, Gibson, Deruded, Edgerly, Wallace, Varnum, and Hare. In the centre of the inclosure the wounded were sheltered, covered with canvas. Major Reno's command had been fighting from Sunday noon, the 25th, until the night of the 26th, when Terry's arrival caused the Indians to retire. Up to this time Major Reno and those with him were in complete ignorance of the fate of the other five companies which had been separated from them on the 26th to make an attack, under General Custer, on the village at another point. While preparations were being made for the removal of the wounded, a party was sent on General Custer's trail to look for traces of his command. They found awaiting them a sight fit to appal the stoutest heart. At a point about three miles down the right bank of the stream General Custer had evidently attempted to ford, and attack the villages from the ford. The trail was found to lead back up to the bluffs and to the northward, as if the troops had been repulsed and compelled to retreat, and at the same time had been cut off from regaining the forces under Major Reno. The bluffs along the right bank come sharply down to the water, and are interspersed by numerous ravines all along the slopes and ridges, and in the ravines, lying as they had fought, line behind line, showing where defensive positions had been successively taken up and held till none were left to fight, lay the bodies of the fallen soldiers. There, huddled in a narrow compass, horses and men were piled promiscuously. At the highest point of the ridge lay General Custer, surrounded by a chosen band. Here were his two brothers and his nephew, Mr. Reed, Colonel Yates, and Colonel Cooke, and Captain Smith, all lying in a circle of a few yards, their horses beside them. Here, behind Colonel Yates's company, the last stand had been made, and here, one after another, these last survivors of General Custer's five companies had met their death. The companies had successively thrown themselves across the path of the advancing enemy, and had been annihilated. Not a man had escaped to tell the tale, but a story was inscribed on the surface of the barren hills in a language more eloquent than words. Two hundred and sixty-one bodies have been buried from General Custer's and Major Reno's commands. The last one found was that of Mr. Kellegg, the correspondent of the 'Tribune.'

The 'New York Herald's' correspondent says: "I write from the scene of Custer's magnificent but terribly fatal charge from a plateau, on which but a few hours since I saw at a glance 115 heroic soldiers of the 7th United States cavalry lying where they fell at the hands of a savage foe, cold and dead. Near the top of a little knoll in the centre of this plateau lay Custer himself, and it touched my heart to see that the savages, in a kind of human recognition of human clay, had respected the corpse of the man they knew so well. Other bodies were mutilated. Custer's was untouched, a tribute of respect from such an enemy more real than a title of nobility. He lay as if asleep, his face calm, and a smile on his lips. Near him were eleven dead officers."

Notwithstanding the cruelties committed by the Indians —who have a decided predilection for pegging their male captives "spread-eagle" fashion on the ground, lighting a small fire over their stomachs while in that position, and almost invariably treating the females with still greater barbarity even as regards physical torture—they have unquestionably real and just cause of complaint. Their territory has been annexed; they have been defrauded in the most shocking and scandalous manner by agents appointed from Washington, who were supposed to attend to their interests; and in their different wars against the United States they have occasionally had tribes almost or quite annihilated by men who spared neither age nor sex.

No one with the smallest particle of humanity can uphold

such treatment, and Englishmen are apt, when talking on the subject, to refer to the superior condition of our tribes in Canada, and proudly descant on the merits of a humane and generous policy, which treats the Indian as a subject, and not as a noxious reptile who should be civilized off the face of creation.

This comparison between ourselves and the Americans is, however, neither fair nor generous, the conditions respecting the peculiar position of the respective tribes of Indians in the two countries being widely different. In "the Dominion" they inhabit land which nothing but immense labour and the expenditure of capital can ever render available for agricultural purposes. Their territories are almost absolutely valueless, owing to the density of timber and dearth of labour required to clear them. In fact, we do not want the land occupied by our Indians, yet we make a virtue (while criticising the Yankees) of permitting them to use it.

With the Americans it is different. Much of the land occupied by Indians is of the very highest agricultural value. I have frequently hunted over miles and miles of magnificent country, which remains entirely unoccupied, simply on account of the danger settlers would incur from close proximity to such disagreeable neighbours, and when it is remembered that owing to the unproductive nature of the Red man, who lives entirely by the capture of wild animals, and does not even breed cattle for his support, that at least a thousand times the acreage occupied by a "white" is necessary for his support, one will see that the position of the Americans is by no means as easy as our own.

The national wish of the United States is most unquestionably to treat these people fairly, though the means they adopt are wrong in every respect. An often quoted though much to be deplored maxim, particularly in the vicinity of the Sioux, is, that "No Injen is a good Injen until he is a dead Injen," and under the existing state of affairs the proverb is literally true.

If the Americans really wish to preserve these people whose lands they have arbitrarily possessed themselves of, there is only one possible method of doing so, and it should be done at once. An accurate register of all young children and births should be kept at the reservations, and for these young children there should be compulsory education. As they grow up, agricultural schools should be added; land should be taken up and tilled by their labour, and all the male Indians who have been educated at the schools, and taught Christianity, compelled, if necessary by force, to work and become self-supporting. This work should be superintended by people sufficiently well paid to induce men of probity and character to accept the situation. The surplus money derived from this source (and it would be considerable, were the plan properly carried out) should be applied solely for purposes of ameliorating the condition of the tribe—in fact, from the time the Indian child went to school until he had his own farm, his house, and possibly had married and had children of his own, and given the very strongest proofs of the improbability of his ever relapsing into his native barbarism, he should be entirely and solely under the control of the State, and almost a slave, except that whatever he succeeded in making would be entirely for his own benefit.

The grown-up Indian of the present might be permitted to die out quietly. As well attempt to teach a hippopotamus algebra as a "Buck" or "Brave" civilization. Continue, therefore, to feed him on the reservation as of old, and keeping him out of mischief as much as possible, devote attention solely to his children.

This plan requires time, patience, and much determination, but it is the only one that will ever succeed; and, if adopted, in thirty years from now the old Indians will have mostly disappeared, and the reservations might entirely be handed over to their reformed children, who will have become an agricultural or pastoral race, and require their nurse-tenders no longer.

www.ingramcontent.com/pod-product-compliance
Lightning Source LLC
LaVergne TN
LVHW020121110826
845151LV00001B/236

* 9 7 8 1 4 2 5 5 4 1 1 5 6 *